*Her Place in*
*the Woods*

Books by Helen Hoover
Published by the University of Minnesota Press

*The Gift of the Deer*
Illustrated by Adrian Hoover

*Great Wolf and the Good Woodsman*
Woodcuts by Betsy Bowen

*The Long-Shadowed Forest*
Illustrated by Adrian Hoover

*A Place in the Woods*
Illustrated by Adrian Hoover

*The Years of the Forest*
Illustrated by Adrian Hoover

# Her Place in the Woods

The Life of
Helen Hoover

David Hakensen

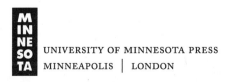

UNIVERSITY OF MINNESOTA PRESS

MINNEAPOLIS | LONDON

The University of Minnesota Press gratefully acknowledges the generous assistance provided for the publication of this book by the Hamilton P. Traub University Press Fund.

Portions of this book were previously published in "A Paradise Lost: Helen Hoover and Gunflint Lake," *Minnesota History* 64, no. 1 (Spring 2014): 34–44.

Published by the University of Minnesota Press
111 Third Avenue South, Suite 290
Minneapolis, MN 55401-2520
http://www.upress.umn.edu

ISBN 978-1-5179-1168-3 (hc)
ISBN 978-1-5179-2025-8 (pb)

A Cataloging-in-Publication record for this book is available from the Library of Congress.

Printed in Canada on acid-free paper

The University of Minnesota is an equal-opportunity educator and employer.

34 33 32 31 30 29 28 27 26 25     10 9 8 7 6 5 4 3 2 1

*To my parents, for introducing me to the woods,*
*and to my wife, Kim, for helping me enjoy it.*

*Into the forest I go, to lose my mind and find my soul.*

—John Muir

# Contents

# Prologue

THE DRIVE DOWN THE GUNFLINT TRAIL was a quiet, almost somber affair. After two months of peace, quiet, fresh air, and excitement about the future improvements they planned for their simple log cabin in the woods, the thought of a twelve-plus hour drive back to Chicago was bittersweet. Ade and Helen Hoover had arrived in late July 1954 at the height of summer's curative powers—warm temperatures, quiet breezes, and a sun that still hung high in the sky. The cabin, nestled in the tall, virgin pines on Gunflint Lake, had provided the relief Helen hoped would get her ailing husband Ade back to health after a slow recovery from surgery.

Neither one talked much as the car wound its way toward Grand Marais. And neither one was looking forward to returning to work. Helen had been able to get a two-month leave of absence from her metallurgy job after successfully completing a large project. She had asked for more time, claiming her husband could use it convalescing in the north woods, but was denied. Ade had been on extended medical leave from a textbook publisher where he was an art director. Helen's mother, who lived with them, had died the year before, so nothing was keeping them in Chicago.

Helen broke the silence. She started offering reasons they should quit their jobs and move to the cabin. The year before they had bought a second cabin next door, so now they had room for their furniture, clothing, and other household items. Helen wasn't tied to her job with the project behind her, and Ade had been on leave from his job for some time. Plus, from the time she was a young girl, she had envisioned a day when she would live somewhere in the north woods and write.

As Helen built her argument, Ade began coming around to the idea, but he still felt they needed more time for planning and to think through the financial ramifications. But Helen thought these justifications were only delaying the inevitable. He could do freelance artwork like he had done at home. Helen thought she could try her hand at writing, something she had put off for years as she focused on her career. Her enthusiasm for their collective ability to make the change started to work on Ade, and he, too, saw that if they didn't do it now, they would only be older and less able to make the move later.

Once they arrived in Grand Marais, Ade drove to the local telephone exchange building where they could place a long-distance call. Helen retrieved her address book from her purse and dialed her boss in Chicago.

"Mac, I guess I'm calling to say goodbye," she said. And with that, Helen resigned her position at the farm implement company. Now she and Ade would pack their apartment in Chicago and get their personal belongings moved to Gunflint Lake, starting a new chapter in their lives. While they did not have a solid plan, Helen knew that something would turn up.

# 1

# A Charmed Beginning

*Ohio, 1910–1929*

ON A COLD WINTER NIGHT in Greenfield, Ohio, a much-anticipated baby was about to be born. Thomas and Hannah Blackburn eagerly awaited the arrival of their second child. Their first, Thomas, died after only three days in 1907. Helen Drusilla Blackburn was safely delivered on January 20, 1910, at home, a two-story, twelve-room brick house. Her birth was a relief to both parents, and given the circumstances, it was assured she would be a child to be doted upon.

After sixteen years of marriage, Hannah, age thirty-eight, had given birth to a healthy baby girl. Her husband, Thomas, was fifty-three years old, and both had come of age in the Victorian era. His family had settled in Ohio, having moved from Virginia. Hannah Gomersall came from a large family in Cincinnati and was the oldest of eight children. Her father, John, was a woolen maker born in England who emigrated to America with his wife, Elizabeth.

Helen was named for Hannah's sister in Cincinnati. Her middle name, Drusilla, was given in honor of Thomas's mother, a woman who had achieved a measure of notoriety in Greenfield. In 1864, the town, then a quiet trading center located in the southwest part of the state, had a Main Street populated by saloons. Public drunkenness had become an increasing problem and of concern to the town's more prominent families. One day, Drusilla's eldest son, William, was walking along Main Street and killed by a stray bullet fired from one of the saloons. No arrests were made, and when it was evident no one would be held accountable, Drusilla and the other women of Greenfield were outraged. They told the mayor they were going to take possession of all the liquor in town and

1

asked that he provide a place to store it. The mayor was amused and did not take them seriously; he suggested they might "return the liquor to Mother Earth from which it came."[1]

The women were indeed serious and did just that. Marching from the Free Soil Church, they formed a procession and marched up Main Street, stopping at various saloons and ordering the proprietors to turn over their liquor. When the saloon keepers locked their doors, Drusilla led the charge. The women broke windows, stepped inside, and then used hatchets, axes, and hammers to break bottles and roll kegs outside, emptying their contents into the street. All told, half a dozen establishments lost twenty-five hundred to three thousand gallons of liquor. Warrants were issued for the arrest of fifty-seven women; they pleaded not guilty and were eventually cleared of most charges.[2]

Drusilla's feisty spirit and sense of justice would live on in young Helen and serve her well in the future. Little did Helen know that moral integrity and standing up for what she thought was right would be traits that she would lean into throughout her life. At the same time, as Helen noted years later, "the little town where I grew up was full of Victorian houses, great trees from the original forest, and people with circumscribed minds."[3] That, too, would be a cross for her to bear in relations with her mother and others she encountered throughout her life.

Helen's father was a factory foreman at the American Pad & Textile Company, holding a key position in the organization. The company had been founded by entrepreneur Edward L. McClain, who in the 1880s had invented a horse pad that prevented the collar from irritating the neck of the animal. McClain's pad was adjusted at the bottom with a flexible metal hook that slipped over the edge of the horse collar and held it firmly in place.[4] McClain worked on his idea at his father's harness shop, perfected the design of the metal hook, and then manufactured the first pad in 1881. By 1887, the company was producing 300 dozen pads a day and employing 250 workers. For the next several decades the company grew, and its pad collars could be found in nearly every harness and saddlery shop in the United States and Canada. McClain's success led him to build for the city in 1912 a state-of-the-art high school, which to this day bears his name.[5]

Thomas and Hannah pampered their new daughter, relieved she was healthy. Hannah recorded every detail of Helen's growth in a baby biography book, noting pets she had, including a pony stabled at the back of their large lot at 323 South Street in Greenfield. Thomas purchased a camera so he could record her childhood moments, with the usual shots of Helen playing or standing in the garden. As was common for the well-to-do at the time, Hannah had Helen sit for a studio portrait each year.[6]

Helen's love of animals came at an early age. In addition to the pony, she had at least three dogs and two cats during her childhood. Helen and her father set the leg of a rooster that had been trapped, and she kept it in a cage in her backyard. When the rooster recovered and grew big enough for the family to harvest, Helen's flood of tears forced her father to reconsider. He traded the healthy rooster for another that they had not become attached to, easing Helen's objections.[7] Helen was also excited when a pair of screech owls nested in their basement, encouraged by her father who left an open window as he welcomed their mousing abilities. The owls reared three young and protected the furnace room from any domestic intrusions. Their occasional calls in the night echoed through the duct work of the house in a ghostly manner, captivating Helen.[8]

Given the large home and Thomas's position at the pad factory, the Blackburns were considered prominent citizens of Greenfield, and Hannah made sure that her daughter had access to the best of everything. Helen often took the train with her mother to visit relatives in Oberlin and Cincinnati. Being an only child, she loved to play with cousins and appreciated the aunts and uncles who doted on her. Hannah, being the oldest of eight siblings, was the matriarch of her family.[9]

Helen's enrollment in kindergarten in 1915 was so emotional for Hannah that Helen's aunt had to take her to school on the first day. It was also during this time that Helen's initial urge to write came about when she read the mystery *The Circular Staircase* by Mary Roberts Rinehart, *Little Women* and *Little Men* by Louisa May Alcott, and the Edgar Rice Burroughs novel *Tarzan of the Apes*. Helen recalled later that she was always scribbling, and her mother was chasing her outside to play with other children. "Since I was older mentally and very near-sighted, I was hardly a success at games. This was no disappointment because I liked to read and write and think."[10] Although there is no record of her having been tested during her school years, Helen claimed later in life that she had a very high IQ, which made it less difficult for her in school.[11]

For an only child living in a privileged family in Greenfield, the cultural opportunities were boundless. At age eleven, Helen enrolled in dance classes at the Eagles' Hall. At her mother's insistence, she also started piano lessons, which she would enjoy all her life. Daily practice and recitals where she played difficult pieces with aplomb made Helen a sought-after pianist at school and church, and she entertained her mother's social clubs. She played both classic pieces and contemporary music, including jazz and ragtime, popular in the 1920s when Helen was coming of age.

Helen further elaborated on these tranquil days in a letter to a friend toward the end of her life:

> Being "lonely" as a child was right for me. My interests were years ahead of my age & I couldn't see across a room. Together that cut me out of physical games & gave me little interest in parties. After I begged my father for glasses at 13, after I happened to look through some that fitted my eyes, things might have changed. However, my parents, having been teen-agers in the 1870's & '80's, banned dancing, "mixed parties," automobiles, etc. So I settled back to read & study.[12]

Helen's father, a hunter, believed that something familiar to a child was not dangerous. He therefore taught his daughter how to handle guns when she was barely old enough to lift his .22 rifle. One summer during her youth, a neighbor's grandson boasted about his abilities with an air gun. Helen, not wanting it assumed that as a girl she was not capable of shooting a gun, shot and killed a red-tailed hawk, collecting a two-dollar bounty from the county office, since hawks were considered a nuisance. While she was proud to have bested the boy and be the recipient of her parents' praise for her marksmanship, she realized the graceful bird she watched every day from her bedroom window would fly no more. It would be something she regretted later in life.[13]

Reading, especially mysteries, was something Helen really enjoyed. During Miss James's seventh-grade study hall, she was absorbed in a detective magazine held between the pages of her geography textbook—until the teacher approached from behind and removed the magazine, depositing it in the trash. When Helen returned to the study hall after class to retrieve the magazine, Miss James was waiting, and Helen made "ill-advised" remarks about her father's position in town, the school board, and how the teacher should not have a role in her choice of reading materials. In turn, Miss James assigned Helen an extracurricular paper that would take a half-hour to read aloud entitled "Our Western National Parks."[14]

Helen anticipated disliking everything about national parks by being forced to write a paper about them. But her attitude changed as she did her research and started to compose her paper, becoming more interested in the natural world of trees, rocks, and waters. As required, she read the paper to her class, and at the end she couldn't resist a parting flourish: "Some day I intend to live in one of the parks where there will be no one to bother me while I read and write about what I see."[15]

When Helen moved up to McClain High School in 1923, she found plenty of academic and extracurricular pursuits to hold her attention. Classwork was graded on a scale of 75 to 100 percent, and Helen earned no grade less than 92 percent in any subject. She took English her sophomore and junior years, Latin and music all four years, and the required algebra, plane geometry, advanced algebra, chemistry, and physics. She continued her piano playing, serving as a pianist for the orchestra as well as the Epworth League, the youth group of the Methodist Church the family attended. She was in the operetta for three years and the glee club for six years. She also won first prize in the Sophomore English Classes Scrap Book Contest.[16] Despite her reluctance to play outside and be physically active, Helen participated on the girls' basketball team in her freshman and sophomore years, as well as girls' baseball. She was also busy with other endeavors, being elected to the National Honor Society her senior year, joining Quill and Scroll, and being a member of the Alethean Society, which promoted literary education, for which Helen served as a critic. She excelled in debate.[17] She was also active in the journalism department and was on the staff of the school annual, *The Dragon*. In a bit of early writing, Helen authored the class poem, voicing the usual appreciation to teachers, a recognition of knowledge gained, and an acknowledgment that the high school had prepared its students well and was sending them into the world brimming with optimism for the future.

Helen also had a busy social life and circle of friends, many of whom shared the same interests. Two of her best girlfriends were Virginia "Ginger" Caldwell and Lillian "Sprousie" Sprouse. Helen's nickname was "Drusy"—short for her middle name, Drusilla—and the three palled around together, giving parties and luncheons for each other, which were reported in the society columns of the Greenfield newspaper. Summers included hiking and going on picnics or swimming at the local country club. Saturday afternoons were spent at the matinee movie theater, which in the 1920s added sound to the moving picture and quickly grew in popularity.[18]

Helen was so coddled in her upbringing and her parents were so Victorian in their attitudes that she was not allowed to go to school events or private homes at night unless one or both of her parents went along.[19] For a while Helen was allowed a boyfriend, one who was carefully screened by her mother as to background, hobbies, and church affiliation. It also proved convenient that he had an older brother, who, with his wife, accompanied them if they planned to go farther afield than the high school football game.[20]

There was no question Helen would go on to college, and her mother's choice was for her to become a teacher of classic languages, a logical profession for women during that time.[21] Helen chose Ohio University in Athens, about eighty-five miles east of Greenfield and easily accessible by train. Helen had wanted to study literature and creative writing, so she compromised and chose to major in Latin when she entered school.[22]

Helen jumped into the hubbub of college life, moving into Boyd Hall, a girls' dormitory on campus. Even though Helen's social life at home was tightly controlled, she was now able to engage in activities befitting the emerging rebellious youth of the 1920s. Gone were the long curls of junior high, as Helen was now sporting a bob cut hairstyle. Her shoes were high heels worn with sheer silk hose; dresses were shorter than what she wore in high school. She and her girlfriends would linger outside the dormitory, touching up the orange rouge and Tangee lipstick that were all the rage, jingling their long earrings as they eyed the boys, who in turn were looking the girls over.[23]

Hannah sent long letters to Helen, reporting on happenings in Greenfield, as well as seeking advice and opinions from her daughter. She would pose questions, numbering them, and noted that if Helen answered all of them, she would receive extra spending money. She also reminded Helen that any grade less than an A was not acceptable.[24]

Despite having more freedom, Helen was also bitterly homesick, as was her roommate, who contracted scarlet fever and was sent home while Helen was quarantined to her room. Not wanting to stay on campus only to be sequestered, Helen took the train home and had hoped to surprise her parents. Instead, her mother, assuming the worst from an unexpected visit home, thought she had been expelled. Helen was stunned by her mother's talent for conjuring up disaster. Once Helen returned to school, she discovered her mother's behavior had cured her of any homesickness, and she focused on her studies.[25]

During that freshman year, Helen dated Brian Andrews,[26] five years her senior. He was a science major she met while waiting to check out laboratory equipment. He was lanky, fair-skinned, and fair-haired, and she was immediately smitten. He picked her up in his new Whippet Coupe with a rumble seat after the Christmas holiday to drive her back to school. They continued going out until he disclosed to Helen that he had previously contracted tuberculosis. His cough had returned; his doctor said rest and care would clear it up, so he was leaving school and not returning until he was better.[27] Brian's plan was to work until he got well, and he promised that when he got settled, he would come back for her.

Helen finished her first year of college uncertain about her future with Brian. She came home to Greenfield for the summer and planned to return to Ohio University in the fall to continue her studies.

On July 3, 1928, a hot, sultry summer evening, Helen decided to sit and play the piano while her father read the paper and her mother engaged in small talk about the church's plan for a mission in Africa. As Helen played, the phone rang, and her father took a call. He returned to the room, grim-faced, and said he was taking the morning train to Cincinnati to see his broker. The previous March had been the beginning of the "Great Bull Market," with stock prices rising until the Great Crash in October 1929. But June 1928 had seen a small falloff of the bull market, precipitating the call from Thomas's broker.[28]

At eight in the morning on July 4, Thomas suffered a heart attack. By nine in the morning he had died. Helen's devastated mother had to be put to bed under sedation. While the rest of Greenfield celebrated the holiday with picnics, parades, and fireworks, Helen, with the help of a neighbor, struggled to make funeral arrangements for her father.[29]

Following the funeral and burial, her father's lawyer disclosed that the stock market falloff had been serious for Thomas Blackburn. There was very little money left: the house was heavily mortgaged, and his life insurance policy had lapsed. This came as a shock to both mother and daughter. They considered Thomas to be a smart business executive in addition to being a respected pillar of the community.[30]

The little good news was that they had enough money for Helen to return to school for one more year. She did so in the fall of 1928, this time staying in a private rooming house in Athens in the fall, and then another one in the spring. A private residence at college afforded her the opportunity to do whatever she wished without the interference of a dormitory monitor or her overprotective mother.

At the end of Helen's first semester, her academic counselor suggested that she give up her mother's idea of teaching classic languages and go into the sciences. He had seen her aptitude for the latter and in her saw potential. Helen switched her major to chemistry, recognizing she was making her first important independent decision. And she knew that by studying in the sciences, she would have a better chance at work than if she had pursued teaching Latin and Greek.[31]

Following Helen's return from Ohio University with no money to continue, there was little opportunity for employment, as she only had two years of college. Helen and her mother fretted about what to do next, eventually coming to loggerheads in a "council of war," as she remembered it years later. Helen thought it best that they sell their furniture, elaborate furnishings, and the expansive house, get what they could for it, and find a new location to start over. Hannah's plans were different; she insisted they should go and stay at the family home in Cincinnati where Hannah's sister and brothers lived; they would take them in, and Helen could seek secretarial training there. In the meantime, they could rent out the Greenfield house and return later.[32]

Helen could see the future her mother envisioned: following the same prescribed activities, playing piano for her mother's groups and clubs, and listening each evening about that day's bridge party, missionary meeting, or papers read at the club. Each event attended by the same small circle of friends with small-town attitudes and morals, all while trading insinuating gossip. Helen had no intention of becoming an old maid putting on her own hen parties in the evening while following in her mother's footsteps in the same social clubs and groups.[33] In this sense, Greenfield was not much different from Gopher Prairie, the fictional rural town of Sinclair Lewis's *Main Street,* satirized for many of the same conservative and narrow-minded values that existed in Helen's hometown.[34]

Helen also bristled at the thought of becoming "poor relations" to her aunt and uncles in Cincinnati, with their lives dependent on them. She wanted a place where they could build a life of their own, and the two went round and round discussing alternatives. Finally exasperated with Hannah's obstinance, Helen suggested her mother could go stay with family because she was going to set out for Chicago. Hannah, hysterical at the thought of Helen going to Chicago by herself, insisted she better go along and look after her daughter's welfare in the wicked city.[35]

# 2

# Grit and Perseverance

*Chicago, 1929–1937*

IN THE SUMMER OF 1929, Helen and Hannah left Greenfield and took the train to Chicago, arriving at the Central Station on the Chicago lakefront opposite Grant Park. It was one of the large railroad stations people disembarked from when arriving in the Windy City, and it was considered by many to be the most beautiful. The red-brick Romanesque-style structure resembled a castle accented by a 225-foot clock tower.

Located across from the train station was the YWCA, where Hannah hoped to stay while they sorted out their future. There were no rooms available, so they moved over to the elegant Blackstone Hotel, and Helen wryly observed that her mother was acting as if their status in life had not changed. But she also knew the stay at the hotel would need to be temporary given their precarious financial situation.

While Hannah would look back forlornly on the past, Helen sensed something special in Chicago. To her, the city pulsed with life and energy. It so differed from her life in Ohio, where she felt nothing ever happened and there was little opportunity for her.[1]

Looking out her hotel room window, Helen excitedly watched people hurrying to work on the sidewalks below. She was reminded of something her counselor at Ohio University, Dean Wells, told her when encouraging her to shift her studies into the sciences. Typically, students were required to take one class in economics and one in sociology, but recognizing Helen's intellect, he released her from taking those courses. "If your circumstances at home don't change, you won't need them. If they do, you're the type to get that knowledge from living." Helen would find herself meeting and competing with all kinds of people in a world that would be far more different from anything she could imagine.[2]

Helen started to look for work, leaving applications at employment agencies she found through the telephone directory. Hannah was aghast that her daughter could not find employment, but Helen understood why. In these early days of the Depression, her well-to-do appearance worked against her, as well as not having the qualifications to do anything. She knew she was good at chemical analysis from her two years at college, but no one was seeking "female laboratory help." She was literate but could not type, further limiting her options. She was told she would make a good proofreader, but that required union membership, which was difficult to obtain.[3]

Mother and daughter also needed to solve the problem of where they were going to live. Furnished apartments were too expensive; they couldn't afford to buy furniture, so instead Hannah looked for a room to rent while Helen looked for work. Helen was nineteen years old and her mother fifty-eight.

They found a sparsely furnished first floor kitchenette apartment in a building a few blocks from the busy intersection of Wilson and Broadway in the Uptown neighborhood. The bathroom was down the hall. The proprietor was an understanding woman who gave Helen information on stores in the neighborhood, directing her to a reasonable delicatessen around the corner. She even brought in a table lamp for them to use, making the room cheerier. Helen noted how well the woman had sized them up.

Helen slept on the sofa. Her mother, with breathing troubles, chose to sleep in a large chair. Once they settled in for the night, Helen heard mice under the bed; she also woke up with a rash. Upon closer inspection, Hannah discovered bedbugs and was off to the building manager. They were relocated to a new room while the furniture was fumigated.

Once that episode was behind them, Helen focused on finding work. She could call employment agencies, but pay-phone calls cost five cents; she remembered there was a branch post office nearby and postcards were only one cent. She decided on postcards and sent them to agencies. She also stopped in at employment agencies, with no luck. The phone in their apartment hallway rarely rang, further discouraging her. Feeling less and less hopeful about searching the newspaper want ads, she found a neighborhood paper with an ad for a company downtown seeking general office work, no experience required. She took a streetcar and applied for a job at the Henry Paulson Co., which handled mailings of advertising circulars for its clients. Dave Adams, one of the co-owners, saw in Helen a hard worker with great potential. She was hired. The pay was fifteen dollars a week, and Helen worked Monday through Saturday, from seven in the morning to six in the evening, with a half-hour for lunch. It would be tight, but Helen and her mother could get by. Rent was $5.50 a week and the streetcar $0.84; that left $8.66 for food, clothing, and all their other needs.[4]

On her first day of work, Helen joined other women at a long table to assemble the mailers and stuff them into envelopes, seal them, and affix a stamp for mailing. She caught on right away and turned out mailers quickly. While the work wasn't difficult, it was repetitive. Helen tried to make friends with coworkers, but she was not welcomed by the group. She thought it might be because she wasn't from Chicago, or perhaps because she was a fast learner; regardless, lunch breaks were difficult, so she took to going out. Helen discovered the main library, where she checked out books, particularly the mysteries she so enjoyed reading back in Greenfield. She also stopped in at a dime store and bought some stationery so she and Hannah could write to friends back home. Helen thought this would give her mother something to do during the day while she was away at work.

Expecting her mother to be pleased by this gesture, Helen instead found Hannah indignant at the thought of communicating with their friends back in Greenfield, risking their shaky status with those they knew. Hannah's reasoning was that people came to Chicago now and again. If their friends came to look them up and saw their diminished station in life, Hannah would be embarrassed. Hannah forbade Helen from writing to anyone back home.

Helen corresponded anyway, sending a note to her college boyfriend Brian Andrews. She wanted to explain her abrupt departure from Greenfield and hoped his health was on the mend. Those carefree days at college provided Helen with warm memories of better times.

In October, Helen was asked to run the hand-operated Addressograph machine. The other co-owner of the company, Jed Adams, did not care for Helen; she did not sign out when she left the floor and took too much time in the restroom. He knew she had some college experience, so he left her to figure out how to operate the equipment. That's when Jake Moskowitz, the shipping clerk, stepped in to introduce himself and give her a crash course in operating the Addressograph. Once Jake felt confident of her abilities, she was on her way.

Given the challenging economic times, Helen dug in and worked hard, wanting to make sure she was perceived as worth keeping on should there be a need to let people go. She had mastered the Addressograph and had completed her day's quota by three in the afternoon, shifting to help the others with stuffing and sealing the circulars. She grudgingly earned the respect of others because she was willing to help them for the benefit of all.

During a break, Helen asked Jake why she was not welcomed by the other women. He laid it out simply: "It's what you are: a lady, good manners, perfect English, college education, expensive clothes. They think you are a rich bitch holding down a job other people need, while you see how the other half lives." He noted that Dave Adams recognized her potential and had paid high, by his standards, to get her.[5]

The worsening economic situation finally had a significant impact. The company announced it was cutting everyone by six hours' pay and laid off five workers. Now Helen would receive $13.64 a week, essentially eliminating any chance of finding a better place to live.[6]

While Helen struggled with social engagement at work, interactions with her mother became more challenging. Hannah complained of the conditions under which they were living, ascribing it to Helen's stubbornness in moving to Chicago. This was frustrating for Helen, who took the streetcar downtown every cold, damp winter day, usually working with a cold and slight fever. If she was even fifteen minutes late arriving home at night, Hannah would rant. Helen's temper was short and her optimism frayed by the reduced paycheck. During the Saturday afternoons that Helen now had off, she entertained herself by going to the library to keep a distance from ugly scenes with her mother.[7]

Helen and Hannah's neighborhood reflected the economic challenges of the day. Tenants in the apartment building moved out; in one case, two people were replaced by five in one room. Panhandling and petty crime began to appear on the side streets, and the building proprietor needed to keep doors locked to prevent break-ins.

However, the difficult times had their upside. Vacancy signs started appearing in apartment building windows, affording Helen the opportunity to seek better accommodations. On a Saturday excursion she found a likely spot, at 847 Sunnyside Avenue, on a wide street of three-story apartment buildings, which appeared to have front lawns and shrubbery. Greenery would be nice once winter was over. The apartment was furnished and had a living room, kitchenette, and tiled bathroom; the last was a bonus, considering they were currently walking down the hall to use a shared bathroom. There were windows to the street and side, providing adequate ventilation. At thirty-two dollars a month it was more than they could afford, but the building manager indicated Helen and her mother were the type of people she wanted in the apartment building. With a little negotiating for a year's lease, which gave them a month free, and the opportunity for her mother to help the manager answer the office phone a few days a week, they struck a deal at twenty-nine dollars a month.

Proud that she had found an apartment, Helen hurried home to share the good news with her mother. Instead, Hannah burst into tears, not believing that her daughter was capable of finding a suitable place while also berating her for not being content with where they were living.

Despite this outburst, they moved to the new building, and seeing that it was indeed a better apartment, Hannah's mood brightened. She immediately took a liking to the building manager, and the idea of working in the office to answer the phone and have access to the goings-on in the building pleased her to no end. Helen celebrated by buying Christmas cards that could carry their return address, and she sent them off to friends and family, including her college beau Brian.

By spring of 1930 Helen had not heard from Brian or any of her friends from home. She wondered about his health and was surprised he had not written since she had shared a return address. She wondered what had changed, given he was so confident in declaring he would seek her out once he was settled. She hoped he had not had a change of heart.

As summer approached, mother and daughter found ways to break the routine. On Saturday afternoons after work, they would take a picnic lunch to the park down the street or go to the expansive Montrose Beach just beyond so Helen could swim in Lake Michigan. Sometimes Helen would take in a matinee. The stifling heat of a Chicago summer was another first for Helen and Hannah. Accustomed to cooling nights in Greenfield, the concrete of the buildings and the blacktop of the streets retained the heat in the city.

Over the July 4th holiday, the building where Helen worked was shuttered for three days. When she arrived for work on Monday the acrid air was suffocating. The reason for the stench became obvious when Helen located a dead rat under the Addressograph machine. Jed Adams happened upon the scene and saw Helen, who was revolted by the discovery. Never really taken with Helen, Jed ordered her to throw it out the window and get to work. Helen was furious. She had put up with enough of his abuse. Standing among her coworkers, she scooped up the dead rat with a piece of cardboard and threw it at Jed, striking him in the chest. Helen thought he was going to attack her, but instead he ran out the front door. While the room caught its breath, Johnny Polanski, one of the men who unloaded crates and had been standing behind her, assured Helen the brothers wouldn't fire her. If Jed had come for her, Johnny would have intervened on her behalf. He, too, had seen enough of Jed's intimidating behavior over the years and was looking for his own chance to settle the score. Helen had now earned the respect of the women she worked with. The incident never came up again, and Jed kept his distance.[8]

Helen now fell into a routine and actually enjoyed the long, dull hours of work. She gradually made friends with one of her coworkers, Marya Stike, who asked if she was willing to double-date with her and her boyfriend Frankie, who had a friend. Marya said her boyfriend's buddy was quiet and intelligent, and she thought he would be a good fit for Helen. Plus, he had a car. Despite her doubts and the fact she had still not heard from Brian, Helen decided it would be a fun evening out.

On September 13, 1930, Marya, Frankie, and Helen's date pulled up in an old touring car. He was introduced as Adrian Hoover—or Ade, as he preferred. Helen sat in front, and as Ade drove he pointed out various landmarks to Helen, using the informal tour guide routine as a way to break the ice. He had bought the car at a junkyard for five dollars, and with a liking for cars and things mechanical he had done the work to get it running. Given her technical background, Helen was pleased she could ask questions that didn't sound too dumb, as she was interested in his knowledge of engines. Ade worked as a set-up man on screw machines at Stewart–Warner, a company that made instrumentation equipment.

The four spent the evening at a local roadhouse, with Ade and Helen making small talk while her coworker and boyfriend bickered. At the end of the evening, Ade dropped off the other couple, and Helen and Ade picked up some hamburgers at an all-night restaurant and drove home. Ade didn't think much of the date and doubted Helen would even want to go out again—but she gave him her phone number when he asked.

When Ade called two weeks later, Helen was thrilled. Ade admitted it took him that long to work up the nerve to call. On a Sunday he showed up trimmed and pressed, making an impression on Hannah with his appearance and politeness. They were off to the Lincoln Park Zoo for a leisurely fall afternoon wandering around, eating popcorn and peanuts and feeding the squirrels.

Ade originally told Helen he had been orphaned, but as they got to know each other and he felt more comfortable with her, more of his story came out. His parents divorced when he was eight, and he had not seen his father, William, since. His mother, Eusebia, could not support Ade, so she left him in the care of various orphanages while she went to secretarial school and looked for work. Ade started working at eleven years old, delivering newspapers in St. Louis. In 1922, when he was twelve, he was sent to live with an uncle in Seattle, where he also delivered newspapers and worked picking apples in Wenatchee. Eventually he found his way back to Chicago looking for better work.[9]

Once in the city, he scraped around doing all sorts of odd jobs. He worked as a Western Union messenger until his bike was stolen. He labored three summers for an ice man, worked at a plant that assembled radio sets, and in between jobs plucked chickens. He was interested in electricity and wanted something in that field but couldn't find the right job. Ade even assembled roller bearings at the International Harvester foundry, working in the stockroom. He did what he could to get by and bought a series of cars that he fixed and kept running.[10]

Ade wrote letters to Helen after every date, often hand-delivering them to her place of work. He did this nearly every day for the seven years of their courtship. Helen did the same, firing off short notes and flirtations while on break at work. She would post them in the building's lobby mailbox.[11]

While Ade was aware that his writing, spelling, and grammar were not great, he was good at drawing and wanted to be an artist. Helen encouraged him, and they both talked of ways he might be able to attend school for this talent, even though he had no money.

They spent Saturday and Sunday afternoons driving through the various ethnic neighborhoods of Chicago, taking in the shops and markets. They explored all parts of the city, from quaint communities to the magnificent homes on Michigan, Calumet, and Prairie Avenues. They ventured into the industrial parts of the city as well, from the rail yards to the factories. Ade even drove her by Al Capone's headquarters on Twenty-Second Street, where armed guards hung around the entrance. When the weather turned cold, they visited free indoor places like the Art Institute of Chicago, the recently opened Adler Planetarium, and the new Shedd Aquarium.

Hannah seemed to like Ade, and Helen had him join them for Christmas dinner, with her mother presiding over a fancy meal. Ade lived by himself and eked by on his $12.60 weekly salary, but he was not able to eat well, much to Helen's concern. When possible, they had him over for meals on Saturday or Sunday nights.

One Saturday after Helen arrived home from work, Hannah confronted her. The manager at their former apartment building had brought over a message with the name of a man and a phone number. Hannah demanded to know who he was, assuming the worst. The number was a downtown exchange and Helen didn't recognize it. Hannah thought otherwise, ripped up the note, and flushed it down the toilet. "I forbid you to return calls to strange men!" she exclaimed.[12]

Helen was incredulous. She went out the door to call the apartment proprietor and learned it had been someone who had received Helen's name from an employment service. They were urgently looking for someone for a proofreading job that paid twenty dollars a week. Could she come by immediately?

Helen caught the "L" train downtown, arriving at the Builders

Building on South Wacker Drive. The man who had called was with the Audit Bureau of Circulations. She filled out a brief application and was given a sample of papers to check for errors. Noting she quickly and accurately proofread the document, the employer said, "Fine. We run eight to five Monday through Friday and eight to noon on Saturday. We have a lot of rush seasons, so pay 50 cents for supper and Saturday lunch; 75 cents for Sunday if we need to call you in. I'd like you to start Monday."[13]

He asked about her giving notice, but Helen shook her head. "They'd be startled if anyone gave notice. I'll be here."

By the time Helen left, the weather had turned into an all-out blizzard, and it took two hours to reach her stop. She slogged several blocks in knee-deep snow and finally reached home, cold, wet, and exhausted.

Hannah looked at her disheveled daughter and announced, "Drunk, of course!" and again assumed the worst. All Helen could do was laugh and tell her mother she had gotten the job at better pay and went to take a hot shower. Hannah's hysterics had once again ruined what should have been a moment to celebrate.[14]

Helen made her way through the snow to the office on Monday morning, thrilled to do a job that was more suited to her abilities and paying six dollars more per week. She loved the professional atmosphere downtown. The office had windows with a view of Lake Michigan. The building had a small lunch spot in the lobby and a candy and snack shop as well as a newsstand. Plus, as she soon learned, her colleagues respected her professionalism.

Helen's new boss, Mr. Johnson, introduced her to colleagues and press operators, then handed her a stack of proofs to review. The work required close attention because there were many figures and place names to check, but in general Helen adapted quickly. At the end of the week when she received her first paycheck, she felt rich. Helen had hoped to keep some money for herself, but Hannah had already gone through most of the savings they had from Ohio, so to avoid an argument she went along with giving her mother more.

The following week, Helen came home to find her closet empty of several of her work dresses. When she asked if her mother had sent them out for cleaning, Hannah replied that she threw them out. "You're working in a nice office now and your clothes are out of style. Skirts are longer and showing your legs to your knees is an open invitation since you say you'll be coming home at all hours. You can buy new ones."[15]

Helen bristled at this attempt to control her, especially on matters of fashion. In order to afford new clothes, and not willing to carry lunch, Helen got some retribution by telling Hannah the money would need to come out of the food budget. Helen got three new dresses, and the two of them subsisted on a dinner of cornmeal, oleo, and salt for several weeks.

Ade and Helen continued to explore the city, checking out the ethnic neighborhoods and enjoying the variety of foods one could find. One Saturday afternoon Ade introduced Helen to pizza at an Italian deli off an alley downtown. As they waited for it to be prepared, they got to talking about food. Ade indicated there were all sorts of different and exciting foods at the neighborhood church festivals, whether they were Italian, Polish, or German. Helen thought it was all so exotic, confessing that during her upbringing in Ohio anything much farther afield than beef, fried chicken, and potatoes was considered fancy. Where she was raised, Helen explained, there were distinctions between people in her parents' social group (mostly people of English heritage) and other groups who were "different"—meaning poor, Black, or foreign. Helen noted that even the Irish were considered suspect because they were Catholic. Second- or third-generation Germans or French were acceptable, especially if they were Protestant.

Helen related that her father never had a car, given he was employed by a company that made horse collars; he thought they were a passing fad. If they needed to go somewhere like Cincinnati, they took the train. She also told Ade about the age difference between her parents and how they had come of age in the Victorian era. With all of the changes following World War I, everyone was "so fixed in their ways and so sure the hometown was the center of the universe that they couldn't have changed had they wanted to."[16]

Ade's car was dependable in warm weather, so on a spring Sunday he and Helen took Hannah and a picnic lunch to one of the forest preserves just outside the city. While Helen and Ade enjoyed these excursions away from the sooty, crowded streets, Hannah was more guarded. She disliked the blue-collar families who also gathered at these parks and declined future invitations to go along.

That w s welcome news for Helen and Ade and provided the opportunity ⌐ extend their trips farther out of the city. One day they went for lunch at Lake Geneva in Wisconsin, about a two-hour drive north. Another time they drove south to Joliet, passing by the state penitentiary. Sometimes they went to the south side of Chicago to watch molten slag being poured at the steel mills, or they visited Calumet Harbor to glimpse the large ore boats being unloaded. These diversions were inexpensive, and they provided privacy and time together.[17]

On Sunday, September 13, 1931, on the anniversary of their first meeting, they started out early in the morning to what Ade described as "his special place," more than a hundred miles away.

"We'll want plenty of time," Ade said. "You'll know what I mean when you see it."[18]

Several hours later, they arrived at White Pines Forest State Park, due west of Chicago. The area was home to the southernmost last stand of old-growth white pine in the region, and their trunks rose majestically above the bluffs of the Pine and Spring Creeks that pass through the park. It was a serene location to wander about, with a pine cone and needle-cushioned earth. Ade and Helen enjoyed lunch on a rocky bank at the base of a large pine tree.

"When I was in seventh grade, I wrote a paper about national parks and read about trees like this," Helen recalled.

Ade replied, "Once I stayed with an aunt and uncle who homesteaded near Seattle. I saw lots of evergreens, some larger than these. I thought I'd like to live in the woods for a while."

Helen sighed. "That would be wonderful."

"Well, why don't we . . . some day?"

"Yes. We'll do that."

Ade then reached into his pocket, produced a small diamond ring, slipped it on Helen's finger, and proposed.

The following Friday Ade was laid off.

✳ ✳ ✳

If Hannah noticed Helen's engagement ring, she said nothing of it. Ade found a cheaper place to live, and they cut back on their driving adventures. In December when the car needed expensive repairs, Ade opted to sell it for twenty-five dollars, reasoning the money would buy lots of bus and train tokens.

Helen's apartment manager received a console radio for Christmas and gave Hannah her old table model, providing hours of pleasure for her mother and much-needed entertainment for Ade and Helen, who couldn't get out as much now. Other entertainments included jigsaw puzzles, which Helen obtained from the lending library in the Builders Building where she worked. Hannah's youngest brother, Edward Gomersall, moved to Chicago as part of his job as a regional manager for Fox Films and provided free movie passes for two that could be used at neighborhood theaters. Hannah and a friend used those passes during the week, and Helen and Ade took full advantage of them on evenings and weekends.

One spring day in 1932, Hannah took ill, and Helen had the apartment building manager send for a doctor. He diagnosed a mild gallbladder irritation, prescribed medication, and admonished Hannah to eat less rich food. Ade, who had been waiting in the apartment office downstairs, was showing signs of malnutrition, and the doctor asked to have a word with Helen. He told her that the man she was seeing did not look well and needed to eat more.

Helen gently told Ade what the doctor said. He admitted he wasn't getting much to eat but hadn't wanted to bother Helen, given she had enough problems with her mother. He had been eating at Salvation Army soup kitchens and sleeping in "L" stations until he was chased out. He eventually found a place to stay when he ran into an old friend who said his parents would take him in. Ade wanted to help pay his way, but without a job he was not able to contribute, so Ade slept there but declined to accept any food.

Ade had worked odd jobs up to this point, cleaning windows and picking chickens in the market, and he hoped for a laborer job on construction of the new State Street subway station in downtown Chicago. He had also learned about a job at an agency that made advertising mats, which are short feature stories designed to look like a newspaper article;

he could start as an apprentice, making three dollars for five days of work. Even though it was less pay than his previous job, Helen encouraged him to try his hand at drawing to see if it was something he could turn into a career.

By this time, the Great Depression was having a bigger impact on Chicago. Men looking for work stood in lines outside employment agencies. More people were seen selling apples on street corners (a common occurrence) or simply panhandling for change. Shack towns started to show up on vacant lots and in parks, and the homeless huddled under bridges and slept in alleys and parks. Businesses closed, banks failed, and factories cut workers and hours.[19]

Helen experienced a 10 percent pay cut, and the weekend meal expense for overtime was eliminated, but she was grateful to have a job. Ade came for dinner on Sundays, so Helen had some sense of relief in being able to keep him fed, although she wasn't so sure he was eating well the rest of the week. They scraped by as many did during the Depression. Helen would stand in line for hours just to get a cheap pot roast for dinner; she bought broken cookies at a discount and two-day old bread for much less. To earn back some money, Ade rented out his "L"-train pass to others going around town doing errands.

There was little left over, but they would pinch pennies so they could indulge in a candy bar at the movie theater or an ice cream cone. Small pleasures gained in importance, and Helen appreciated the little treats more than the big ones.

Franklin Roosevelt's election in 1932 had brought significant change. When he took office in March 1933, he began working with Congress to enact sweeping legislation to address the country's Depression. Beer came back in the first hundred days of the administration, with full repeal of Prohibition in December.[20]

One day after work while walking in the Loop, Helen bumped into George, an old college friend who had been a fraternity brother of her boyfriend Brian. After a round of greetings, they ducked into a diner to catch up over coffee. George was trying to get back to Iowa, having had no luck finding work in Chicago. The conversation eventually turned to Brian, and George asked what had happened between them. Helen said she had sent him a Christmas card but had never heard from him. George said that Brian had written back, suggesting he come visit for Christmas, but the letter had been marked "return to sender."

"That was just before he died," George added. "He really loved you and wanted to marry you and take you with him."[21]

Helen was shocked. She had no idea Brian had died. But as difficult as the news was, she was grateful that she finally knew what had happened to him. It also hinted at why she had not heard back from others that she had sent letters to. She suspected that her mother, always worried about appearances, must have confiscated the mail when Helen was at work.

Helen returned to the office to calm down and compose a plan of action. She now knew her mother had run interference on the mail, as she had originally threatened to do. Rather than confront her at this point, she decided to send a letter from work to her cousin Janet, another person she had written to, who was Hannah's goddaughter. Janet and Helen had been close until they were sixteen, when something happened that fractured the relationship between them and their mothers. Helen didn't know what had caused that rift. Still, Janet had wished Helen well in her move to Chicago, so Helen had reached out that first Christmas but received no response.

A week later, Helen received a reply. Janet was pleased to hear from Helen and provided an update on her life. She also shared the story of what had caused the rift between their families. Janet had confided to Hannah that she had kissed seven boys, which when passed along as gossip to Hannah's circle of women friends implied the girl had been intimate with seven boys. Janet's parents understood that was not possibly true and immediately knew Hannah had helped spread the gossip. They forbade further contact between the cousins and the two families.

Helen was mortified. She had been oblivious to all of this at the time, likely shielded by her mother with some sort of concocted reason for the falling out. There was no point in bringing up the revelation now; Hannah would only get hysterical and deny it. Helen worked over everything in her mind, trying to grasp the lengths to which Hannah would go. Her mother had been old-fashioned, even puritanical, about morals and intentions, always placing events in the worst possible light. Helen now recognized that her mother was "secure in the belief that anything she did or said was for the best, and therefore right."[22] Helen decided to be wary lest a row with her mother scare Ade away. While she doubted Hannah could come between her and Ade, her mother certainly had been clever in estranging Brian from Helen.

The summer of 1933 afforded Helen and Ade another diversion: the Chicago World's Fair, held on the occasion of the city's centennial. And after Prohibition lifted, the couple spent time in the city's beer parlors and evenings exploring various drinkeries. Helen relished being away from her mother; Hannah resented her for it.[23] Ade was now doing free-lance artwork, and they had a little more money to expand their leisure time. They went to places like the Aragon Ballroom to hear the orchestra and to the Palace Theater where they could see vaudeville. By the summer of 1934 they were able to enjoy the second year of the Century of Progress, as the World's Fair was called.

While the couple continued to entertain themselves roaming the city, Ade bought a car for twenty-five dollars, giving them an opportunity to venture farther than before. Ade went to work doing illustrations for the telephone company's Yellow Pages and by 1936 had received enough of a raise for the two to start seriously discussing marriage. Seeing that they had a combined income of $52.50 a week, they went to City Hall to get their marriage license. They would be married by a judge there, avoiding expense and the fuss they expected from Hannah. They started to look for an apartment that would be suitable for all of them, deciding to make their home somewhere on the north side, near Lake Michigan for its parks and beaches, and the "L" for transportation into the city.

Just after Christmas, Helen discovered Hannah holding her purse and the marriage license. "You simply cannot marry that factory hand!" Hannah exclaimed. Helen reminded her mother that at age twenty-six she was no longer a minor and could marry when and whom she chose. She took the license and told her mother to never make a derogatory comment about Ade again and to stay out of her purse and her private life.[24]

The next time Ade came for dinner, Hannah was ready to try and take the upper hand. She informed Helen and Ade that it would take at least a year for her to find a suitable place for them to live, with furniture that would work for all of them. Before she could get any further, Ade cut in and told her the new apartment was going to be their apartment and Hannah was going to be their guest. Helen and Ade would tend to the details, and he hoped she would find it suitable. While Hannah's eyes held contempt for Ade, Helen could not have been happier to have him intervene and stand up to her mother.

Helen's uncle Edward, the Fox Film representative, and his wife Claire lived at 1120 Lake Shore Drive and offered to host the wedding at their spacious apartment. Helen and Ade wed on February 13, 1937, and moved into their new apartment at 1210 Jarvis Avenue, a block from Jarvis Beach on Lake Michigan. The unit was a few steps down from street level, making it easier for Hannah. They furnished their three-room apartment with bargain furniture, a chair-bed for Hannah, a sleeper sofa for their bedroom, and a deposit down on a baby grand piano for Helen. They even added a telephone.[25]

Ade's work continued to improve, and he started to get evening overtime hours, which he gladly took. Helen spent her spare evenings writing, hoping she could get something published. Most of these were short episodes, character studies, and some hard luck "slice of life" stories of several thousand words.[26] None appear to have been published, and Helen had little initial success until through a mutual acquaintance she met Jack Lally, the religion and literary editor for the *Chicago Daily News*. He offered to look over her samples at his after-work haunt on Randolph Street. It was here that Helen sold her first piece of writing, a short story for the Chicago Daily News Syndicate for which she was paid five dollars.[27]

While it wasn't much, it was a start.

# 3

# Marriage and Metallurgy

## Chicago, 1938–1953

BY 1938, WHEN ADE HAD BEEN EMPLOYED LONG ENOUGH to earn some time off, he, Helen, and Hannah went to Cincinnati so Helen's relatives could meet their new in-law. From there Helen took Ade to Greenfield, Ohio, to show him the house where she was born, McClain High School where she had been a student, and other sites around the town.[1]

Once back in Chicago, the Hoovers settled into a placid routine of working and exploring the city in their free time. With their double income they could afford to splurge and bought a used car, a 1935 LaSalle sedan, a less expensive but sporty and agile cousin of the Cadillac. Much more reliable than their previous Nash, now they could tour the neighborhoods in style and comfort.

Helen continued to write, developing characters and crafting short stories with different plotlines. Most were amateur in their themes and approach, but they kept her thinking about ways to write dialogue and develop a story arc. It is not clear whether any of these were submitted to her friend at the Chicago newspaper, and there is no record any were published.[2]

The Hoovers took their first vacation to Mexico in 1939, and on that occasion splurged and purchased an 8 mm Kodak movie camera, which had been introduced in 1932 for the home market. This was the beginning of a new hobby for Ade, making films of visits to Michigan, the Ozarks, Cincinnati, and street and park scenes around Chicago. Once shooting was done, Ade mailed the film to Kodak where it was developed, then returned.[3]

By the summer of 1939 they were at last ready to begin their search for the idyllic cabin in the forest that they had dreamed about for so long. Not surprisingly, Hannah objected, thinking that cabins were for sportsmen, not for a civilized, modern married couple. Helen fretted about whether her mother could stand to be alone for the two weeks of vacation, but Hannah's doctor said he'd check in on her. Hannah, who was now sixty-seven, was in no shape to go along anyway and was likely peeved that Ade and Helen wanted to spend time by themselves.[4]

Helen and Ade left the city without a plan, heading to Madison, Wisconsin, and then took side roads toward the national forests in the northern part of the state. They found tourist cabins near Wisconsin Rapids where they stayed their first night, enjoying steaks at a nearby roadside restaurant.

They pressed on, spending the rest of their vacation driving on dirt and gravel roads, seeking old-growth pines like they had seen at White Pines Forest State Park where Ade had proposed. They didn't have much luck, instead finding second-growth evergreens and lots of aspen and poplar trees. The logging days of the last century had left a fair amount of cutover land, and either the axe or forest fire seemed to have taken the ancient pine that they so desired to live among.[5]

Ade and Helen spent their next summer vacation in 1940 continuing to look in the national forest areas of Chequamegon, Lac du Flambeau, and Nicolet in Wisconsin, but again without much success. While they found plenty of the old-growth pines they wanted, most were on federal land, which they could not buy. Ade reasoned that if they found a forest area they liked, privately owned patches likely existed nearby.

In the summer of 1941, they set out again for parts of Wisconsin and Michigan, determined to find a place. They started making inquiries during their travels, asking gas station attendants, lunch counter wait-resses, and other locals where they could find the old-growth pines. Most didn't understand what the Hoovers were looking for, so they weren't much help. Helen was discouraged and began to think they were chasing a pipe dream; Ade was more optimistic and suggested they get off the main highways and on to more side roads.

On their final day of exploring, Ade went down a side road, travel-ing into the woods before coming upon an old log cabin from which a man emerged and asked if they were lost. Ade said they were looking for "virgin timber" and the road had looked promising; they were looking to find a place among the tall trees that resembled the days before settlers.[6]

The man said he was surprised they had found him, as he did indeed own the only piece of uncut land in the area; his grandparents had settled it and only cleared an area for the cabin. He took the Hoovers deep into the woods to show them ancient pines and spruce, some towering two hundred feet into the air. He left them to wander around while he headed to town. They were in awe of this beautiful parcel of land, and even though it was not for sale, it gave them hope that there might be a place for them somewhere.

$$* * *$$

During this time, the threat of the United States entering the war in Europe was building every day. While America had not committed to fighting directly, it had an obligation to provide munitions and war materiel to its allies. In the Far East, Japan had been on the march with its own expansionist plans, first invading Manchuria and then other parts of China and southeast Asia. In America, isolationists were desperate to keep the country out of the war, calling President Roosevelt a warmonger and believing he was in league with "international bankers" and big business interests that had profited from World War I. But as country after country fell, Roosevelt increasingly made it clear that Adolf Hitler would not stop in Europe and that America would eventually be threatened. It was just a matter of time.[7]

Sunday, December 7, was snowy in Chicago, and Helen and Ade convinced Hannah that taking a drive out to the country with a picnic lunch that they could eat in the car would be a way to enjoy the bright day. When they came home that afternoon, they learned the Japanese had attacked Pearl Harbor. Like most Americans, they were shocked. They also recognized that Ade would soon be called to serve. He started taking night courses to study electricity. Helen decided to brush up on chemistry and enrolled at DePaul University.[8]

Helen continued to work at the Audit Bureau, but she also knew that with men going off to war there would be opportunities for women to fill other jobs. In February 1943, Helen left the Audit Bureau to take a position at Pittsburgh Testing, an analytical laboratory. She was the first woman to work in the chemistry lab but felt at home because it reminded her of the days in the lab at Ohio University.

Ade joined the Navy and left Chicago by train in November 1943. He spent some time training at various posts around the country before being shipped out. He was an electrician's mate on the USS *Cahaba*, which was commissioned in January 1944 and sent to the Pacific theater to support combat operations as a fueling ship.[9]

Helen took to her new job quickly, analyzing the content of materials to make sure they met standards. She worked with about a dozen men who kept a close eye on her work. Her boss, the chief chemist, knew Helen had majored in chemistry and physics in college and allowed her to analyze anything that came into the lab. She tested steel, cast iron, aluminum alloys, brass, and coal, among other materials. The hours were long, from morning to after midnight, and usually Saturdays, Sundays, and holidays as well. The work was so intense she even stood while eating, a sandwich in one hand and a beaker of acid in the other.[10]

Hannah objected to Helen's long hours and thought she should stay home evenings and keep her company, but Helen resisted, telling her mother she needed to do her part to support the war effort, plus they needed the extra income that came with overtime. Helen was also taking night courses in biology and was just fine not having to spend any more time with her mother than was necessary. These studies did not necessarily help her in her work but proved to be something that piqued her interest and challenged her mind.[11]

Ade regularly wrote to Helen from his ship, and Helen kept all his letters from the war, which were carefully hand-lettered but written with little information other than the food they ate and the daily routine. They arrived in batches and were often dated months before they were received and had the stamp of passing the Navy's censor.

In her letters to Ade, Helen used sentimental greetings, such as "lamb," "sugar plum," "angel-pie," "dearest sheep," and "honeybunch."[12] In June 1944, Ade came home on leave in Gulfport, Mississippi, so Helen caught the Panama Limited train from Chicago and met him at the Roosevelt Hotel for a reunion. She must have brought the 8 mm camera they owned, as there are movies of New Orleans and the French Quarter restaurant the Court of Two Sisters, popular among servicemen there.[13]

In March 1945 an opportunity for work at another company came along, and Helen moved to the Ahlberg Bearing Company, where she took over chemical and metallurgical control. Again, she was in an environment dominated by men. She assessed equipment, kept the lab clean and organized, and ordered supplies for the steel analyses and microscopic studies that she was expected to do. Under the direction of the machine shop foreman, she learned how to drill her own steel samples for analysis.[14]

One day she was shown the damaged rings on a faulty piece of machinery; the metal was wearing out too fast, and the company could not afford the machine to be down. One of her colleagues indicated they had tried using other types of steel, with no luck. Helen shared that she was aware of a relatively new alloy called beryllium copper; it was expensive but durable. When she tried to take a sample of it, she needed to use diamond dust to cut it. Given those properties, she surmised it would last a long time but had no way of knowing for sure. The shop foreman was impressed.[15]

As she started to interact more with her colleagues, she became less self-conscious about being one woman among many men. Helen identified with many of them, as she had come to know their world when she and Ade explored the working-class neighborhoods of the city. She remained in contact with many of these colleagues later in life. Still, because she was a woman, there were some who didn't want to work with her. The factory manager resented her theoretical knowledge, and the production manager propositioned her when they met. She kept her distance from him.

As the war wound down in 1945, Helen found a rhythm in her work. Following V-E Day in May and particularly V-J Day in August, it was only a matter of time before Ade returned home. On December 3, 1945, she received a call from him that he was back in the country, and she met him at the Chicago train station a week later.

The war's end meant that men would be returning to their jobs and the women who had replaced them would now be expected to return to their prewar lives. Helen's laboratory and shop work had been successful, so she was asked to stay on. She was thrilled because she enjoyed metallurgy and knew her work would continue to be important in the changeover from wartime production to peacetime products. She found the job challenging and enjoyed applying her theoretical knowledge. Helen endured ribbing from some of the returning workers who had fought in the war, but she had also earned the respect of the older workers who had remained at the company.[16]

As a female metallurgist, Helen was a bit of a curiosity in the field, and when sales and manufacturing associates from suppliers visited the facility, they were introduced to her. On one of these occasions she learned from a French metallurgist touring the country about a heat-treating method called *austempering*, a process that uses molten salt rather than oil or water in the quenching, or rapid cooling, stage. Austempering had been successfully applied to other metals but not yet tried on the high-chromium, high-carbon steel used in the manufacture of bearing races. (Bearing races are smooth, hardened rings that guide and support rolling elements, such as balls, in a bearing assembly.) The French visitor also shared that U.S. Steel Corporation was experimenting with the method. Helen thought the process might help solve a problem she was dealing with at Ahlberg, so she called the chief metallurgist at U.S. Steel's Gary Works in nearby Indiana to see what she might learn.[17]

That call led to Helen making her first airplane trip, flying to Philadelphia to meet with one of U.S. Steel's metallurgists, who for the next several days proceeded to school her in salt-bath heat-treating procedures. What she learned would indeed be promising back at Ahlberg; when she returned, they set up an area in the plant to apply the new heat-treating processes.

During this time after the war Helen and Ade began once again to consider finding a place in the north woods with that elusive timber. In addition to exploring the northern areas of the region, Helen was also reading books by authors who had left comfortable jobs and conventional lifestyles and moved to the woods. These "back to the land" narratives captured readers' attention during the mid- to late 1940s, serving as a pleasant diversion from the challenges of the war. Helen likely read these best sellers as she later referenced them in letters to literary agents and friends. They included Louise Dickinson Rich's *We Took to the Woods*, published in 1942 and a popular best seller that took a lighthearted approach to the author and her husband moving to a remote lake in northern Maine in the 1930s and the trials and tribulations they encountered living there.[18]

Helen also read *The Egg and I*, a humorous memoir written by Betty MacDonald, telling the story of a newlywed husband and wife moving to a rural chicken farm on the Olympic Peninsula in Washington, published in 1945.[19] While the author was not particularly forgiving of her husband in the book, it was yet another example of a popular work of nonfiction that showed how a married couple could give up a conventional lifestyle and go live in the country.

In 1947, John Rowlands published *Cache Lake Country*, an account of a year in the woods of northern Ontario where Rowlands had worked as a lumber company scout. This, too, was a book that captured Helen's attention, and she and Ade were particularly impressed with the pen-and-ink and woodcut illustrations by Henry B. Kane prominently featured throughout the text and in the margins. In addition to the author, the book's main characters were the illustrator Kane and an older Cree Indian named Chief Tibeash, both of whom resided on nearby lakes. Arranged as a monthly diary, the book is part folklore, part philosophy, with lots of wisdom about self-reliance and living in the woods.[20]

While these books certainly fed Helen's imagination, she and Ade were also influenced by Sam Campbell, a popular nature writer, filmmaker, photographer, and lecturer who was a fixture in the Midwest and beyond. Campbell came to prominence in the 1930s and 1940s for his work promoting an appreciation of nature and conservation, as well as vacation destinations in northern Wisconsin and the Upper Peninsula of Michigan, for the Chicago and North Western Railway. Campbell was dubbed the "Philosopher of the Forest," worked out of his home in Three Lakes, Wisconsin, and had a tremendous following.[21]

Campbell spent the summer months at the "Sanctuary of Wegimind," his island cabin on nearby Four Mile Lake. There he observed and interacted with the wildlife while not allowing guns or firearms, which he believed allowed him to get closer to animals. He domesticated a pair of porcupines, who he called Salt and Pepper, and filmed himself playing with them. He would then return to the city in the fall and set up a schedule of lectures in the greater Chicago area, extolling the beauty of the wilderness, sharing stories of the animals he came in contact with, and showing films of the Sanctuary and other places he visited. It was a busy schedule; in one January to May time frame, Campbell delivered seventy-eight lectures to church groups, scout troops, parent-teacher groups, and conservation clubs, his capable wife Giny operating the film projector. He also authored many books on woods animals for children and several books about his nature philosophy for the adult market.[22]

Although there is no record of Helen and Ade attending one of Campbell's Chicago-area lectures, they were so anxious for guidance on finding a suitable place in the woods that Helen wrote to him through a work colleague at Ahlberg Bearing who was a friend of the conservationist. Campbell responded to her letter in June 1947, cautioning her to be aware of inflated prices in the north woods, but also asking her to be more specific about what she was seeking. Though additional correspondence wasn't saved, Helen was not shy about reaching out to the wilderness expert himself to get his opinion about where they should be looking.[23]

That summer the Hoovers traveled to the area around Iron Mountain, Michigan, where the Ford Motor Company owned a forest for production and recreational use. The company maintained a sawmill there to supply wood; it was a typical company town. Although the area was beautiful, Helen thought the town a bit sterile, with its simple houses and orderly downtown. In many ways it reminded her of the insular atmosphere of her childhood home of Greenfield. She surmised they would not be happy there.

\* \* \*

Labor tensions increased at Ahlberg Bearing, followed by a strike. Staff in the shop were not happy, and the heat-treating process Helen had helped set up was in disarray. In the spring of 1948, she decided it was time to leave. Helen was able to take some time off before finding another job in metallurgy. Ade had started working as a promotional art director at the elementary school textbook publisher Scott, Foresman and Company, which produced the very popular Dick and Jane series of reading primers that were a mainstay in American elementary education for decades.

Now with some time off, Helen thought she would try her hand at cooking, something she had let her mother do for years while she and

Ade worked full-time. She had been given a casserole recipe from one of her work friends that seemed easy enough; while her mother was visiting a neighbor in the apartment building, Helen started to prepare it. When Hannah returned, she was so upset to see Helen in the kitchen that she became hysterical. Helen was stunned at the response and tried to quiet her. That only made matters worse, and in a fit of pique Hannah locked herself in the bathroom.

Ade came home to the unfolding scene. He asked if she had ever seen her mother act this way. Helen said she had not. Ade volunteered he had seen this behavior in Hannah before and convinced Helen the best thing for them to do was go out for dinner; when they returned, all would be fine. That's indeed what happened. When they came back, Hannah was sitting outside with one of her neighbor friends, acting as if nothing had occurred.[24]

The two decided it was best for Helen to return to work, which she gladly did. She applied to several technical employment agencies, but to no avail. Most didn't believe they'd be able to place a woman in an industrial job, despite her experience. She called several acquaintances at other companies, given her knowledge of metallurgy, metallography, and chemistry, as well as laboratory work and all-around technical troubleshooting. When one company learned she had not completed her college degree, the employment manager was blunt: a man without a degree could not get hired, so a woman without one was even more out of the question.

Frustrated by the lack of progress, Helen remembered a shop manager contact she had at International Harvester Company, the farm implement manufacturer. She called to make inquiries and explained the details of the heat-treating project she was trying to get off the ground while at Ahlberg Bearing, hoping it would impress him. He was indeed interested and told her of a new research center the company was setting up in the suburbs to develop better manufacturing methods. He gave Helen the name of the person running the labs and said to use his name in getting an appointment, advising her to skip going through the personnel department.

Helen was able to get in and see the lab manager, who promptly asked what she could do. She offered a summary of her metallurgical work and he seemed impressed, but there were no openings except in the physics department. Helen didn't have that experience but said she could learn. The manager already had enough people with knowledge; his challenge was not having enough people who could apply knowledge to practical problems. He also noted the person hired would need experience working with equipment. Helen rattled off a list of machines she had worked with, noting confidently that she could run them better than most men.

The manager was impressed with Helen's confidence and hired her at a salary just under $2,000 a year. Her starting position was less than what she was making at Ahlberg, but she took the job because it was work she knew she would enjoy doing. Ade was pleased that she found something in a large company but was apprehensive about her having to prove herself all over again in a male-dominated organization. That was true enough, Helen agreed, but she had been hired by a man in management who took a chance on her. She was up for the challenge and knew she could do the work. She started on February 17, 1948.

On her first day she learned about the fifty-year-old problem with disc harrows, a farm implement used to break up the soil and prepare the ground for planting. Due to problems with the steel used in their manufacture, the discs were prone to breaking—not just when they came into contact with rocks, stones, or other soil materials, but also when the equipment was dropped on hard clay.[25] Some solutions had been found to alleviate the breakage, but they involved a super-alloy steel that used expensive materials such as chrome and nickel. This was not economical for International Harvester, which was manufacturing for the mass farm market. They were investing in research to find a less expensive solution to this long-standing problem. Broken discs meant downtime for farmers, when planting the season's crops was a critical and time-sensitive endeavor.

After six months, Helen was allowed one week of vacation. She and Ade had been doing some research for their next trip and had little time to spare, squeezing their cabin hunting into one week. Their plan was to drive straight through to Duluth, Minnesota, and then venture farther north to Ely and Hibbing, where Helen wanted to see the open-pit iron ore mines.

They hadn't made plans on where to stay, instead driving until dark and seeking a motor lodge or tourist cabins along the highway. At breakfast the next morning they told the proprietor of their plans to drive beyond Duluth. He encouraged them to first go up Highway 61 along Lake Superior, as the fall colors would be spectacular. If they still wanted to get to Ely, there was a state highway that would connect them.

Helen and Ade followed his advice and took Highway 61 up the North Shore. They must have enjoyed the scenery, as they did not turn to head north to Ely but continued on to Grand Marais. As each mile passed, they were awestruck at the beauty of the landscape. This part of Minnesota and the land to the north in Ontario was part of the vast Laurentian Shield, a section of ancient continental crust exposed by the glaciers that formed this region of lakes and hills eight to twelve thousand years earlier. Left behind was granite, basalt, and gabbro; the retreating glaciers created a maze of lakes, muskeg bogs, rivers, and streams that would define the region's geography.

The Sawtooth Mountains rose along the shore of Lake Superior, and the changing aspens, maple, and birch presented a colorful palette against the dark green of the pines. After driving northeast along the lake, the Hoovers reached a crest overlooking Grand Marais and the harbor below. They checked into a motor lodge in town and got settled.

After making inquiries at the U.S. Forest Service office about the sort of remote woods and a cabin they were looking for, they were directed up the Gunflint Trail.[26] This route dated back to the time when indigenous people used it as a footpath to move from their hunting and wild rice grounds to the shore of the great lake where they lived part of the year. Starting in the late 1890s the trail gradually expanded from Grand Marais and was used by early mineral prospectors and then logging companies. By the 1920s it had been expanded to accommodate automobiles. But it wasn't until the late 1930s, when the Civilian Conservation Corps completed the last portions of the road, that there was a passable route to the end, some fifty-plus miles from town.[27]

The Gunflint Trail started as a blacktop road and rose quickly into the hills above Grand Marais, providing a beautiful vista of Lake Superior as the Hoovers ascended. Ade quickly realized the drive was going to be a bit nerve-racking as they encountered construction work on the road, which only narrowed as they went farther north. The trail had blind spots and sharp turns, and it took time to travel the forty-plus miles to Gunflint Lake. As they drove, they came to a section of white pines standing as a sort of gateway to the wilderness beyond. These were some old-growth trees that had not been harvested earlier in the century when most of the area had been logged. Helen and Ade took this as a positive sign and saw the potential of the area, with its wild feel.[28]

Closer to their destination, the Hoovers came to the top of a ridge and saw ahead of them what they would learn was Magnetic Lake and the western end of Gunflint Lake, with the hills of Canada beyond. It was a stunning view after driving so close to the edge of the forest.

Given that it was already late in the season, most of the resorts were closed and the summer tourists had left. When they arrived at Gunflint Lake and turned down the road to the Gunflint Lodge and pulled in, they were surprised to find little activity there. A CLOSED sign hung on the building, leaving both feeling deflated, but they decided to check it out as long as they were there. Walking toward the deserted lodge, they met the owner Justine Kerfoot, who came out to see who had stopped by. The Hoovers could see the wide lake, docks, and the gracefully sloping hills beyond. It was an idyllic setting. There wasn't any old-growth timber, but the boreal forest felt exactly like what they were seeking.

Justine had grown up outside of Chicago and had come to Gunflint Lake in 1929 when her mother, Mae Spunner, was seeking to buy the lodge. After securing her daughter's commitment to help run the resort during summer vacations, she made the purchase. Mother and daughter made do following the stock market crash that year, and they were able to keep the lodge going despite financial challenges. In 1932, Bill Kerfoot, who had been a previous guest, showed up looking for work, was hired, and helped Justine run the resort. In 1934 they were married and eventually had four children.[29]

Justine offered the Hoovers coffee and cookies, and when they asked if any cabins in the area were for sale, she directed them to a place a few miles farther east. The composition of the woods changed as they drove down the side road, the stands of young birch giving way to big pine trees like those they had seen years earlier on other travels. They found the place for sale and turned down a steep driveway toward the lake, arriving at a log cabin nestled among the pines. This was the setting the Hoovers had been looking for.

Walt Yocum, the owner, was indeed planning on selling the cabin.

After introductions, the Hoovers indicated they had been directed from the lodge. Yocum was originally from Kentucky and had built the twin-gabled cabin in 1936, which was of a unique design for the area.[30] As Walt took Ade outside to show him the property, Helen was introduced to Walt's wife Adelaide, who gave her a tour of the inside. Helen could see that the cabin was in tough shape; bare wooden floors and no running water, though there were electric lights. Adelaide was not shy about her enthusiasm to have a buyer. She related that Walt liked living on the lake during the summer and doing business as a guide, but he got bored in the winter, and she missed going into town.

Small, efficient cabins had become popular in the 1920s as the automobile and improved highways extended vacationers' ability to travel to undeveloped wilderness areas and build their own getaways. Minneapolis architect Chilson D. Aldrich capitalized on this trend with his popular book *The Real Log Cabin,* which offered plans and advice on how to achieve one's own idyll in the woods.[31] Some of Aldrich's cabins still stand today in northern Minnesota.

The Yocum cabin was of simple log design, consisting of two large rooms—one that included a living area and the kitchen, the other a bedroom with a closet. It had a basement that was anchored on two sides by the slope of the hill and contained an assortment of discarded wood, an old barrel stove, tin cans, and other trash. There was an icehouse by the lake and several outbuildings used for storage, plus a wind generator for electricity.

The cabin definitely needed work, but the Hoovers were eager to buy something, and this place had much of what they were looking for. After considering the pros and cons, they decided to purchase it and spend the rest of their vacation assessing what work needed to be done. That way they could make plans over the winter for fixing up the place the next summer. They returned to Chicago, excited at having finally found their place.

There is speculation in Helen's later correspondence to friends that being awed by the beauty of the location and the fact they were from Chicago—and therefore likely not skilled in choosing a cabin—made them easy marks for a quick sale of a less-than-worthy structure. What is unknown is how much the Hoovers actually paid for the cabin, as the deed for the property lists the sale as being for one dollar on October 30, 1948. In her draft manuscript "A Little Place in the Woods," Helen notes that Yocum wanted $4,000 dollars for the cabin, which would be in line with prices at that time.[32]

✳ ✳ ✳

International Harvester's operations were much larger and more hierarchical than Helen's previous employer, Ahlberg Bearing. She soon realized that in her former position she had much more freedom and the ability to gain more experience with less structure, working with a wider variety of testing equipment and other machines typical of an industrial shop.

This previous experience came in handy one day when a rush sample of metal arrived in the department for Helen to analyze. The sample needed some machining, but there was no way she would be able to get a work order until the next day. Her two coworkers could write themselves an order to do the task, but neither one knew how to operate a lathe to get a sample. When Helen volunteered, both looked at her in disbelief. She also offered that she was capable of taking drillings and doing other related tasks. With that, she took the work order to the machine shop foreman, who was suspicious she could actually run the lathe. He watched her closely, and she got the sample she needed.[33]

Helen enjoyed working on the various shop machines and demonstrating to the men that she knew her way around the lab equipment. She was once engaged enough that she was also able to have some fun that caused a kerfuffle in the highly corporate International Harvester culture. While using the photo magnifier one day on a metal sample, she found a pattern in the image that closely resembled the outline of a clown. She took a print of the image, wrote up a clever caption with some arcane technical language that amounted to an inside joke for metallurgists, and submitted it to the *Journal of American Society for Metals,* a trade magazine. She thought anyone in the field familiar with an image from a photo magnifier would get a chuckle from it.

A few months later the journal published the image and caption, noting the submission came from the research lab at International Harvester.

The corporate public relations people were not happy that an employee had bypassed the proper channels to submit to a trade publication. Calls were made to her supervisor, and she was called into a meeting with her boss and representatives from headquarters downtown. When she explained that it was meaningless humor that other metallurgists would know was absurd, it didn't help matters. Helen thought she was giving a plug for the thoroughness of the work performed in the company's labs; management took a different view. While her boss was more forgiving and mildly amused, it was another reminder to Helen of the rigid corporate code of behavior she was expected to follow.

In the spring of 1949, the Hoovers took a quick vacation to Gunflint Lake. Earlier that winter they purchased some land adjacent to their property from Russell and Eve Blankenburg, long-time area residents and retired resort owners who had owned much of the land on the south side of the lake, so they needed to finish the paperwork in Grand Marais.[34]

When they returned to Chicago, a series of events made for a difficult year for Helen, Ade, and Hannah. Helen recognized that one of her colleagues must have flagged the trade journal submission to her supervisor. She felt she was being watched, but not knowing who the accuser was, she could not talk with anyone about it. She understood that although it had been harmless, it was against company policy, and a jealous colleague wanted to put her in her place, or worse, see her fired. It reminded her of a troubling experience when she was at Pittsburgh Testing that contributed to her departure there. That incident was different, as it involved individuals who were known to her and was done out of petty jealousy; this seemed more ominous.

This situation went on for four weeks, stressing Helen, and when her boss cleared things up, she came down with pneumonia, followed a month later by a mild nervous collapse. Ade had an operation on his throat from which he did not recover properly and was laid up in the hospital for two months. At the same time, Hannah collapsed and was also hospitalized. By the time Ade and Hannah came home, Helen had discovered she was pregnant. Following the stress of work and the worry of caring for two individuals on the mend, she had a miscarriage. Helen was so emotionally devastated from the experience that she began to stutter off and on for the next three years.[35]

Following this sequence of maladies, the Hoovers looked forward to their first full vacation as owners of the cabin in northern Minnesota. In Helen's mind the cabin had sat snugly and locked up all winter, awaiting their return. When they did arrive, however, it was not the idyll they were expecting; after sitting for months all winter and the spring thaw, the cabin smelled of mildew. As they worked to open windows and let in some fresh air, they noticed mushrooms growing on the ceiling and a slow drip of moisture from the beam above them. Dampness in the basement had warped the floors.[36]

The next day they inspected the basement, coming around to the side and entering through a door in the foundation. There was a small gully leading up to it, with a steady trickle of water. Inside, it was a jumble of wood planks, an old washing machine, and a rusty old barrel stove that had been there since they bought the place. More ominously, there were acid-filled glass batteries used for the wind generator sitting precariously on a shelf. Ade scooted Helen out while he secured them. Helen retreated upstairs. Later, after Ade had surveyed the basement, he came back upstairs. "I hate to tell you this, but we've really bought a dog."[37]

They spent most of their vacation time cleaning and making lists of items they would need to bring on their next trip. And they needed advice on how to shore up the basement wall to secure the foundation. One of the nearby lodge owners recommended a local handyman, Charlie Boostrom, who lived about twenty-five miles away. He and his wife Petra had started Clearwater Lodge in 1915, and after many years catering to guests, they sold it a few years prior to the Hoovers' arrival.[38] After a certain amount of convincing, likely by Bill Kerfoot, Boostrom came to look at the basement and promised to make improvements over the winter, telling Helen and Ade it would be repaired when they arrived the following summer. Having that issue resolved, they returned to Chicago, believing they had the problem fixed.

Getting Boostrom to lend a hand was an example of how resort owners and residents looked out for each other on the Gunflint Trail, sharing skills and expertise. Boostrom had come to the area in 1911, first working with a mineral prospector and then for forestry surveyors and logging operations before building a lodge so he could guide fishermen and deer hunters. At the time, the area was still fairly undeveloped, with most resorts only having electric plants to provide power during the day and a wood-burning cook stove to prepare meals.

Years before prospecting, logging, and the start of lodges and resorts, the area was opened to trade and commerce by voyageurs, first the French in the late 1600s and then English, Scottish, and American colonists in the late 1700s. These traders pushed west from eastern Canada and the Great Lakes, first in hopes of finding a passage to the "Western Sea," and then to trap beaver, mink, fox, otter, fisher, marten, bear, wolf, and wolverine to be sold in Montreal and trading company posts across the region.[39]

By 1951, Helen was able to move over to the metallurgy department at International Harvester, having proven her abilities with equipment no one thought a woman could handle, such as a lathe (used for precisely machining hard materials) and the tensile machine (used for measuring the strength of a metal sample). She had worked with similar equipment at Ahlberg, including a photo magnification machine. The range of metals and the sampling required were varied and complex, challenges Helen eagerly embraced. When not testing samples, she used her downtime to better learn the department's equipment. The research center had finally been tasked with trying to solve the fifty-year-old disc harrow problem that every farmer, blacksmith, metallurgist, heat-treater, and mechanical engineer in the business had not been able to solve.

The testing and analysis of the properties and strengths of various metals were followed by technical reports that needed to clearly explain the findings. Helen found writing reports on her observations an enjoyable part of the job, although they did not allow for much creativity. Given the importance of each project and the need to write clearly for management up the line, she felt she was up to the task.

The following year Helen was promoted in the department as her work on the disc issue continued, with experiments using the austempering process she had learned about at her previous job. This was a new approach for International Harvester, and Helen's testing of steel hardness proved to be making headway. She was aware of work the U.S. Navy was doing testing the failure of steel on World War II ships and made inquiries on how the company could apply the results of similar testing on its steel. At the same time, Helen was invited to present a paper on the subject at the annual meeting of the American Society for Testing Materials in late June 1953. The paper, titled "The Measurement of Directional Strength in Straight and Cross-rolled Strip Steel by the Navy Tear Test," was published in the society's journal that summer.

* * *

On Gunflint Lake, Charlie Boostrom had fixed the cabin's foundation problem. When the Hoovers arrived for their summer vacation in August 1953, they faced the usual tasks associated with opening the cabin after a year of it being shuttered. One day, while at one of the lodges, conversation with the owners turned to the amount of work the Hoovers put into their short vacations and how they needed a chance to actually sit down and enjoy the place without having to think of all the chores and improvements that needed to be made.

One of the lodge owners asked if they had heard the place next door to them was for sale. The Hoovers said they had not and admitted to not even having met their neighbors, understanding they kept to themselves and wanted privacy. The lodge owner said the neighbors, Robert and Alice Morrissey, had just arrived that day, and he offered to arrange a meeting. They owned a restaurant chain and lived in Minneapolis.[40]

The cabin just to the west of the Hoovers had been built in the early 1920s and included a fair amount of lake frontage. There was a path that went from the Hoover cabin to the Morrissey place, and Helen and Ade took the short hike through the woods the next day to call on them. The grounds were immaculately well-maintained, and the house was low and wide, clad with wood siding and painted a gray-green with cream shutters and bright scarlet doors. A round stone chimney rose through the middle of the roof, and a screen porch stretched across the lakeside. The Morrisseys were in their midsixties and pleased to meet their neighbors. While Ade and Robert walked the property and talked about a price for the cabin and land, Helen and Alice toured the inside, which was furnished with antiques. The tiny kitchen shared a wall of round rock that was the backside of the fireplace, which faced the living room. The bedrooms were small but cool in the shade of the trees.

It was apparent the Morrisseys were pleased to meet the Hoovers, and after hearing more about the troubles they had since purchasing their cabin with a small creek running through the basement, they concluded the sale was meant to be. The parties agreed to terms, and the Hoovers now owned a second cabin, six hundred feet more of lakeshore, a few antique pieces of furniture, and several outbuildings, including a carport by the side road, all for $7,000. The sale closed on August 27, 1953.[41] How the Hoovers could pay for a second cabin is unknown, although records indicate they had a mortgage payment through the late 1950s. Likely it was a five-year contract-for-deed arrangement with the Morrisseys.

Helen and Ade returned to their jobs in Chicago where Hannah's health continued to decline. She died of congestive heart failure on Friday night, October 9, 1953, at age eighty-two. Helen planned the funeral for the following Tuesday and returned her mother to Greenfield, Ohio, to lie in the cemetery next to her husband, Thomas, who had died twenty-five years before.[42]

Helen and Ade must have been relieved. Hannah had been a difficult presence in the household for years, with her petty criticisms and emotional outbursts. Helen felt duty-bound to care for her mother regardless of how insensitive and rude she could be. After the war, as Hannah's health declined, they reached an accommodation, and the three of them coexisted as best they could. Helen and Ade found time to enjoy the city out of the apartment, and once they purchased the cabin in 1948 they looked forward to several weeks alone each year.

For Helen, Hannah's passing brought her closer to the possibility of moving to the north woods. All she needed to do was convince Ade it could be done.

# 4

# Bears in the Basement

## *Gunflint Lake, 1954–1957*

WITH HANNAH'S PASSING, nothing was holding Helen and Ade to Chicago. They had many discussions about quitting their jobs and moving to Gunflint Lake, particularly now that they had ample space for their furniture and belongings with two cabins. On January 20, 1954, Helen's birthday, she floated the idea to Ade of moving to the north woods, noting that they were both now forty-four years old and that if they truly wanted to do it, they better get at it sooner rather than later. In earlier discussions about one day leaving Chicago, Helen had used her fiftieth birthday as a marker, since she would then qualify for a reduced pension from International Harvester, but if they waited, the challenge would only be greater given their age.[1]

Ade was concerned with Helen's ability to walk away from her work. She was nearing the end of the successful disc harrow research project, and with that behind her, there undoubtedly would be other projects the company wanted her to take on. She was good at what she did and was well paid. The work was stimulating and challenging, and Ade could not envision her being able to simply turn off the intellectual curiosity.[2]

Helen thought otherwise. She believed that what she was working on was not critical, and, typical of someone who was bright and intelligent, surmised that anyone with half a brain could do it. And she was growing weary of "men and machinery."

They continued to discuss a move to Gunflint Lake, believing if they could leave their jobs by summer, they would have time to fix up the log cabin and prepare it for winter while living in the newly acquired "summer" cabin next door.

There was also the issue of finances. Ade figured they had enough saved for three or four years of living expenses, but they would also need to supplement that with some form of income if they were to live there permanently. Ade thought he could find some freelance drawing and illustration work similar to what he was currently doing. Helen was interested in trying her hand at some type of writing now that she had the time; perhaps mysteries, or even stories about nature. It was a plus that she had been writing reports that made technical information understandable to company executives. She may have even remembered that school essay on national parks she was forced to write as punishment for reading a detective magazine in study hall.[3]

While Ade was concerned about Helen's ability to leave her high-performance job, Helen was equally concerned about Ade's health. Following minor surgery to his throat the previous fall, he had been slow to recover, forcing him to take a leave from work indefinitely. Helen didn't realize how bad off he was until coming home from work one day in the spring to see Ade struggling to carry groceries up the four steps to their apartment building. The gritty air of industrial Chicago did not help his recovery, and getting him out of the city and to the north woods where he could relax and benefit from clean air was a primary motivator for Helen.[4]

Helen sought a one-year leave of absence from her job so she could get Ade out of the city and healthy again. Management was skeptical about a leave of that duration and arranged for Helen to meet with the company psychiatrist, believing that several sessions with him would bring her around. The psychiatrist was convinced that Helen was merely tired from the stress of the disc harrow project and was trying to escape into a fantasy from her childhood. He also believed that she would be unhappy in the extreme cold and isolated conditions of the north woods; she was used to being around people, comfortable in an urban setting, and needed the mental stimulation that came with her technical position. In other words, it was best she stay at the company.[5] Helen was amused that International Harvester was going to such lengths to convince her that she was incapable of living in the woods. To her, the interactions with the company psychiatrist were a mental game, and she was determined to outsmart him and her bosses.[6]

Helen didn't receive the year's leave of absence she requested, so she settled for the two months they offered to nurse Ade back to health.[7] While Helen trained her replacement, Ade spent time sorting and packing. Moving from a ten-room apartment with years of acquired belongings, including a baby grand piano, was no easy task. Additionally, they did not own the clothing they would need to live in the north woods year-round.[8]

It's unclear if Helen quit her job before retreating to their cabin that summer. In numerous author biographies, interviews with newspaper reporters, and correspondence with friends over the years, Helen indicated that they started the two-month leave beginning July 23, 1954. Her end date of employment at International Harvester is listed in company records as September 21, confirming a two-month leave.[9]

In her book *A Place in the Woods*, Helen notes having to return to Chicago after two months, the trip having accomplished the goal of getting Ade rested and healthy again. As they reluctantly drive home toward Grand Marais, Helen realizes she'd be happy if she never saw the inside of a laboratory again. They again discuss their respective ages and that, if they're going to live in the woods, they should do it now; they could manage the financial aspects as well. The chapter ends with Helen calling her boss in Chicago from the local telephone exchange to quit her job and say goodbye.[10]

Helen very well could have planned all along to quit at the end of her leave, given that International Harvester and its company psychiatrist were convinced her need for the extended leave was just a passing fancy. Since they had begun packing their belongings and getting them ready to be moved to their two cabins in northern Minnesota earlier in the summer, it's entirely possible she never intended to return. Quitting long-distance removed the unpleasantness of doing it in person and enduring the continued protestations of company officials.

Regardless, by the summer of 1954, the Hoovers had decided to move permanently to Gunflint Lake. Now they needed to get settled, await the arrival of their belongings from Chicago, and prepare the log cabin for the winter. One challenge of relocating in the fall was the closing of the area resorts and the disappearance of seasonal neighbors who could provide valuable tips on living in the woods and help when the newcomers needed it.

As to the matter of money, Helen knew that she was going to get a refund of some insurance from her company and the balance of her reduced pension. In August, she received $200 from her two uncles in Cincinnati, Robert and Bruce Gomersall, as a gesture to help get them started. In late September Helen received the company insurance refund of $42.50, and early in October the Hoovers transferred $500 from their bank in Chicago. At the end of October came a refund from her company totaling $187.08, and in November two refunds came from the John Hancock insurance company totaling $932.58. Helen also sold some technical reference books she had used at work, which netted $300.[11]

The income helped defray a considerable amount of expenses the Hoovers incurred to get supplies for their new life. They bought an airtight stove from the Montgomery Ward catalog (noted in her check register by its nickname of the day, "Monkey Wards"). They also purchased boots, coats, wool pants, hats, gloves, long underwear, and sleeping bags from L. L. Bean and Eddie Bauer, mail-order companies known for their rugged outdoor gear.[12]

In the late fall, Ade arranged to meet with a business prospect in Duluth who was going to offer him a $10,000 contract for artwork that Ade could do from their new home, sending the finished work by mail.[13] This would be significant income, given that the average household income in 1954 was $4,200.[14] And it would be a comfortable amount of money to hold them over and help cover the costs of fixing the log cabin, buying food, fuel, and other necessities they would need for the winter and beyond.

One thing the Hoovers did not consider was the lack of a nearby source for food. The closest grocery store was in Grand Marais, more than forty-five miles down the Gunflint Trail. Some of the staples they could get from nearby resorts, but those would not be available once they closed for the season. Helen asked the resort owners how the locals managed. During the summer, she learned, trucks brought up food from town, supplying resorts and residents who had accounts with the grocery stores and wholesalers. After the tourist season ended and resorts closed, such deliveries were discontinued. One resort owner told the Hoovers that they could put in a large order for the entire winter and have it shipped before the end of the season. Smaller items could be sent by U.S. mail from town once they established an account with a grocery store.

Food storage would be another challenge. The log cabin had no refrigerator; the Yocums had simply stored food in the cool basement. The wind generator that came with the cabin was unreliable and incapable of providing consistent power. In the summer this was a problem, but in the winter they could improvise and freeze some items in an old storage locker. Without a butcher nearby, they would need to purchase canned meat from the grocer. Ade did not hunt or fish, so adding wild game to their diet was not an option.

Helen and Ade quickly realized that the mail would be their lifeline to the outside world. Their mailbox, like others on the south shore of Gunflint Lake, was located at the intersection of their side road (County 50) and the Gunflint Trail, about three miles west of their property.

After getting somewhat settled and enjoying several warm fall days, the Hoovers planned to get to town to make a deposit at the bank, lay in a supply of groceries, and pick up the airtight stove they had ordered, which had arrived at the post office. On November 2, they were surprised when they awoke to a winter wonderland of nearly a foot of snow, something they had been told could be expected any time after mid-September. They drove into town taking care to navigate the still-unplowed road, following a single line of ruts.

Ade dropped Helen off at Ed Toftey Company, one of the grocery stores in Grand Marais and the closest thing to a Chicago supermarket. The store had plenty of packaged goods, and Helen loaded up on a variety of foods. She also found a selection of canned meat and tried as many as she could since fresh meat would not be an option given their distance from town. Helen inquired about having bread sent up by mail, but the store clerk quickly dispelled her of that idea, noting that at twenty-four cents a loaf and postage of twenty-nine cents, it made little sense. Despite not having much experience baking, Helen decided that using local resort owner Peggy Heston's bread recipe would have to do.[15]

While Helen stocked up on groceries, Ade loaded the airtight stove and picked up additional supplies at the hardware store for repairing the roof. He bought kerosene for the lamps and white gas for the lantern. The two then stopped at Humphreys, the department store that carried clothing and other essentials, and were able to buy long underwear and wool socks that would be helpful to have before their other supplies arrived from the catalog companies.

Loaded down with groceries, fuel, and warm clothes, the Hoovers headed back up the trail, encountering a road that was in worse shape than when they came to town several hours earlier. While coming over a blind hill—common on the old Gunflint Trail then—they collided with a car nearly head-on. The other car was driven by a young man traveling with his fiancée. Both cars were heavily damaged. Ade was slammed into the steering wheel, and Helen was pinned to the dashboard by the force of groceries and other goods in the back seat shifting forward. Ade was able to extricate himself and, with the help of the other driver, pull Helen out through the back door. Fortunately, no one was severely injured, but a passerby took Helen and the other woman back to town to be checked by a doctor. Ade and the man stayed to make sure no one crashed into the accident scene. Once in town, the passerby notified the sheriff and arranged to have the Hoovers' groceries retrieved from the car and sent up to their cabin.

Helen and the woman were checked out by the doctor, and the men eventually arrived in town to be examined as well. Helen had a bump on her forehead from hitting the windshield, and her legs and ankles were stiff; the young woman from the other car seemed only to have a few scratches. The other driver was also fine, but Ade had four detached ribs, which meant he could not lift anything heavy for weeks. The two men met with the sheriff. The other driver had no insurance, and given his young age, basically no money, either. While the Hoovers were properly covered, they did not carry collision insurance, so there was nothing to cover their loss. Their Chevy was seventeen years old with a book value of less than fifty dollars.[16]

When they returned home, Helen realized she was more injured than she had thought. Her arms were bruised deep purple from her elbows to her shoulders; her knees were beginning to swell. They recognized how serious the accident had been. What they had thought were minor injuries were still painful and would cost them in time and energy, a true problem given all the work they needed to do to prepare for winter.

The local garage mechanic said the car could be salvaged at a significant cost, but they did not have the money to fix it. The bigger disappointment was that without a car, Ade did not have transportation to Duluth to meet with his prospective client who had promised a contract to do artwork. Due to the storm, the roads were barely passable, the phones were out, and they were unable to get a message to the prospect. It was a major setback for their anticipated income and suddenly cast concern over their livelihood.[17]

The accumulation of challenges these first few months worried Helen, and she recalled years later that she had reached a low point of their brief time living in the north woods. It was not lost on the Hoovers that locals had bet they would not make it through the winter. Their main source of potential income was gone, Helen's pension check had not yet arrived, and expenses were far more than they had anticipated. Although discouraged, Helen adopted an optimistic motto that "something will turn up," borrowing the phrase used by the character Wilkins Micawber from *David Copperfield*, one of the books she had been reading that had been left behind in the summer house by the Morrisseys.[18]

Even with Ade not physically able to do much, they spent the rest of November tightening up chinks in the log cabin and tending to other tasks before the onset of their first Minnesota winter. They had enough funds to buy eight-foot logs from one of the local neighbors, which could then be cut up and split as they needed it. Fortunately, Ade had cut enough firewood for them to get through his time being laid up, but he would soon need to get back to chopping wood. Helen fetched water from the lake and carried in firewood, tasks too hard for Ade to do. It's not clear why they didn't ask some of their neighbors for help, but they probably did not know enough people yet to feel they could impose. And some of the neighbors they did know had left for the season.

As Ade healed from the car accident and the disappointment of the lost work, one way they could make a living came into clearer focus. While in Chicago, Ade had used his artistic talents and free time to make wood jigsaw cutouts of his own design, such as letters, numbers, and animals, painting each to give them an individual quality. He had several orders from friends to fulfill for Christmas. It would provide some income while he recuperated, but this was not a long-term solution.[19]

Helen thought more about writing. She had done some back in Chicago in the late 1930s, but those efforts had been for fun and lacked commercial appeal, despite her having sold a piece to a newspaper syndicate. Working long hours during the war, going to school at night, and caring for her mother had left little time to pursue writing. Besides, Hannah would have felt Helen was paying her no attention, so focusing on writing would have been impossible. Since moving north, Helen had little time with all the daily chores and getting situated, especially with Ade laid up. However, with winter setting in, writing was now a distinct possibility.

It occurred to Helen that people might find it interesting and amusing to read about how they lived now in contrast with the life of convenience they had just left behind, so she wrote a letter to *National Geographic* magazine pitching the idea. They sent back a brief reply inquiring whether she had a camera so she could shoot to their specific requirements. All the Hoovers owned was a simple box camera, which would not provide the quality necessary. That seemed to be the end of that idea.[20]

As the days moved closer to Christmas, Helen realized that with all the distractions of the accident, getting firewood cut and stacked, and preparing for their first winter away from the city, she had not given any thought to sending cards to their friends.

The stark reality of a Christmas with only the two of them hit Helen hard. It would be entirely different in the woods, with none of the hustle and bustle of the city, the decorated department store windows, and holiday office parties. The solitude of the quiet snow-covered woods would be their new Christmas. Coupled with the challenges they had experienced thus far, and the lack of steady income weighing on their minds, it made for a depressing holiday. Without a steady source of income, there was always a nagging feeling that they might not make it through the winter and would have to return to Chicago and start over there. The Hoovers realized they would need to revert to skills learned during the Depression years if they were to make it through.

Their gloom was soon broken by a flood of Christmas cards and letters from family and friends eager to know how Helen and Ade were getting along. The joy of receiving these letters made Helen realize she needed to write back—not only because she was grateful for the news from people, but also to let them know they were safe, healthy, and following their dream. She thought of creating a monthly "north woods" letter that could provide insight on the usual (and unusual) facts of their surrounding new life. The mail generated many questions about the cabin, the lake, and the wildlife in the woods.

Ade liked the idea and thought that if they had a mimeograph they could easily create something that could be inexpensively reproduced in quantity. The mimeograph is a low-cost duplicator that was a forerunner to photocopying. It combines a stencil with an ink roller, forcing ink over the stencil image onto paper. It is hand-cranked, perfect for a cabin without electricity.

Both Hoovers had worked with a mimeograph before—Ade in his art director position and Helen back in her days at the Henry Paulson Company. Fortunately, the movers had packed their Chicago telephone directories, so Helen was able to write to several office equipment supply houses to get catalogs with pricing and information about new and reconditioned machines.

Eventually Helen contacted a Duluth sales representative from a mimeograph manufacturer. She described their unusual situation and what they hoped to do, and he was able to come up with a mimeograph and related supplies that was within their meager budget. The good news was that he could ship it to Grand Marais in two days; the challenge was trying to get the machine from town up the trail. Luckily, one of their neighbors had been flagged down at the freight office and agreed to bring it out to the Hoovers.

Ade set up the equipment, organized the stencils and paper, and got the mimeograph operating. Helen asked him to create a woodsy illustration that could be used around the edges of the paper. Ade sketched a snow-covered balsam tree that ran up the left side of the page, and a doe, fawn, and snowshoe hare on their path with the lake and the Canadian shore across the bottom. He used a stylus to create the image on the stencil; the delicately etched drawing was the ideal image to accompany the letter. Helen wrote a general roundup of how they were adjusting to their new life, offering observations of their day-to-day activities, and answering questions that friends had posed in their correspondence.

The letter went out to their list of family and friends, and the Hoovers were delighted to get return notes. Helen noticed two themes that ran through much of the correspondence: people commented on the simple beauty of the illustration Ade had created, and Helen's letter had elicited more questions about their move and new way of life, particularly living among such diverse and plentiful wildlife.

Ade's illustration had inspired one of their first efforts at making a living. Helen reasoned that Ade could create a variety of nature-themed designs that could be used on notepaper, letterhead, bridge tallies, and place cards. It would be easy enough to buy a selection of paper and envelopes by mail from the Duluth company that had provided their equipment and supplies. And the mimeograph would serve another important function: they could create direct mail letters to promote their crafts and notepaper business.

The winter proved to be harder than the Hoovers had anticipated. They had not estimated their food well, so they resorted to lots of starch and sugars to hold them over. Cornmeal pancakes with brown sugar syrup became a staple, as they were filling and provided energy, but they were also high in calories and fat. There were no fresh vegetables, only canned. Helen learned to bake bread, which was again inexpensive but full of carbohydrates.

Living in a cabin with cold temperatures and deep snow was something they had never experienced before. In Chicago, winter was a nuisance to be endured. If there was a major snowstorm, others dealt with snow removal, and eventually life returned to normal. In the north woods, coping with winter's harsh elements became a matter of life and death.

The Hoovers had no running water, and therefore, no indoor plumbing. The lake provided the fresh water they needed for cooking and cleaning. Ade cut a hole in the ice to draw buckets of water and covered it with a piece of wood. Although he hoped the covering would prevent the hole from freezing over each night, it didn't; he had to chop the hole every time he went to draw water. They had an outhouse, or privy, as Helen called it.

The cabin had a small oil furnace, so the airtight and the cook stove provided additional heat in the log cabin, but it was still cold despite their efforts to tighten up the cabin for winter. They landed on a routine for keeping the cabin relatively warm at night. Ade went to bed early, and Helen, being more of a night owl, read well into the night. Ade would fill the airtight with wood before he got into bed and read, providing heat for the early evening hours. Helen would then feed the stove before she turned in, often between midnight and one in the morning, which would extend the heat a few more hours. When they awoke in the morning, it was not uncommon that the temperature inside would be around freezing; Helen later remarked that on those very cold mornings there would be a thin layer of ice on top of the water bucket.

Fortunately, Ade had purchased a secondhand chainsaw from one of the nearby resort owners in the fall, providing an easier way to cut firewood for the seemingly inexhaustible amount of fuel the airtight and cook stove demanded.

\* \* \*

One late winter day there was a rap at the door. Helen opened it to find a well-dressed and sophisticated-looking gentleman carrying a variety of leather cases. He introduced himself as Volkmar Wentzel from *National Geographic* magazine, apologizing for not calling ahead but realizing when he arrived in town the Hoovers had no phone. Helen had thought the reply about not having a suitable camera had ended the magazine's interest, but apparently it did not. In addition to being caught off guard— Helen was concerned about what she felt was her dowdy appearance and Ade's growing beard—the cabin was dingy from being closed up all winter and smelled of fireplace smoke. They hardly looked presentable, particularly to such a worldly traveler.

The Hoovers escorted their guest around the grounds, scouting possible outdoor scenes. Wentzel took photos of Helen cooking, Ade feeding wood into the airtight, and the general layout of the cabin. He took many photos and passed along to Helen that his editor thought she would do a fine job writing up a short article to accompany the photo spread. She was encouraged that a letter alone had impressed an editor at *National Geographic* about her writing abilities.[21]

A sizable order for some of Ade's jigsaw handicrafts soon arrived in the mail. The income allowed them to purchase additional groceries that could be brought up by the mail truck. They splurged and bought ground beef and bacon; when it was delivered the following week, the grocer had included some suet and a bone. The suet would feed the birds, providing entertainment; the bone might attract a fox, which the grocer noted would be a good mouser.[22]

The Hoovers looked ahead to spring and the prospect of planting a garden and getting some chicks through one of the resort owners, who had suggested they would be easy to keep and would provide eggs. Fresh eggs appealed to Helen and Ade after a winter of powdered milk and powdered eggs. What's more, the addition of several chickens would bring another level of animal entertainment.

The return of warm weather also brought increased frequency in the mail service, and Ade would be able to use the runabout boat that the previous owner had included with the cabin sale. The purchase of a second-hand outboard motor allowed Ade to travel to Gunflint Lodge, where he could dock and walk a shorter distance up the road to the mailbox rather than the three miles it took in the wintertime walking by snowshoe or on foot once the road was plowed.[23]

Neighbor Peggy Heston dropped off the chicks. Ade set to the task of building a pen for them, as they would likely not survive without some protection from predators. Using scrap lumber, Ade created a decent-size coop and run area and enclosed it in chicken wire.

Myrl and Peggy Heston owned Heston's Lodge, located east of the Hoover cabins on the south side road. The Hestons purchased the lodge in 1943 and were originally from Chicago. As a family, they had traveled through Grand Marais to Ontario to fish and hunt, and they were familiar with the area. When the couple saw a for-sale ad for the resort in the local paper, they jumped at purchasing it. They were among the first to offer the Hoovers help in adapting to life in the north woods.[24]

While Helen and Ade were getting the chicks settled, there was a knock on the door from an unexpected visitor. Introducing himself from the U.S. Weather Bureau, Leo Jeske was checking to see if they would be willing to have an official rain gauge installed in their yard. He sheepishly noted that he intended to come earlier, but some of the neighbors thought the Hoovers might not make it through the winter. The task carried with it a stipend of $3.50 per month. Ade quickly agreed, noting forty-two dollars a year was real money to them.[25] The end of May brought a much-needed infusion of cash in the form of a $547.90 tax refund. Its timing could not have been better, as the Hoovers' checking account balance was down to $13.67.[26]

As tight as the finances were, Helen and Ade always intended to feed the birds and other animals that gathered in their yard. Neighbors had initially supplied them with some suet and corn, but once they began attracting more birds and small animals, it became a never-ending task to feed the various critters assembled in the yard. They started to regularly buy corn, sunflower seeds, suet, and graham crackers.

The summer of 1955 was spent taking time to fully unpack the boxes and furniture the mover had hurriedly dropped in the fall. They had shipped up most of their household goods, including hundreds of books and records, plus a phonograph. And Helen could finally play the baby grand piano that had been moved to the summer cabin.

With the return of the resort owners, people were anxious to check in and see how the Hoovers had survived their first winter. Some were frankly surprised, considering they did not eat game or fish, which they could take for the price of a license (or poach, which was widely done in remote areas as it was the only way to put food on the table). The stories of how they endured the cold, losing the car, Ade being laid up for several months with broken ribs, and the fact they fed birds and animals but had little food for themselves only added to the Hoovers' mystique.[27]

In occasional visits to the Gunflint Lodge and Heston's Lodge, Helen would spend time in their lobbies, reading various magazines and newspapers. After scanning a copy of *Audubon* magazine on one such visit, Helen realized there was ample material outside her cabin door that she could write about. Given her general understanding of nature and years of writing reports in the laboratory, she thought there might be an opportunity to do some observational nature writing of her own.[28]

Observing animals in nature was one reason they moved to Gunflint Lake. Helen was intent on learning how humans and nature could co-exist. While logic would suggest that feeding wildlife in their yard was a form of domestication, Helen and Ade saw it as a chance to help the animals, particularly in winter, which in turn provided them opportunities to study animal behavior and learn more about how they interacted with each other. The knowledge Helen gained from watching the animals—an extension of what she did in the laboratory back in Chicago—would become important as she began to consider writing about all that went on right outside the cabin windows.

In addition to magazine writing, Helen was starting to think that their experience moving to the forest might lead to a book, although up to this point she had never attempted something of that magnitude. Despite their lack of funds when they arrived at Gunflint Lake, Helen had continued to receive *Writer's Digest,* a magazine for aspiring writers she had subscribed to in Chicago.[29] She likely saw one of the prominent ads that appeared on page three of every issue touting A. L. Fierst, a New York literary agent, whose promotional sales pitch was likely irresistible to an aspiring writer like Helen. Seeking input and guidance, she sent Fierst a letter. Although no copy of this initial correspondence exists, he must have offered some measure of encouragement because Helen began to seriously consider writing a book based on their move and all the mishaps they subsequently endured.[30]

That summer, International Harvester contacted Helen to wrap up some unfinished business for her work on solving the disc harrow problem. Helen had received a patent for her discoveries in the austempering process, and her former bosses needed her to assign those patents to International Harvester so they could protect the intellectual property that was now the basis of their new manufacturing process. She was invited to Chicago to receive a commendation for her work but replied she wouldn't be able to attend as there was no one else to feed the chickens. She signed the appropriate papers and returned them by mail.

The interactions with International Harvester caused Helen to reflect on her work there. It provided an impetus to send a letter to management suggesting they consider ways of providing specialty compensation for "creative scientists" who labor on behalf of the company but are often thwarted in their abilities by the strict rules of the corporate environment. Helen made a well-articulated argument suggesting a bonus or royalty to keep these kinds of scientists engaged.[31] The reply from International Harvester vice president Ralph C. Archer grudgingly acknowledged that they had been trying to address that issue but were continually getting tripped up by the fact that they could not always reward individuals for innovations that were, in effect, a team effort. Archer also took the opportunity to suggest that Helen could "again return to an active life in business to which you could greatly contribute." He further indicated that her ability and talent was not being fully utilized living in the woods.[32]

The exchange of correspondence validated for Helen the reasons she had chosen to leave. Archer's letter implied she was foolish to be wasting her time in the woods, echoing the sentiments of the company psychiatrist, and was equally condescending in its tone about Helen's idea of royalties or special compensation for engineers and scientific staff. The response was typical corporate platitudes and the patronizing expectation of employee conformity that drove Helen from the company in the first place.

Helen channeled her frustration into two short stories that she hoped to sell to business or farm journals. The first, "The Fugitives from Our Laboratories," was a fictional yet autobiographical account of working in the confines of the corporate setting. She expertly articulated the structure of a research department not unlike International Harvester's and notably used the pronoun "he" throughout to describe the challenges the "creative scientist" faced in working in an environment where conformity to rules was rewarded and stepping outside of one's assigned task was considered insubordinate. The article built a strong case, arguing that forcing creative types into managerial harnesses was counterproductive to scientific inquiry and that those capable of making creative breakthroughs—idealists such as herself—would not be rewarded in such an environment and ultimately end up leaving the company. Notes in her ledger indicate she tried submitting it to several business magazines for publication, but the 3,700-word story was too narrowly focused and read like a manifesto for freeing scientists from unnecessary rules so they could do what they thought was best. The writing was likely more cathartic than anything else.[33]

In "From Field Failure to Factory: How Industrial Research Works for the Farmer," Helen provided an easy-to-follow yet technical narrative of how the disc harrow problem was assigned to her, the research she undertook to solve it, and the challenges she encountered along the way by the usual corporate naysayers and doubters. For the purposes of this fictionalized account, these colleagues represented in Helen's mind conformists who were obstacles to scientific inquiry. In this telling, the protagonist is a female scientist, and the narrative also introduces a range of internal critics with monikers such as "the Diehard," "the Up-and-Coming Young Man," "the Oldtimer," "the Conservative," and "the Metallurgist" to illustrate the various characters who got in the way. In the end, it is of course the creative scientist—an untrained woman, no less—who solves the problem none of the aforementioned naysayers—all men—believe could be solved. By then, the protagonist is disillusioned with the corporate hierarchy and moves to the woods once her work is finished.[34]

As with the first story, "From Field Failure to Factory" has a feeling of settling old scores and having the last word—which in a sense Helen did, by receiving a patent for the austempering process. More likely, writing these two articles was a way to finally put closure on this chapter of her life and move on, especially since she was not successful in selling them.

Helen turned her attention back to the notepaper business and decided to make inquiries by mail to gift shops, resorts, and grocery stores in the Grand Marais area to see if they would be interested in selling the nature stationery that Ade was creating. Coupled with the requests from friends following the late holiday letter, the Hoovers thought they might make some money by putting Ade's artistic talents to use. Operating their business as Hoover Handcraft, they offered a variety of items for sale. Helen created crochet patterns and instructions for making several items that could be sewn together. Ade designed stationery, note cards, bridge tallies, and place cards as well as wood picture plaques and jigsaw-cut letters and numerals, either painted or stained. The range of items offered belied that it was a husband-and-wife operation.

The Hoovers created a catalog in 1955 for friends and another for the gift shops, resorts, and other stores. For retail customers, the folksy catalog copy noted the "shop is in connection with our home. Ade prepares our designs, I work out the crochet, and we make our 'handmades' together." The copy in the wholesale catalog featuring Woodland Stationery was more direct: "These items sell. They go like hot cakes in gift shops . . . and national mail-order trials have been most successful." The Hoovers even provided a Dun & Bradstreet reference to allay any fears they were not a going concern.[35] Given their precarious financial situation, the Hoovers must have relied on their long-standing credit history from their days in Chicago.

The six-page catalog, designed by Ade and mimeographed, offered dozens of items, including notepaper and his hand-painted wood animal and letter initial pins, as well as the promotional items Helen procured through her uncle, Bruce Gomersall, who was in the advertising specialties business in Cincinnati. These included plastic "Handi-Hats" and five-comb family sets for thirty-five cents each or three for a dollar. Helen's crochet patterns were priced from fifteen to twenty-five cents. Woodland notepaper was sold in four designs of twenty-four folded sheets and envelopes for seventy-five cents. It's not clear how the Hoovers fulfilled the variety of handmade items they offered, but they were likely created once an order was received. All these transactions could be conducted by mail, making it an ideal home business for their circumstances. Whether it could produce enough income for them to live on was another matter.

One fall day in 1955, the deputy county sheriff appeared at their door and served the Hoovers with a summons and complaint from the man who they had the car accident with the previous November. He was demanding $800 for damage to his car, even though at the time he admitted to having no insurance. This came as a complete surprise, and the Hoovers quickly consulted a local attorney to help straighten out the situation.[36] Their lawyer filed a counterclaim for $10,300 for damages to their vehicle and lost income on the art contract since totaling the car prevented Ade from getting to the meeting in Duluth. This quickly brought the situation to a close, and both parties withdrew their claims. In the meantime, gossip along Gunflint Lake rumored that the Hoovers had initiated the lawsuit against the driver and that Ade was at fault.

Helen later included the accident and subsequent lawsuit in her book *A Place in the Woods* but downplayed the dispute as a simple misunderstanding that got cleared up at a meeting between the Hoovers and the driver in the lobby of one of the resorts. In actuality, the driver was put up to filing the complaint by some local people who thought the Hoovers had money and would be quick to settle. The episode, recounted by Helen in a letter to their attorney, was another example of how Helen and Ade were treated by locals.[37]

As the Hoovers began to prepare for their second winter, they had a better idea of what to expect, but having enough food was still a challenge. Without a car to get to town, one of the local resort owners suggested they estimate their needs for the winter and order their food from the Duluth wholesale food supplier in the fall before shipments for the season ended. Buying in bulk would save money, but they would also need to pay a large bill upfront. Fortunately, they could use their business, Hoover Handcraft, to qualify for a wholesale purchase. Helen requested a catalog from the supplier and went about determining how much food they would need from fall until spring.

This presented another challenge: where to store the cases of canned and packaged food that would be shipped to them. It helped that they had two cabins; the summer house was not insulated, so dry goods not affected by the cold could be stored there. Items at risk of freezing would need to be kept in the log cabin, which was heated but smaller than the summer house. This meant cases of food were stacked in every nook and cranny of both places. The additional weight in the log cabin was such that Ade needed to add structural support to the floors.

Finding room for the addition of dozens of cases of food would be no small task given the size of the winter log cabin. It had two rooms, one 17 × 12 feet and the other 24 × 12 feet, with the latter divided in half by a stove. In the smaller room they kept nearly a thousand books crowded around the walls on shelves that Ade had built from scrap lumber. There were windows on the north and west sides of this room, which faced the darkest parts of the woods. On the south side, where there was the most light, there was no window; the previous owner had hoped to build a fireplace on that wall.[38]

Half of the larger room was taken up by the kitchen, which required a person to walk across it to get anywhere in the cabin. There was a small window on the south side, where Helen attempted to grow some plants in winter. Ade's worktable was situated in front of the north window facing the lake, between the door and the living room, where it got all the drafts in winter. The other half of the larger room included more books, a worktable for Helen and her typewriter, about a hundred phonograph records, the phonograph, and some furniture. The Hoovers slept on a daybed and a studio couch, which proved more practical than a bed. The room also included a rocking chair, and clothes were piled where they would fit. In addition, this was considered the "work room" where they had set up the mimeograph, another table for production, and reams of paper and boxes of envelopes for the note card business.[39]

To say the log cabin was cramped would be an understatement.

Ade had been working on restoring the power plant that had been inoperable shortly after they bought the log cabin. Having worked as an electrician in the Navy and being an all-around handyman, Ade tinkered with it and hoped that they could at least generate enough electricity for lights so they did not have to rely solely on kerosene. On December 1, Ade felt that he had worked out all the technical quirks and decided to give it a trial for a couple of hours. The plant was in the old icehouse by the lake, which Ade had converted into his work building. They had electricity for several hours, which proved to be much better for reading and working in the evening. Ade felt confident he had fixed that problem.

That evening they decided to turn in at about eight in the evening. Later that night, Ade awoke and heard what he thought were tree branches breaking. The snapping sound got louder, and Ade went outside for a look; he thought it might be deer coming around the cabin. When he opened the door, he saw the work building in flames and yelled for Helen. They both ran to the lake, which was not yet frozen, and hustled buckets of water to extinguish the fire, working for several hours to save the building. Exhausted, they surveyed the damage. The building was still standing and was not a total loss; Ade had rescued the outboard motor they had purchased, but the power plant was ruined. It was yet another frustrating setback as they adapted to life in the wilderness, with only themselves to rely upon.[40]

As winter approached, Helen had started to write short stories about the animals she was observing. She did not know how or where she would sell them, but she was finding plenty of material in observing the birds they were feeding, as well as the smaller creatures that appeared in and around the cabins.

The winter of 1955–56 brought heavy snow, but the Hoovers were better prepared this time. The summer and fall had brought more time to make necessary repairs to both cabins, cut more firewood, and get into the seasonal rhythm of life in the wilderness.

Always an avid reader of mysteries, Helen thought that some of her writing might also be aimed at this genre and decided to join the Mystery Writers of America, a professional membership organization. She wrote to see if she would qualify and had an enthusiastic response from the executive director, Dorothy Gardiner. That struck up a friendship that served Helen well in many ways. Gardiner was herself a successful author of historical fiction and well connected in publishing circles. In Helen she found a smart, educated woman who shared her love of mysteries and writing. They began exchanging letters on a regular basis, with Gardiner sending extra books she received from publishers and providing tips and advice about writing.

As they got to know each other better, Helen must have confided her desire to write about nature, as they did not discuss how she could break into the mystery market. Gardiner offered advice on how she could sell her nature stories, both in the juvenile market, of which Helen had little knowledge, and the general market, where she might make real money. Helen provided ideas of where she thought her work could sell, and Gardiner pushed her to think confidently about her writing.

Inspired by their correspondence, Helen started to write short stories about animals and nature for the juvenile market. She reached out to magazines such as *Children's Activities* and *Humpty Dumpty's*, both popular titles aimed at young readers during the postwar years. Gardiner subtly mentioned Helen in the membership newsletter *The Third Degree*, noting her life in the woods as a writer and mentioning how many stories she had submitted for publication. These news items made it seem as if Helen were a peer of the organization's more accomplished members, which certainly didn't hurt her chances of being recognized by possible publishers.

During the 1950s, the market for nature stories was rich, with a variety of magazines publishing them. There were of course magazines for conservationists and those who enjoyed nature, such as *Audubon,* the magazine of the National Audubon Society; *Nature Magazine,* published by the American Nature Association, later merged with *Natural History;* the *Living Wilderness,* published by the Wilderness Society; and the *Atlantic Naturalist,* a publication of the Audubon Naturalist Society of the Central Atlantic States. There were also several literary and general interest magazines that featured nature stories and offered reviews of nature books. These included popular titles such as *The Atlantic Monthly, Harper's,* the *New Yorker,* the *Saturday Evening Post, Saturday Review,* and sometimes *National Geographic.*

While the *New Yorker* was considered more literary and erudite than other magazines during this time, editor William Shawn had been enchanted with Rachel Carson's book *The Sea around Us,* her exploration of the sea that combined factual observation with the wonder of discovery.

The *New Yorker* serialized the book in 1951, one of the first nature stories to receive such prominence in the magazine. The book appeared on the *New York Times* best-seller list for more than eighty weeks and won the coveted Burroughs Medal for excellence in nature writing. Shawn thought Carson a first-rate author and wanted to introduce her to America.[41]

There were also the "big three" outdoors magazines for hunting and fishing enthusiasts, a genre that had been popular in America for decades but boomed in the 1950s alongside men's magazines and an increase in hiking and camping. Competition between *Sports Afield, Outdoor Life,* and *Field & Stream* was fierce, reaching nearly three million readers in combined circulation. While Helen doubted her writing was a precise fit for these magazines, she did wonder whether her stories' emphasis on conservation might appeal to their readers.[42]

Helen continued to sketch out her autobiographical manuscript about two urban dwellers who spent years searching for a cabin deep in the boreal forest. The challenges they faced and the misfortunes that befell them added to the story line. At this point the story was more of a chronological narrative, combining observations of animals and nature with the hardships of adapting to living without the conveniences of their city home. Composite characters represented the many people who helped them, such as lodge owners, neighbors, and a local trapper.

In December, after reading a story in *Ellery Queen's Mystery Magazine* that had originally appeared in *Humpty Dumpty's,* Helen thought some of her nature writing could be good material for children and sent a note of introduction to Alvin R. Tresselt, *Humpty Dumpty's* editor. Tresselt was himself a successful children's author, having written *White Snow, Bright Snow,* with illustrations by Roger Duvoisin, which won the Caldecott Medal in 1948.[43] Helen noted in her letter that she was a former metallurgist from Chicago and proposed a monthly feature "about our wild neighbors, their habits and doings, our contacts with them, and their relations to each other and the sharp environmental changes they must meet." She signed off with mention of not having access to his magazine in her part of the world but that she would be happy to write something for his consideration.[44]

On Christmas Eve, Helen heard the howl of a wolf outside the cabin and went out to listen; in its eerie call she heard a loud "Nooooooooo-ellllll!"

The call gave her an immediate idea for a children's fairy tale, loosely based on the Norwegian legend that all animals can talk on Christmas. She sat down at the typewriter and quickly dashed off the story and finished it Christmas Day. Called "Great Wolf and the Good Woodsman," it tells the tale of a woodsman who twists his ankle and falls in his cabin, unable to get help; the deer, squirrel, and chickadee, whom he feeds, are worried that without a warm fire he might freeze to death. They contemplate how to help him, and in keeping with the legend, the wolf overhears their concerns and tells them he will go to the lake where another man lives and tell his dog to bring the man to the cabin. The wolf reaches the cabin where the dog lives. The dog rouses his owner and coaxes him to the cabin, where the woodsman is rescued. The moral is that we all have good things in us, and the reader is asked to listen carefully for the wolf howling "Noooooooooo-ellllllll!" on Christmas night. Helen thought "Great Wolf and the Good Woodsman" would make an enchanting children's story. She set it aside so she could work on it more in the new year and hoped to submit it to one of the children's magazines.

Meanwhile, Tresselt replied quickly with some sample issues of *Humpty Dumpty's*, but Helen wasn't convinced she was right for the magazine. Despite her uncertainty, she sent him several stories written on speculation, and he offered feedback on how to tailor them to the magazine's three-to-six-year-old audience. Tresselt clearly liked her writing style, and her correspondence was written in a genuine and conversational tone the New York editor found refreshing. As their letters continued in frequency, they were fast becoming friends, and Helen soaked up all the advice he offered about writing for young readers.[45]

One of the stories Helen wrote on speculation for *Humpty Dumpty's* was "Mr. Bear's Surprise." In it, the animals of the forest come together to get a Christmas tree for the bear that hibernates in the winter. The animals deliver the tree to Mr. Bear, waking him from his slumber, and the bear is grateful for their thoughtfulness. Helen wanted the message of the story to be the importance of doing something nice for others. Tresselt said that it was not a fit for *Humpty Dumpty's*, but he was encouraged by her effort just the same.[46]

When *Humpty Dumpty's* passed on "Mr. Bear's Surprise," Helen sent it to *Children's Activities* that spring. They accepted it for the December

1958 issue, for which they paid on publication. While she was delighted with the sale, it would still be more than a year before she would see the fifteen dollars they offered.

Among the animals that appeared as the Hoovers fed the visitors in their yard was an ermine, a sleek member of the weasel family whose fur color changes with the seasons. Helen was intrigued with this fast-moving mammal and its sly way of taking apart the suet cage at night to get at the food. She spent several weeks observing "Walter," as he was now called, at first from the cabin window, and then outside, sitting patiently by the cabin door with food in hopes of earning the weasel's trust. Eventually she did, and it sat on her lap while she fed it. Ade captured the moment in a photograph taken with the box camera they had brought with them. In January, Helen submitted a story about Walter to *Audubon*. The editor, John K. Terres, returned it with suggestions for a new introduction and a light rewrite of some parts. She submitted the revision, and they accepted it in June and paid her fifty dollars. She had now sold a story to one of the leading nature magazines in the field.[47]

It occurred to Helen that an ad in *Audubon* promoting their wildlife notepaper business might appeal to the magazine's readers. She placed their first classified ad in the March–April 1957 issue, promoting "Woodland Wildlife Notepaper . . . authentic scenes look handdrawn." The ad offered a sample packet with twenty-four sheets of notepaper and envelopes for a dollar. While the $3.15 cost of the ad was not insignificant for the Hoovers, the audience was perfect for Ade's fine wildlife drawings and hopefully worth the investment.[48]

Between the sales to two juvenile periodicals and a well-respected nature magazine, Helen was encouraged by her initial success. But it remained to be seen whether it would be enough to sustain them. The notepaper business continued to show promise, so if her writing and Ade's artwork could bring in enough money, they might not have to return to Chicago, proving their success to all of those who bet against them making a life in the woods.

\* \* \*

In May 1957, Helen learned that a great-aunt in Cincinnati had taken ill. Helen felt it was important to go and be of help to her maternal aunts and uncles. All were single or widowed and lived in an old mansion that Helen had remembered visiting from her youth. This would be the first time she had left Gunflint Lake since the car accident in November 1954, just months after they had moved there permanently, and she anticipated being gone for a few weeks.

Helen hoped the trip would give her time to continue working on the manuscript about two urban dwellers moving to the north woods. Unfortunately, the visit exposed the idiosyncratic life of her mother's siblings. Her two uncles, Bruce and Robert, talked incessantly, the television always on in the background. Helen had planned to write twelve to fourteen pages a day, but she couldn't concentrate enough with all the interruptions. She was able to get just one or two pages completed each day, and only after everyone had turned in for the night. Instead of trying to write during the day, she explored the attic of the house with its old trunks and clothes, things she remembered from her childhood visits, and conjured up some mystery storylines that she could turn into something later.

The Hoovers wrote to each other nearly every day, with Ade sharing news about what was going on at the lake and Helen sending observations of her bachelor uncles and their quirky behavior. The mail was delivered twice a day in Cincinnati, so it was easy to send letters back and forth. Helen excitedly told him she had been working on a scene based on the real-life fire that burned down the Gunflint Lodge in 1953, but with her own fictional twist of the main character, Jenny, finding the body of an escaped mental patient in the ruins.[49]

When Helen returned from Cincinnati, she was pleased with her magazine sales and began to write more nature and juvenile stories for submission. She composed the story of an injured mother mouse who raised her brood under the large cook stove with the help of the Hoovers feeding them. She offered it to *Nature Magazine* with three illustrations by Ade accompanying the piece. This one sold relatively quickly, and she was paid fifty dollars. She submitted several other short stories that fall and waited to hear of their acceptance.

On a beautiful September day, the Hoovers took out their boat for a ride around the lake, taking in the sun and fall colors. On their return, Ade caught sight of the yellow heating oil truck on the side road by Gunflint Lodge. It was a reminder they had not stocked up on oil for the coming winter. Concerned that with the lodge closed for the season the oil man would not be back, Ade visited a neighbor down the way who was staying for the winter. The man indicated that the oil man did not come up the trail in winter, but he would be happy to sell Ade some oil at retail prices, which were higher at this end of the trail. Ade would need to go to his place and transfer the oil into containers and haul it back to their cabin.

Ade and Helen thought this was somewhat unneighborly, but they went along because they needed the oil. They would have to be careful given the high cost, but they could manage. Helen tried to imagine why a neighbor would not be more accommodating, and she recalled one of the locals who had referred to the Hoovers as "kooks" the previous year. The impression must have made the rounds and stuck with some people.[50]

In between writing short articles for money, helping Ade with the growing notepaper business, and other tasks, Helen finished the manuscript she had long been working on. Having been encouraged by A. L. Fierst, the New York literary agent she corresponded with in 1955, she packaged up the three hundred–page plus manuscript on November 17 and sent it off for his review.[51]

The manuscript, titled "A Little Place in the Woods," was the autobiographical story of Helen and Ade's decision to find a cabin and eventually move from the city to the woods. Helen wrote it under a pseudonym, Jennifer Price, and used different names for themselves: Jenny and Don. As in her future books, she makes composites of people in the area and also assigns them pseudonyms. The writing is fairly straightforward, and she relates amusing as well as frustrating tales of adapting to their new life. Her description of the log cabin and the subsequent travails with the spring running through the basement and the effort to get the foundation walls secured are recounted in all their maddening detail. The "summer" cabin purchased from their neighbors in 1953 is also rich in its description of the yard, plants, and its furnishings, some of which they were able to purchase.[52]

Many actual incidents that occurred during their first couple of years appear in the draft: getting their furniture and belongings situated in the two cabins, gathering firewood and fixing up the roof, learning to keep the cabin warm with the airtight and the kitchen's cook stove, and going to town for groceries and supplies with the subsequent car accident. She also includes Ade losing his art contract, starting the notepaper business, the weather bureau man showing up to offer them the job of measuring the temperature, rain, and snow, and getting chickens from one of the resort owners.

The manuscript also notes Helen's realization that she can write about nature and describes some of the early efforts to submit pieces to nature and children's magazines. Other day-to-day interactions include neighbors who cut ice for them, the man delivering heating oil, and a visit across the lake by boat so Ade could get his hair cut by a Métis woman named Awbutch Plummer, who worked for Justine Kerfoot and was part of a settlement of indigenous families who lived on the Canadian side of the lake. The manuscript ends on this scene, with the Hoovers looking back across the lake at their cabin, which after a brief summer shower, is illuminated by a rainbow that ends on their shore. They take it as signal that they will be staying.

# 5

# The Buck with the Generous Heart

*Gunflint Lake, 1958–1962*

**ALTHOUGH HELEN CONTINUED TO MAKE SOME MONEY** from her stories and the notepaper business was doing well, both activities took considerable time, often leaving the Hoovers exhausted. They still struggled to make ends meet and had mortgage and insurance payments to make, supplies to purchase for the business, and food to buy—especially in the fall when they needed to lay in a large grocery order to get by until spring. And of course, the corn, seeds, and suet for the birds, squirrels, and deer they were intent on feeding was also a considerable expense in winter.

Helen's stories were each selling for between fifteen and fifty dollars, but there were as many rejections as there were sales. In 1957 (her first full year of writing), she sold four stories, for an income of $185. There were the weasel and fisher stories for *Audubon* and the story of the injured mother mouse that she sold to *Nature Magazine.* She was able to do a slight rewrite of the weasel story for *Frontiers,* another nature magazine, which paid thirty-five dollars.[1]

The notepaper business was labor-intensive and took much of their time. As early as 1955, they produced catalogs promoting the designs and other promotional items they sold. Helen wrote promotional copy for the catalogs, and Ade created new notepaper designs each year. Drawing the stencils for each design was time-consuming, and it needed to be fit in between all the other chores and repairs that filled his day. Expenses were high as they needed to keep a variety of paper and envelopes in stock to fulfill the catalog offerings.[2]

Ade also created custom stationery for local businesses. These included stencils for the Wedgewood Motel in Grand Marais as well as for St. John's Catholic Church, personal stationery for a New York literary agent, and Christmas notepaper with woodland scenes for customers looking for something unique for their holiday letters. The Hoovers offered a holiday card with a patch of birch bark covered with a small pine bough attached by a red string.[3]

The notepaper business lost $831 in 1957, so it was good that Helen's income could offset the losses. The business started to do better in 1958, likely with the help of the classified advertising in *Audubon* magazine. By the end of the year, the losses were only $320.[4]

In early 1958, the Hoovers received a notepaper order from Winnifred (Winnie) Hopkins of Milford, Delaware, likely a result of the classified ad. This was the start of a long friendship by mail that would serve Helen well years later when she was writing her final book, *The Years of the Forest*. In their correspondence, Hopkins mentions several times that she kept all of Helen's letters to reread, and Helen noted that someday she might want them back if she ever wrote a book. Indeed, that is what happened, and the letters provide insight into the daily life of the Hoovers spanning several years.[5]

In February, *Humpty Dumpty's* editor Alvin Tresselt accepted Helen's fable-like story about the Christmas wolf, "Great Wolf and the Good Woodsman." She was paid fifty dollars, and the story, published in December 1958, would be the first of her writing to appear in the magazine. Tresselt wanted to see more of her nature writing, believing they might be able to make room for those types of stories. Having written the "Woodsman" story almost as a lark, its acceptance boosted her confidence.[6]

Helen had been writing through the previous fall and now had several articles accepted. In its "This Happened to Me" feature, *Outdoor Life* published her submission about her firing a gun at two wolves attacking a doe, which she submitted under the byline "J. Price, Grand Marais, Minn."[7] This was the first time she was able to sell to a mainstream sportsman's magazine. She also sold stories on the Canada lynx, flying squirrels, and shrews to *Audubon, Canadian Audubon,* and *Frontiers* magazines, respectively.

Helen revisited two articles she had written about her days at International Harvester and decided to send them around to business magazines for consideration. She pitched "The Fugitives from Our Laboratories," her missive about disrespect shown to scientists and creative engineers, to *Nation's Business*, *The Atlantic Monthly*, and *Harper's*, but all of them passed on it. She sent a variation of this same story to *Life* magazine, but it was rejected there as well.[8]

At this point Helen was writing and sending out as many articles as she could, knowing some would hit and others would not. Although not big moneymakers, her monthly animal stories for *Humpty Dumpty's* were each paying thirty dollars and were a steady source of income. What became apparent was that her stories about nature and animals were having more success being accepted than her submissions to business and mainstream magazines.

In addition to her nature writing, Helen was also a gifted letter writer. She had the skill of adjusting her letters to the interests of each recipient. For Winnie Hopkins, she offered a friendly, conversational style, offering insight into the wildflowers that grew in their yard, the latest antics of the animals, the types of birds they were feeding, and brief glimpses of her nature writing for children. There were also references that filled in their routine, such as Ade's three-mile walk to the mailbox, how they got their food in winter, the books she enjoyed reading, the bread she baked, and other minutiae of their daily life. Most of the writing was upbeat, with an occasional reference to hardship; Helen was wise enough not to invite pity. She also asked about her friend's vegetable and flower gardens and offered opinions on health issues when asked.

In the case of Alvin Tresselt, there was the usual discussion of editorial suggestions, rewrites of stories, and topics for future submissions. Tresselt, like the Hoovers' notepaper customers, friends, and old coworkers from Chicago, was curious about their north woods existence and worked in questions asking how they managed in such a remote location, how they tolerated the weather, and how they kept from getting bored; this, too, provided opportunities to share insights about their lives. Tresselt and Helen's relationship became closer as they shared points of view on conservation issues and other topics of modern life, including current events, the threat of nuclear war, and even some national politics (both had been for Adlai Stevenson in the 1956 presidential election).

They shared an easy relationship as Helen opened up and Tresselt became fond of both her intellect and the quality of writing she produced for the magazine. He admired how she and Ade lived away from the pressures of urban life, which as a New York editor he dealt with every day. His letters reveal the hubbub of someone in the publishing industry, with details about the daily commute between Connecticut and Manhattan, family activities, business travel, and the corporate pressures of overseeing several magazines for children, as well as being an editor at Parents' Magazine Press.

Helen's correspondence with Dorothy Gardiner was similarly focused on shared mutual interests. Initially Helen wrote to inquire about membership in the Mystery Writers of America, but after exchanging letters she learned that Gardiner was also a successful author. In turn, Gardiner recognized a kindred intellectual spirit from their correspondence and became a great source of information on the publishing world. As Helen continued her output of short stories for the nature field, Gardiner offered encouragement and was a cheerleader when Helen received a rejection letter or was unable to sell an editor on a story idea.

Despite the vigor with which she wrote, a recurring complaint Helen made was that she was forever behind on her correspondence and had to clear the backlog of several dozen letters or it would hinder her ability to focus on writing and other tasks.

Helen kept carbon copies of her most important correspondence, such as those with her editor Tresselt. However, when it came to personal letters, she couldn't afford to use the carbon paper, making copies of her personal letters rare. Helen also wrote letters in longhand, so no copies of those exist. That's why the trove of letters Helen received back from Winnie Hopkins is so helpful at understanding the Hoovers' day-to-day life.

The winter lingered in 1958. Despite their careful planning the previous fall, the heating oil ran out, forcing Helen and Ade to burn trash, rags, worn rugs, and even an old mattress, along with wood to maintain the heat.[9]

While the late winter also impacted their ability to order food that spring, there was enough to feed the birds and squirrels. Helen would also save scraps from their meals to feed the various animals that were now regular visitors. Besides genuinely wanting to help in the bitter winter, feeding them also kept the animals in the yard so Helen could watch them and study their interactions. Her natural inquisitiveness and observational skills afforded her a perceptive view of animal behavior that informed the nature stories she was writing, while the animals in the yard provided ample subject material.

In the spring of 1958, the Hoovers' poorly balanced diet caught up with Helen; she developed scurvy. Helen promptly ordered lemons from the local grocer, who sent them up by mail.[10] This wasn't the only time that a poor diet plagued Helen. She wrote to Tresselt that she had been "tired and crabby" for three months, and when she cut her hand on a metal can lid, she bled "pink liquid." After consulting an old hemoglobin comparison chart—only a former scientist would have one of those lying about a cabin—she realized her blood iron was down to 40 percent. She promptly ordered liver and bottles of iron from town and felt better in a few weeks. "Here is an example of the hazards of living in isolation," she wryly admitted in a letter.[11]

Spring brought about new activity along the lake as cabin owners returned and the lodges planned for the opening of the fishing season. The oil deliveryman stopped in to check on Helen and Ade and replenish their supply after the long winter. The Hoovers were relieved to see him and related how they had run out of oil and resorted to burning trash and other junk to keep warm. He asked why they hadn't let him know they needed more oil when he was up in February, and they shared the story of the neighbor who told them there were no deliveries in the winter. Annoyed by this ruse, the deliveryman asked what they had paid. When told thirty cents a gallon, he said he would have sold it to them for just over eighteen cents a gallon and offered to bring up some used oil drums to store it. The deliveryman was curious why they had not written during the winter to let him know they needed oil. Ade sheepishly explained that they didn't know his name. "You could address a letter to the 'oil man,'" he said, "and it would have gotten to me." The Hoovers realized they had yet again been subjected to the unfriendliness of some neighbors, but also understood they still had a bit of the city about them.[12]

As Helen pondered additional ideas for articles, she decided that a story about a north woods Thanksgiving would be fun to write up. As the basis for her story and the recipes accompanying it, she used their first Thanksgiving on Gunflint Lake in 1954. That first autumn, the Hoovers were invited to Gunflint Lodge with some of the local neighbors who had remained in the area after the tourist and hunting seasons. It was a communal meal, and Helen captured the spirit of the occasion. The lodge owners, Bill and Justine Kerfoot, had prepared venison, and others had brought potatoes to mash and ingredients for salad. Helen made rolls in the lodge kitchen. The article included recipes for blueberry rolls and raspberry cream pie, as well as one for mincemeat. She sent it off to *Gourmet* magazine and received an acceptance; she was paid $150, her largest single writing sale to date.[13]

With the coming of spring in 1958, Helen and Ade planned a garden and hoped to grow carrots, onions, and beans, along with flowers. The growing season was short this far north, and of course anything they planted would be of interest to the many animals that frequented the yard. Helen wished to grow root vegetables that might last into the winter, when something fresh would taste good and provide natural nutrition. Ade went about building protection out of old chicken wire and hoped that would keep nibbling animals at bay.

In May, the local newspaper, the *Cook County News-Herald,* carried a front-page article about Helen, calling her a "writer-inventor" who "lives on Gunflint Trail." The occasion of the article seemed to be the official awarding of her U.S. patent for the "heat-treated agricultural implement disks" the previous November. There was also mention of the award in *Farm Implement News* in March. The local newspaper editor must have been made aware of these developments by Helen, as no one else would have known so many details. The article also made note that "many a manuscript had been mailed through the local P.O." and proceeded to offer a biographical sketch lifted from the *Farm Implement News* story.[14]

What is curious about the news article is the motivation for sharing all this personal background at this time. The Hoovers had lived on Gunflint Lake for nearly four years but were still considered outsiders. Did Helen believe a story recognizing her professional achievements would make them more acceptable to local residents? Or was she trying to assert that she and Ade were smarter than people gave them credit for and needed to provide the credentials to prove it? While her motivations were not clear, her ability at self-promotion was evident.

By the summer of 1958, Helen had become involved in a local issue that could have an impact on the area in general and their side road in particular. There had been discussions in Grand Marais about creating a new U.S. border crossing into Canada to make it more convenient than the crossings at Grand Portage to the east and International Falls to the west. The proposal by the town's chamber of commerce was to extend the road on the south side of Gunflint Lake and create an entry point at the far eastern end of the lake. Many locals were opposed to this, as it would increase traffic along the road and spoil the wild nature of the area. While some would welcome the increased commerce, especially business leaders in Grand Marais, others, like the Hoovers and some of their neighbors and resort owners on the Gunflint Trail, were not convinced. Meetings were held and letters in opposition were written to the *Cook County News-Herald*. Helen was more than happy to help organize those opposed to the project.[15] She also sent a letter to George Selke, the commissioner of the Minnesota Department of Conservation in St. Paul, to make him aware of the proposal. She observed that "a road here would be the beginning of the end for this wilderness area, which is particularly unspoiled and readily accessible."[16]

During this time, Helen had been sending *Humpty Dumpty's* short features on a variety of animals. Tresselt had bought most of them, and in July he said that he wanted her to write a monthly nature column for the magazine called "Aunt Helen's Nature Page." He thought her style and voice were very much like someone's aunt, believing it would be a good way to frame the feature for young readers. The column would start the next January; Helen now had a monthly recurring source of income, even if it was nature stories for children, paying thirty dollars each.[17]

With the quick acceptance of the Thanksgiving story in *Gourmet* earlier in the year, Helen decided to submit several more food and cooking stories, hoping the editors would like those as well. A short story titled the "The Apple Butter Kettle" was rejected for its "weak theme." Two others, "Marriage Is a Feast" and her story about the neighbor Charlie Olson who came to cook dinner, titled "Ol' Eric's Plain Cooking," were also rejected. Again, she was clearly doing better with her animal and nature stories.[18]

In the summer, Ade discovered his pet rooster, Crown Prince, had died during the night. Ade had built a coop for the three chickens and created a run for them, complete with chicken-wire protection from the various predators that might show an interest. Crown Prince's death was difficult for the Hoovers. In a letter to her editor Tresselt, Helen noted it was "written through a pall of gloom, cast by the unexpected death of our big old rooster, who was alarm clock, watch dog, protector of the hens, and family pet."[19]

The cooperative power company had been bringing electricity up the Gunflint Trail, and representatives were going from property to property to determine interest and get owners to sign easements to clear the land for the power lines. The Hoovers were skeptical about electricity; they had been getting by without it, and when they wanted something special, like music on a New Year's Eve, Ade could get the old power plant running, and they could enjoy the luxury of listening to records or tuning in to radio celebrations at midnight. When they learned that the clearing required to reach their cabin from the road could be two hundred feet wide, they politely told the power company salesman they were not interested. He tried several angles to get them to reconsider, but as Helen said later, "we decided in favor of the trees."[20]

In the autumn of 1958, *Gourmet* magazine arrived with the "Snow Country Thanksgiving" feature Helen had quickly written earlier in the year. She was also surprised to see her story "Weasels Are Wonderful," about the ermine she had been able to feed from her hand, as the cover story of the November–December issue of *Audubon*. She knew that editor John K. Terres was pleased with her writing, but she did not expect her story to receive such prominent display. She felt this boded well for her fledgling writing career.[21]

Dorothy Gardiner offered writing advice and admonished Helen not to get a literary agent or pay one for a reading fee; Helen didn't share that she had previously sent a book manuscript to a New York agent. Gardiner also suggested she reach out to some major publishers. They occasionally

did books of nature essays, and she would be in a good position to un-
dertake such a project given her work with *Audubon* and the other nature
magazines now buying her stories.[22]

In December 1958, writing to her friend Hopkins, Helen mentioned
the idea of writing a book. In the letter, she provides thoughts on what
she believes is a more realistic perspective on living in the woods from
what was then recognized as the classic of the genre:

> Have thought of doing a book on our woods life but this is a
> problem because of Louise Dickinson Rich's WE TOOK TO THE
> WOODS. Everyone looks to that as a sort of bible and, really, she
> only says exactly what almost everyone says who is in the woods
> and looks at it in the most conventional way. That is probably the
> secret of its success. I enjoyed reading it to no end, but can take
> issue with a lot of things in it.
>
> The truth of the matter is that, unless you are remarkably
> phlegmatic, life in a place like this has moments of hair raising
> terror, mind-numbing glory, heart-wracking sorrow. But, when
> most of the accounts show only the gentler side of it and make
> it look so very much easier that [sic] it is and play upon only the
> emotions that are usually roused in people in less dramatic situ-
> ations, it is hard to try and write something that is true and will
> still be accepted. It is hard to make people believe some of the
> things of beauty than [sic] come and go. It is hard to show that
> observance of violent death, which is the only death wilderness
> things know, has [sic] it in the whole of "I am Alpha and Omega,
> the Beginning and the Ending." The woods is a[n] admixture of
> violence and peace, beauty and terror, wildness and gentleness.
> I have never read anything that really brings that out, that is,
> anything in the popular vein. I'm afraid it would be hard to sell
> because people like to think of the wilderness as a place in which
> to escape from all the struggle of life, while it really is a place of
> constant struggle.[23]

*We Took to the Woods* was a best-selling book published in 1942 and offered many parallels to Helen and Ade's own woods life. Louise Dickinson

Rich was in her early thirties when she and her husband Ralph moved to the remote backcountry area of western Maine near the town of Middle Dam. Rich spent years submitting articles to a variety of magazines, including *Outdoor Life*, the *Saturday Evening Post*, *Good Housekeeping*, and *Woman's Home Companion*, before she wrote her book chronicling their life in the woods. They even had a "summer house" and a "winter house," which is how the Hoovers referred to their own two cabins.

As Helen noted, the book was a joy to read, mostly because Rich could relate to her readers. Each chapter's title was in the form of a question, asking something about living in the wilderness that either a friend or faraway city dweller had asked. While Helen had some quibbles with the uplifting way she portrayed life in the woods, Rich captured for a broad audience the idyllic aspects of living in the country sprinkled with enough hardship so as not to lose credibility by making it seem too rosy.[24]

While Helen contemplated a nature book, her magazine writing continued to pay off. By the end of 1958, she had been paid $638 for more than a dozen stories submitted to children's and nature magazines, a significant jump in income from 1957.[25] "Mr. Bear's Surprise," the children's story she submitted the previous year telling of the forest animals bringing a Christmas tree to the hibernating bear, was published in *Children's Activities* in December, accompanied by the fifteen-dollar payment. It was the first story she sold after moving to Gunflint Lake.[26]

The holiday notepaper business had done well, too, and with Helen's income from writing, it started to feel as if there was an easing of pressure on how they would make a living. Coupled with a holiday check from her aunt Claire Gomersall, Helen and Ade decided to invite their friend Ollor Snevets, a local trapper and guide, to have Christmas dinner with them. Snevets was a fixture in the area, and the Hoovers liked him because he was an independent thinker and self-supporting, traits they found appealing. Helen prepared a holiday feast—turkey with a bounty of side dishes, including mashed potatoes, sweet potatoes, peas, and raw carrot salad.[27]

After dinner and while enjoying dessert, Helen heard breaking branches outside the cabin door. She looked out the window to see an emaciated deer feeding on Swiss-chard seed stalks in the garden, its ribs visible, and its legs trembling. The buck was clearly starving, and as Snevets observed, someone had taken a shot at its head and the animal appeared blind in its left eye. He knew the creature had to be hungry, as a buck would not venture so close to a house and people unless desperate for food. Helen wanted to feed it, and she provided some scraps left over from the meal. Snevets suggested they let the deer poke around the yard to graze on what frozen plants were left in the garden and cut cedar boughs for it to eat. That would hopefully help get the buck healthy.

Thus began several years observing Peter Whitetail, as Helen named the buck, and eventually the doe Mama and their numerous offspring. Helen was captivated by Peter, and the fact that he responded so well to her efforts to nourish him back to health only provided more impetus to learn about this special animal. He returned to the yard for the next several days, and Helen found more food scraps to give him. Ade went into the woods to cut cedar boughs and brought them back to the yard.

Helen had no practical knowledge of deer but continued to feed Peter and some others through the winter. The protection of their large yard gave Helen plenty of opportunity to observe him while he interacted with the other animals. Helen noticed when she was outside that Peter could not see her if she was on his left side, a result of the eye injury. She spent time coaxing him to turn his head fully to the left so he could see that side. Helen believed that without this "training" Peter would be more vulnerable to a predator.[28]

Peter was gradually regaining his health, thanks to Helen's assortment of food and Ade's supply of cedar boughs. The Hoovers purchased corn from town and added sunflower seeds and suet for the birds and squirrels. If Peter wanted more food, he would tap the back step of the cabin or peek into the windows—knowing Helen and Ade were inside—and they would soon produce something for him to eat.[29]

One day in January, Peter came to the cabin in an agitated state. Helen smelled wood smoke, and upon looking toward a neighbor's closed-up cabin, she could see a small campfire that had been started by an ice fisherman. Helen thought it odd that Peter had come to "tell" her about the fire and found his behavior to be curious. She ground up some carrots for him and wished she had more scientific literature about deer.[30]

The beginning of 1959 brought more encouragement for Helen's writing in the form of a ten-page single-spaced letter from the New York literary agent A. L. Fierst. He returned the manuscript "A Little Place in the Woods" marked up with suggestions in the early pages, because "style is of maximum importance at the beginning of a book" and "your writing improved as it went along." He liked Helen's descriptive writing and felt most of her dialogue was credible.[31]

Fierst's primary criticism of the manuscript was that it was not unlike other books in the same genre: husband and wife leave the city for the country and face difficult challenges. While he did not cite *We Took to the Woods,* he did mention *The Egg and I,* the 1945 best-selling book by Betty MacDonald that recounts her husband buying an egg farm on the Olympic peninsula in Washington and the subsequent trials and tribulations they had adapting from city life to raising chickens. Helen disliked the book because of its emphasis on Betty's timidity and her husband's assumption that she wanted to live on a farm. Most readers, however, could identify with the light approach MacDonald used to illustrate her plight, her own personality quirks, lack of farm experience, odd neighbors, and unsympathetic husband, which made for a breezy read. What was left unsaid is that the woman had no choice in the matter; the husband made the decisions, and the wife was expected to go along.[32]

One of the key suggestions Fierst made was the necessity of fictionizing (today we would say fictionalizing), even in a nonfiction book. While "A Little Place in the Woods" was mostly autobiographical and based on real places, people, and events, Helen had fictionized some elements of the story, such as the circumstances of the dead body found in the ashes after the lodge fire. While that was based on a true event of the Gunflint Lodge burning down in July 1953 and a young guest who had died, for dramatic effect Helen had made the victim an escapee of a mental hospital the local sheriff was pursuing. Specifically, Fierst noted, "even if the author is entirely faithful to what was seen and discovered, he is likely to fictionize by probing a character, highlighting a minor conflict of personalities, streamlining actual dialogue, and so on." He noted further that "fictionizing is not only harmless but almost always desirable."[33]

Fierst implied he had shared the manuscript with some publishers, indicating to them the author would be tightening up parts of it. There is no evidence of him receiving any inquiries about a book, and there is also no indication that Helen did further work on this manuscript for him.

Perhaps she thought it best to focus on building her reputation writing magazine articles, as she was now selling them at a good pace. And she may have decided to heed her friend Gardiner's advice not to engage with literary agents.

Peter the buck now appeared in Helen's correspondence. In a note to Hopkins, Helen wrote, "the deer has since adopted us. Every day he trots down to the house and gawks in the windows until we give him corn and suet and crackers."[34] Helen's ongoing curiosity with Peter had presented in her mind the possibility of a story she could submit to several magazines, even some beyond the nature field. She queried her editor John K. Terres at *Audubon,* as well as Russell Lynes, the editor at *Harper's* magazine—someone Gardiner had suggested—but was turned down by both.[35]

The Hoovers had brought their box camera and 8 mm film camera from Chicago, but they rarely used either because the cost of processing film was expensive. However, Helen wanted to take pictures of Peter, not only to accompany letters pitching the deer story but also for Ade to have for any illustrations he might do. Film could be sent by mail to Grand Marais for processing and returned the same way.

Despite Helen's success writing for various publications, she was not feeling up to doing much writing the winter of 1958–59. In May 1959 she confided to Hopkins that "she was under the weather" and had been "dodging a nervous collapse when I came up here, brought on by interruptions to my research work." She shared that the residual chronic problems stemming from her career job—"stomach butterflies, nightmares, and nervous sweats, and such miseries"—still troubled her, so she contacted the town doctor in Grand Marais and received some tranquilizers to help. "You can't imagine how wonderful it is to feel good and peppy after ten years of jitters."[36]

This admission to Hopkins of "jitters" nearly five years after the Hoovers had moved north and ostensibly left those work troubles behind was telling. Helen and Ade's first years of living in the north woods were not easy. Even though they had left the pressure of work and the unhealthy physical environment of Chicago for Gunflint Lake, life was not without new obstacles and challenges. While they ardently believed in their self-adopted motto "something will turn up," the wait between

money coming in and the unanticipated troubles and expenses that arose
were likely terrifying. The mishaps they encountered tested their confidence in themselves, and their initial lack of planning to live in the
woods—and not seeking help from others—often put their lives at risk.
Their naïveté and reclusiveness were the sources of gossip, curiosity, and
mild amusement of longtime residents who were also suspicious of newcomers. Neighbors could not relate to a couple living year-round in the
woods who did not hunt or fish. The fear of failing to make a living must
also have contributed to Helen's chronic nervous condition.[37]

Throughout early 1959, Peter continued to be a presence in the
Hoovers' lives, and his well-being was a source of interest while Helen
was not feeling up to writing. Another pair of deer tracks appeared, and
one day they noticed a young buck accompanying Peter to the yard. Helen
named him Snowboots for his smaller feet; he was likely one of Peter's
offspring born the previous year. Several nights later, the Hoovers set out
more cedar boughs, and after dinner they heard thumping. The doe that
had been so elusive for many months appeared in the clearing, feeding
with two fawns. Appropriately, they named her Mama.[38]

In the spring, Helen's first story for the *Living Wilderness* arrived,
which was the magazine of the Wilderness Society, a national conservation organization that advocated for federal lands protection. The article
was the first of four that would describe each season on Gunflint Lake,
this one about the coming of spring. It featured some of the observational
writing that would become her signature in the future:

> I enter the trail in the everlasting shadow of the trees, their trunks
> rising from the springy brownness of the needle-covered forest
> floor like temple columns, filigreed by palest-green lichens and
> brightened by the emerald velvet of moss. A hundred feet above,
> the evergreen branches interlace, as pine and spruce, cedar and
> balsam, brace each other against the fury of the winds. Here and
> there silver birches, their trunks ragged with bark like shattered
> armour, show high silvery branches, misty with the purple of
> buds and the green promise of leaf-tips. There is no underbrush
> in this dim and shaded place, but scattered green shoots foretell
> future low verdure.[39]

By summer Helen had snapped out of her funk and was writing again—both her regular *Humpty Dumpty's* nature columns and articles for *Audubon, Frontiers,* and other nature magazines. Editor Alvin Tresselt wrote to tell her they were increasing her rate to forty dollars per column, a welcome increase in income. She was flattered to be invited to write a piece for the *Naturalist,* the quarterly journal of the Natural History Society of Minnesota, which Ade illustrated. Encouraged by friend Gardiner, she sent out feelers to other national publications to see if there might be interest in her nature writing.[40] She started a back-and-forth correspondence with John Lear, the science editor at *Saturday Review,* hoping to interest him in something. As she revealed more about their woods life and daily routine, Lear became more inquisitive, especially when Helen mentioned they "order the groceries for the whole winter in one swoop because they come by freight."[41] That elicited curiosity from Lear, and Helen replied with a brief accounting of the seasonal food order:

200 lbs. of white flour with perhaps 15 lbs. each of rye and whole wheat, white and yellow cornmeal, hominy grits, oats, and brown and white rice.

15–26 cases of canned vegetables and juices.

6–10 cases of canned fruits and juices.

10–15 cases of canned meats and fish.

100 lbs. of granulated sugar and 25 each of brown and powdered.

A quantity of necessary miscellany: yeast, salt, baking powder, toilet tissue, wax wrapping paper, powdered eggs, etc.

Occasional luxuries: cookies, salad dressings, molasses, peanuts, gingerale, etc.[42]

While the letters didn't lead to any request for article submissions, the dialogue was instructive in what a national general interest magazine editor would consider in terms of nature writing. Helen absorbed as much as she could from their correspondence and notched it up as another contact that might prove useful in the future.

With the arrival of tourists in summer and increased activity and sounds along the road, Peter and the deer family withdrew into the forest where ample quantities of food were now available and they could freely exist away from visitors. It would also be time for Mama to give birth to fawns, which she would do in a safe and quiet place.

For several years the area around Gunflint Lake had been infested with budworms, which caused defoliation of the balsam and spruce trees, eliminating the cones that were a source of food for squirrels, chipmunks, and birds. In addition to depleting this important food source, the trees were stripped of outer needles in their upper crowns, making them appear as if they would die. Many of the Hoovers' neighbors prematurely cut down trees they believed would die; others asked the U.S. Forest Service and other government agencies to eradicate the budworms with aerial DDT spraying.[43]

Helen was opposed to any sort of DDT spraying, and she complained in letters to the editor of the local paper about the county highway department using DDT to keep the weeds down on the Gunflint Trail and their side road. Being a reader of science and nature magazines, Helen knew of the damning evidence becoming widely known among scientists and conservationists about the impact DDT had on the ecosystem. She had read about the spraying of trees for Dutch elm disease with DDT on the campus of Michigan State University and its impact on the food chain, killing robins that had eaten earthworms contaminated by the chemical.[44]

Bringing her scientific skills to bear on the problem, Helen extensively researched the budworm issue and began writing letters to state and federal officials opposing the spraying, noting the impact the chemical would have on their immediate environment. Foremost was the fact that most residents on Gunflint Lake used that body of water for their primary water source, and runoff containing DDT would likely contaminate it. She wrote to several state agencies, the U.S. Forest Service, and eventually to her U.S. Congressman, John Blatnik, asking them to intervene. Helen indicated that she was a scientist who had been studying the budworm problem for several years. She asked that there be no spraying in her area, as it would impact her research on animal behavior in response to the infestation. Helen got her wish; the area was left unsprayed.

Because the Hoovers gathered weather data for the U.S. Weather Bureau, she was able to track temperature and rainfall amounts that not only informed her research but also proved helpful to the Minnesota Department of Conservation and other agencies in better understanding the budworm issue. The infestation ran its course, and Helen contributed to a better understanding of the budworm's life cycle by correlating weather data to the insect's prevalence over a five-year period. While many residents couldn't grasp Helen's scientific approach, they had to grudgingly respect that she had done her homework. And in the end, the Hoovers still had all their trees.

\* \* \*

Summer 1959 brought visitors up the trail, many of them unexpected, which also likely contributed to Helen being on edge. "I don't understand why people, who would never just walk in on us in town, come in here without even a word of warning," Helen complained to friend Hopkins.[45] Summer was when she needed to spend time in the woods observing plants and animals so she could write. It was also when Ade needed to tend to outside repairs that could only be done in warmer weather. However, the Hoovers discovered one benefit to having visitors: they began renting out the summer house to friends several weekends in the summer and fall. It was another way to help make ends meet.

In the fall, Helen learned that the Metal Treating Institute, a trade association and publisher of the magazine *Metal Treating*, bestowed upon her its Annual Achievement Award for the most outstanding article of 1959, one summarizing her research in solving the disc harrow problem. The award was presented at the organization's annual meeting banquet in Chicago. In his remarks about Helen, the Institute's president noted her colleagues at International Harvester said that "she is a study in contrast. She could operate a lathe or a tensile treating machine—or do beautiful crocheting. She achieved success in what is generally considered to be a man's profession, but (God bless her), she retained the charming characteristics of the normal woman." While Helen did not travel to Chicago to receive the award, she gladly accepted the hundred-dollar honorarium that went with it.[46]

Even though Helen had been working off and on for several years writing "A Little Place in the Woods," she did not disclose to many of her correspondents that she had actually completed an entire manuscript. Dorothy Gardiner was aware of it as she had received some sample writing to critique, but to friends like Hopkins, Helen was more circumspect. "I still have not managed to reach the book stage—it does take a long time and as a rather new writer, I mustn't let any of the short things which will help to get my name out pass me by. When I get around to trying to interest a publisher in a book, I'll need all the publications in all the periodicals I can find to help the deal along."[47]

On Christmas Eve day, while Ade had walked to the mailbox, Helen was distracted by a noise in the yard and stepped out to take a look. There she found a man dressed in hunting gear, despite it being well past deer hunting season. She asked what he was looking for; he replied that he had heard about a tame buck and wanted to get a look. With that, Helen ordered him off the property, which had been posted for trespassers. His response was to point the gun her way and suggest she go back into the cabin.

Caught completely off guard by this display of aggression, Helen retreated inside and quickly loaded a clip into their semiautomatic pistol while keeping an eye on the man from the window. She then went back outside to inquire why he was still there. Noticing Helen had a gun, the hunter quickly left the property, departing in a truck with no license plates. Helen was grateful that her father had taught her how to handle a gun when she was young, giving her the confidence to confront the trespasser. When Ade returned and learned of the incident, he was livid.[48]

Holiday mail usually brought parcels from friends, including boxes of cookies, nuts, and candies, luxuries the Hoovers could not afford. Winnie Hopkins sent food items as well as other small gifts such as hot pads, calendars and notepaper, and even a lemon cake on Helen's birthday. The Hoovers appreciated these kind gestures from both friends and people they hardly knew.[49]

Early in 1960, Peter, Mama, and two young bucks returned and started feeding in the yard. The bucks had likely been born the previous summer, and Peter and Mama brought them back to the safe place where they could feed and rest. One of the bucks greedily ate the corn Ade put out; naturally, that led to him being named Pig. His brother was given the less descriptive name of Brother. The Hoovers delighted in watching the antics of the two bucks as they tussled for feed and Mama attempted to keep them in line.[50]

In the middle of January, a large wolf showed up on the side road near the cabin, and all the deer vanished into the forest. The wolf's tracks were so large Helen thought it looked as if a horse had trotted down the road.[51]

Helen was keeping noted nature writer and conservationist Sigurd Olson up to speed on the efforts of the Grand Marais Chamber of Commerce and others in the area to push forward with a plan introduced the previous year to establish a new border crossing to Canada. Some resort owners and vacation cabin owners realized that such a move would make it easier for tourists and other wilderness seekers to bypass their area and go into the wilder Quetico Provincial Park in Ontario and at the same time ruin what they believed was the unique and unspoiled wilderness of the area. Helen again made these points in a letter to George Selke, the commissioner of the Minnesota Department of Conservation, urging the state to oppose the proposal as the road would cross state-owned land.[52]

It's not clear when Helen and Olson first established contact. She was familiar with his efforts to establish the roadless area in the boundary lakes region and his subsequent work to create what became the Boundary Waters Canoe Area in 1958. Most certainly she knew of his first two books, *The Singing Wilderness* and *Listening Point*, which had appeared in the past few years and received attention in the nature magazines Helen wrote for and read. In response to correspondence about the proposed entry road, Olson shared that he was finishing *The Lonely Land*, which would be published in 1961. Olson indicated he had read Helen's story "Forest Friends" in the *Naturalist* and congratulated her on it; she was not even aware it had appeared in the December 1959 issue.[53]

Helen received a separate acknowledgement of that story from Margaret E. Murie, who was involved in the Wilderness Society with her husband Olaus; the latter was the Society's president from 1950 to 1957. Murie, who lived on a ranch in Moose, Wyoming, near Grand Teton National Park, described some of the wildlife in their area in the same terms Helen used in her letters to friends. Murie also sent along copies of the Society's magazine, the *Living Wilderness*, unaware of Helen's recent feature about the spring season on Gunflint Lake.[54]

In addition to writing new works, Helen revisited previous ones. She believed her short story "Great Wolf and the Good Woodsman," which had been published by *Humpty Dumpty's* in December 1958, might be ideal as a children's book. She was partial to this fairy-tale–like story because of the wolf howl she heard on Christmas night in 1956 that sounded like an extended "noel" greeting. It also allowed her to cast the wolf in a more sympathetic light, which she hoped would educate young readers about its place in the animal ecosystem. She sent the manuscript to several national publishing houses, including Bobbs-Merrill, E. P. Dutton, Charles Scribner's Sons, and Alfred A. Knopf, but none were interested.[55]

As the snow melted and spring approached, the deer grew restless. Peter, Pig, and Brother left the yard, retreating into the forest for the summer months. Mama stayed, and Helen saw from her flanks that the doe would be having fawns. She soon retreated into the forest to find a quiet place to give birth, which she did in early June. One day, Helen was walking on the trail in their yard and came upon an agitated Mama; Helen knew the fawns were nearby, so she returned to the cabin. A few days later the Hoovers observed two fawns feeding with Mama in the yard; Helen and Ade named them Pretty and Fuzzy.[56]

One of the Hoovers' neighbors surprised them with the gift of a gas-powered refrigerator. The neighbors had installed electricity at their own cabin and now had no need for the appliance. This would be the first time that Helen and Ade could enjoy at their own cabin ice cream, cold drinks, and chilled lettuce, which they purchased at the Heston's Lodge store.[57]

What Helen and Ade had not anticipated since they began feeding Peter, Mama, and their family was the arrival of the deer hunting season in November. Certainly, word about the large buck that the Hoovers had fed the previous winter had gotten around to neighbors and lodge owners. While that caused worry, the deer came through the hunting season without any casualties. It was, however, a reminder that there may be problems in the future.

In January 1961, Helen started to work on chapters for a possible book on the plants and animals in their immediate vicinity. She hoped that doing some focused writing on a specific subject might give her sample material to send to publishers. While she continued to contemplate this nature guidebook, it is not certain whether she was also working on revising "A Little Place in the Woods" after feedback from A. L. Fierst.

Feeding the deer family and observing their behavior continued to entertain the Hoovers through the winter. The deer consumed large quantities of cracked corn, oatmeal, kitchen scraps, and even a package of multiprotein food, which they kept for emergencies. It all served to provide the deer much-needed nourishment to supplement the cedar boughs that Ade harvested from the surrounding woods. By now the deer visitors included two years of Peter and Mama's offspring: Pig and Brother, the two bucks that had been with them the winter of 1959–60, and now Pretty and Fuzzy, two does who were born the previous summer.

In a letter to Tresselt in the spring, Helen's thoughts about a book continued to occupy her mind as she shared observations about one that had influenced their decision to move north:

> CACHE LAKE COUNTRY was first issued in 1948 and was one of the factors in making up my mind about living in the woods. You'll hoot, no doubt, but if I were not so dependent on the mail, I'd gladly be as deep 'inside' as [author John] Rowland[s] was. I've seen just two people besides Bill [her nickname for Ade] since Christmas, and the silence is hardly ever broken except by wind. I love it that way. If I could choose the people I should see and talk to, it would be different. But I get mildly beserk [sic] when I listen to hours of gossip, much of it vicious, and try to talk sense with people who haven't the slightest grasp of logical thinking. Have been told I am an intellectual snob![58]

By the summer of 1961, Helen was ready to make inquiries about her book idea. At the suggestion of a friend, she sent some of her wilderness writing to editor Tay Hohoff at J. B. Lippincott. Hohoff was a firm but respected editor held in high esteem in publishing circles. She had just shepherded Harper Lee's *To Kill a Mockingbird* into print the previous year. Lippincott was also the publisher of *We Took to the Woods*, the book Helen felt was a high bar in terms of experiential nature writing, and *The Egg and I*, which A. L. Fierst had mentioned. Given these factors, Helen thought her own experiences and subject matter would appeal to the editor. Hohoff reviewed the samples and provided some feedback; she also wanted to see more writing. Helen appreciated her comments, cited the need to do some juvenile stories in the short term, and would see about sending a manuscript in the fall.[59]

The summer of 1961 was quieter than usual because the forest was extremely dry and concerns about forest fires kept tourists away. Canada had been hit particularly hard that summer, with dozens of fires burning in remote parts of western Ontario. The Hoovers kept a wary eye on the hills beyond the northern shore of the lake for any sign of smoke.[60]

Mama reappeared in the spring, and somewhere near the yard she gave birth to twins once again, bringing the fawns around for feeding in early August. The bucks, named Little Buck and Starface, played in the yard, chasing butterflies and drinking from the nearby brook. Fuzzy was often found in the yard as well, eating among the greenery near the cabin.[61]

In October, Helen learned that her aunt in Cincinnati had died, and the Hoovers made a quick trip there for the funeral. For both to leave was difficult since their chickens, Tulip and Bedelia, needed to be fed and watered daily. Upon their return, the Hoovers discovered to their dismay that a friend who had looked in while they were gone noticed evidence of mice in the cabin and had put out poison. Helen was furious, as most of their friends and neighbors knew that they did not use any poisons or pesticides. The poisoned grain was scattered all over the cabin, and Helen and Ade had the unenviable task of cleaning it all out and watching as Helen's tame mice slowly died, leaving a stench that eventually faded. She had hoped to write a story about her family of mice, but now that was impossible.[62]

Helen received interest from Thomas Y. Crowell, a New York–based reference book publisher that had included one of her early stories in an anthology of *Audubon* magazine articles they had published. In July 1961 she sent them examples of writing with observations of nature, and they asked to see some additional work. In September she sent a sample chapter on predatory mammals and waited for a response; in November she received word that they liked her writing and were interested in having her do a book on nature. The publisher forwarded a two-book contract for $1,000 to be paid in four installments, the first of which she would receive right after the first of the year.[63]

In a letter to her friend Hopkins, Helen described what the adult nature book would be about. "I hope to show the wilderness as it can look to anyone with a couple of guidebooks and a high-school idea of natural history, provided they look at it with reason and common sense. Most of the books I've read are either too sentimental or go all out the other way."[64]

✳ ✳ ✳

The fall 1961 hunting season proved to be challenging for the Hoovers. Word that they had been feeding deer for several years was now known far and wide by lodge owners and others on the trail, so hunters converged on land in their vicinity despite it being privately owned and posted against trespassing.

In October, some of the deer that had regularly fed in the Hoovers' yard during the fall and winter started returning to feed on the corn and cedar boughs. Pig and Brother soon appeared on the path, having grown considerably and showing eight-point antlers. Pretty ambled into the yard, and Mama was there with Little Buck and Starface. Even though the bucks had grown and become independent, Mama still ruled the yard.[65]

While the warm fall days and cool nights gave Helen and Ade the chance to enjoy the growing deer family, they were concerned about the days ahead. Early on the first morning of the hunting season, Helen was startled by a gunshot. She got up and went out to explore, reaching the road as some hunters were driving away with a buck tied to their car. She was sick that one of the deer family had been taken.

Fortunately, once the shooting started, the deer disappeared, and the Hoovers could only speculate as to how many had been killed. In those carefree years following the arrival of Peter and his family, the appearance of hunters likely caught the deer family off guard, given they had not encountered many of them before. Helen was struck by their innocence as they fled the yard on opening day, and she lamented the cruelty of man.[66]

A friend from Minneapolis stopped by to tell them he heard that some hunters had taken two bucks from the Hoovers' land. He provided a name, but it didn't register with them. Then Helen recalled recently having a conversation with someone on the road who innocently asked if she had seen any deer. She had shared that two bucks had been feeding in their yard, but that Peter didn't come around until after the hunting season. It now occurred to her that, due to a seemingly benign conversation with someone she considered a neighbor, word had been passed about the presence of deer on the Hoover property.[67]

The hunting season represented some of the more visible changes to the area that the Hoovers had observed but failed to comprehend. Ade and Helen had limited contact with outsiders, so they didn't perceive having any enemies. They had been feeding the deer for three years without trouble from hunters, so they wondered why people would suddenly behave this way.

Their friend put it to them bluntly. "It's just that there are more hunters. And a lot of 'em won't come back to spend their money if they don't get their buck." He further explained that expanded roads, power, and telephones all contributed to the problem. "They bring these guys who are too green or too lazy to find a deer in the woods and who'd be uneasy unless civilization was at hand."[68]

It took a few weeks to know exactly the toll hunting had taken on the deer family. Over several nights in December some of the deer returned. Particularly troubled was Starface, who had been born the previous summer. He was terrified and bleating for his mother, whom the Hoovers had not seen. Pretty, another of Mama's offspring, appeared to settle the terrified deer until Mama appeared several days later. She did not have Little Buck with her, so presumably he had been taken. Pig and Brother were likely the two bucks their friend mentioned, and Fuzzy had not returned either, also likely shot.

The Hoovers were happy to see Mama return and reunite with Pretty and Starface. The deer were wary, and Ade kept plenty of seed and corn in the yard, especially after several inches of snow fell. Helen kept a watchful vigilance on the yard, anxiously awaiting Peter's return. She knew, however, that with the number of deer that had died, it was likely that a buck of Peter's size would have been shot. Fortunately, her pessimism was thwarted when Peter silently appeared in the yard one night. They put out extra feed and cut plenty of cedar boughs for what remained of the deer family.

The Hoovers had a wistful Christmas, lamenting the hunting season just passed and the changes that were quickly upending the sanctuary they had created for the deer. Helen also had a growing uncertainty about the people they thought they knew. She had felt those who lived in proximity to what she believed was "the morally clean atmosphere of the forest" were better than those who lived among the city's corrupting influences. That was proving not to be true.[69]

While Helen was sad at their losses, Peter and Mama were again in the yard, tending to the remaining deer in their family. Helen tried to enjoy the last days of 1961, as she had a book to write and needed to get started on it right away in the new year.

# 6

# The Restless Writer

## *Gunflint Lake, 1962–1965*

AS THE HOOVERS were getting used to the remaining deer family feeding in the yard, they observed that the animals were becoming skittish and restless. Helen and Ade knew this meant wolves were again in the area, and after several days, the deer vanished deeper into the woods. Helen had by now received the first $250 installment from the Thomas Y. Crowell contract, so the task at hand was to get started on the book, but worries about the unaccounted deer preoccupied her thoughts.

In early 1962, Helen and Ade went on a walk to look for signs of deer on their side road and discovered both deer and wolf tracks crossing the land near their cabin. It appeared that a larger deer, likely Peter, had drawn a wolf away from smaller deer tracks, perhaps those of Starface, with Peter and the wolf trailing off to the lake and the smaller tracks going in the opposite direction. The Hoovers surmised Peter may have found his natural end by a predator while protecting his son.[1]

Sadly, that was not the case. One of their indigenous neighbors from across the lake, likely their friend Awbutch Plummer, reported to Helen that Peter had been shot and left for dead. This act of cruelty stunned Helen, as it indicated to her that someone had killed Peter out of malice.[2] She understood from run-ins with hunters trespassing on their property during the previous deer seasons that there were people willing to spite them for trying to keep hunters off their land. But to shoot Peter out of season and leave him for dead was more than heartbreaking for Helen and Ade. It validated the unease Helen had felt at Christmas, and it forever changed how the Hoovers felt about their home on Gunflint Lake.

For a time, Helen's health was poor. It wasn't until mid-February that Helen was able to get up and about. She claimed in a letter to Hopkins that she was afflicted with "muscular myolitis" (an inflammation of the spinal cord), but it's uncertain how Helen was able to make this self-diagnosis. She claimed to have picked it up in Cincinnati the previous fall when she went there for her aunt's funeral. It was more likely that Helen was emotionally drained from the shooting of Peter and the other deer and could not get up the energy to focus on the book.[3]

In a letter to her editor Alvin Tresselt that spring, Helen lamented the previous hunting season's casualties:

> The three deer left of my eight tame ones come every night. I think Mama has learned that we are the only safe people. If so, she will not have her fawns in the yard any more, as she did the last two summers. The killing of the deer has disillusioned me more than things usually do. For two years they were left alone and, like [a] gullible chump, I thought people were being considerate. Now I have learned that the presence of friends of mine during the hunting season protected the deer, because the shooters didn't want the word to get back to me as to who shot the deer and wrecked my behavior study. However, the word got back indirectly and I knew who to curse in the dark of the moon.[4]

There is no record of who the offenders might have been, but it was another instance of neighbors behaving in ways Helen and Ade could not understand.

Despite these health and emotional challenges, Helen needed to get started on the book for Thomas Y. Crowell. Before she could, however, she needed to finish a story she had promised the editor of *Defenders of Wildlife News Bulletin* on bow-and-arrow hunting. The organization had made it a priority to pursue legislation across the country to try and ban the practice.[5] The article, "With My Bow and Arrow," is an explicit antihunting commentary that begins with Helen describing finding one of the deer that fed in the yard with an arrow in its underside. Although she was opposed to hunting altogether, Helen conceded a high-velocity rifle bullet kills instantly if done properly. She argued that animals shot by an arrow die slowly of internal hemorrhage and only a skilled hunter could kill quickly at close range with a bow and arrow. Helen expressed her philosophy about living things in a broader way that also invoked the presence of the nuclear age of the time:

> Ade and I do not kill things, and this is sometimes called sentimental in a derogatory way by people who seem to feel that kindness and compassion toward any form of undomesticated nonhuman life is weakness. But we see nothing brave in callousness, nor maudlin in gentleness. Respect for life itself is an all-important need of mankind. If men had that respect, the deadly atomic blasts which pollute the air and threaten the world would never have come to pass.[6]

Helen was certainly safe in taking a hard stance on bow hunting with the *Defenders* audience, and she further elaborated on "outlaw" hunters and their illegal practices. The article makes the point that most of the hunters on their property were from outside her area, providing cover to separate them from neighbors who hunted and shot the deer in and around their property. It's apparent that some of the raw emotion in the article was a direct result of the deer lost during the previous hunting season.[7]

After completing and submitting the article, Helen threw herself into the book project, as the manuscript was due by December 1962. The book as proposed would be organized into chapters that included trees, plants, insects, birds, various types of mammals, a chapter on the deer family, and another about the weather, plus a bibliography of source material and an index. The text would provide Helen's observations of each category of plant or animal as seen on walks throughout their property or in close proximity to their cabins. Rather than have it read like a straight guidebook, Helen would combine her storytelling abilities with her observational skills to create a narrative that highlighted the Hoovers' activities living among the plants and animals near the property.

Helen shared with friend Hopkins how she approached her writing. "I work it out more-or-less subconsciously and then sit down and let 'er rip. The only trouble with this is that interruptions play the devil with the delicate mental planning."[8] Helen kept writing, and by April reported that she had about twenty thousand words to go and hoped to have a completed manuscript by June.[9]

Spring was late and cool in 1962, followed by heavy rains, which was exactly what was needed to wash the budworms out of their webs and kill them, leaving only a small natural population. The Hoovers lost only a few trees among the hundreds on their property. Helen was pleased that they had let the forest take care of itself. They hadn't panicked like many of their neighbors, who had cut down trees that would have been only temporarily affected.

For the book, Helen consulted a variety of experts for information and to confirm observations she made in her writing. Relationships she had developed with staff at the Minnesota Department of Conservation and the U.S. Forest Service from her writings and concerns about the budworm infestation proved useful as she worked on the manuscript. She also reached out to academic subject-matter experts at the University of Minnesota and other well-known specialists in their fields. And Helen even had "Mr. Wilderness," as she called Sigurd Olson, read and review the manuscript.[10]

Helen adapted content from magazine articles she had written for *American Mercury, Audubon, Canadian Audubon, Frontiers,* the *Living Wilderness,* and *Nature Magazine,* which proved effective in providing observational and anecdotal material that already existed. Weaving in stories about the animals they fed and observed gave the book a lighter feel than a typical guidebook and made the text more approachable for a mass audience. Mentions of "Walter" the weasel, "Hoppy" the three-footed mink, "Gregory" the groundhog, and all the various deer family members provided engaging storytelling among the factual material.

With field guides in hand, Helen walked the land, checking her notes and observations. She applied her skills from years in the laboratory to make certain her writing was clear and accurate. Helen continued refining the text, typing and retyping pages as she shaped it into a final format.[11]

Before she could finish the manuscript, Helen had to contend with deer hunting season in November. Since the shooting of three deer during the previous season and Peter's subsequent killing earlier in the year, the hunting season had left her even more anxious. Before the deer season opened, grouse hunters shot near their property, rattling Helen and prompting Ade to add "No Hunting" signs on their land. Helen's concentration was interrupted by the shooting, and thoughts of the approaching deer season caused her to work at night and sleep during the day. Ade was always worried about Helen's emotional state and tried to make sure she ate; due to her anxiety, it was not uncommon for her to drop weight during this time.

Helen grew more anxious with each passing day, and when the deer appeared in their yard to feed after an early snow, the Hoovers worried they would be easier to track. Helen had the idea of feeding the deer and then having Ade sneak around the other side of the cabin and discharge his .45 automatic pistol, hoping to scare the deer away before the hunters descended. It worked. The deer vanished when they heard the shot and did not return for some time.[12]

Helen may have been relieved to have cleared out the deer, but the hunters would remain a menace. One morning she heard a car on the road and men talking; she took the pistol, slid in the clip, and walked toward the road to find two hunters on their property. She asked what they were doing; looking for deer, they replied. Helen tried to convince them there were no deer and that she lived on the property, but the hunters were unpersuaded. When she produced the pistol, they quickly left, and Helen followed them to the road to make sure they were gone. She stayed on watch to make certain they didn't return.

Later that evening, their friend, the area U.S. Forest Service ranger, stopped by to check in as he heard there had been some trouble on their road. Helen admitted she chased two men off their property. The ranger had met a local resident who had driven by the Hoovers' place and had seen an agitated woman with a gun in her hand walking down the road. The resident described Helen's appearance perfectly, and the ranger replied, "Oh, that's Mrs. Hoover." While it took a minute to sink in, they were all eventually laughing, understanding the story now making the rounds via the "moccasin wire" would be a deterrent by itself and only add to Helen's colorful reputation.[13]

With the book deadline approaching, Helen finished typing the manuscript on Christmas Eve 1962. Titled "The Untamed Land," she sent it to Crowell for review.[14] The Hoovers once again invited Ollor Snevets for Christmas dinner. What could have been a melancholy holiday re-membering Peter appearing at their door four years earlier was instead an opportunity to look forward and not dwell on his killing the previous February. Mama and many of Peter's offspring continued to feed in the yard, providing somewhat of a legacy, which took away some of the sad-ness for Helen and Ade.[15]

Several weeks later, Snevets was having trouble with his truck and asked Ade to come by his place to take a look. Despite not having a car, Ade was still good at solving mechanical problems, given all of the work he did on the many cars he had owned when they lived in Chicago. After walking over to give it a look, Ade offered some ideas on what was wrong. As a thanks for his help, Snevets offered to give Ade his old Chevy sedan, since he knew the Hoovers had been without transportation for nearly ten years and he didn't need a second vehicle. The Hoovers were dumb-struck by the trapper's generosity.

The car needed some repairs, and Snevets knew a trustworthy me-chanic in town. The cost of fixing it and adding insurance, as well as the cost for gas and oil, would be negligible given Helen's book advance and the future earnings once it was published. It also meant that Ade would have to take a written driver's exam and a behind-the-wheel test, which Snevets said he would take him to do in Grand Marais. Helen, excited by their good fortune, shared news of the car with some of the neighbors. This only seemed to bring out the naysayers, who cautioned Helen that no one ever passed the exam the first time. One woman who had seen Snevets and Ade going to town offered to pick Ade up and bring him back up the trail when he didn't pass. Helen assured her that wouldn't be necessary, and she was all the more pleased when Ade arrived that eve-ning, driving the car from town.[16]

Helen now took some time to catch up on personal correspondence and gave herself a brief break from writing. In a letter to *Humpty Dump-ty's* editor Alvin Tresselt telling him she had finished the manuscript, she reflected on when she felt the desire to write. "At age twelve I knew that I wanted to write, preferably detective or adventure stories, and produced some hilarious examples about ten thousand words each." This was all set aside for school, then college studies, the subsequent death of her father, and then the need to care for her mother and earn a living. "I never wrote a line until around the time I first wrote you. So far as I'm concerned, all those years were waiting years. And now I probably don't have enough time left to do half of what I'd like to do."[17]

By February 1963 Helen was writing again, this time getting six *Humpty Dumpty's* pieces about animals out of the way in anticipation of the manuscript revisions she expected to receive from her publisher. Helen preferred writing ahead on these monthly columns so she wasn't under the pressure of a deadline. Helen learned that her editor at Crowell, Gorton Carruth, was leaving to go to another publishing house. This raised some concerns, as someone who she was not familiar with would be taking up the final editing and preparation of the manuscript for publication.[18]

Having seen some of Ade's artwork via Helen's personal stationery—a line drawing of a Canada goose in flight—Crowell asked if Ade could do illustrations for the margins of the book, as well as a jacket drawing. This was no easy request, as the publisher wanted nearly a hundred small line drawings of the animals, plants, trees, insects, and birds featured in the book. They also asked for a hand-drawn map of the property to use on the book's endpapers. Enthused by Crowell's appreciation of his work, Ade quickly started drawing, recognizing the illustrations would provide additional income.[19]

By mid-May, Helen had been through five rounds of corrections with a copy editor Crowell had retained who supposedly had some familiarity with the subject matter. The copy editor's queries and disagreements about the content were forwarded to Helen through Edward Tripp, Carruth's successor and editor of reference books at Crowell. Helen sent her comments back to Tripp for review and consideration. All of this was handled by mail; in 1963, telephone communication on the trail was less than ideal. The Hoovers were on an eight-party telephone line, and during the opening of fishing and the tourist season in May, the lines were busy with calls to and from the lodges. Besides, long-distance phone charges at this time were expensive, making them impractical. The good news was that mail delivery came twice a week in the spring.[20]

Helen thought the copy editor had gone overboard on changes, quibbling over Helen's description of fiddlehead ferns and taking issue with whether squirrels could swim. "Right now, I doubt that I'd open the book if it were miraculously delivered to me in advance," she grumbled in a letter to Tripp. Helen attached a four-page, single-spaced response to the suggested changes, using her own sources and references to correct the copy editor's immoderate demands.[21]

A biographical introductory chapter that Helen thought might help the reader better understand how the Hoovers moved to the north woods and why she undertook the book was eliminated, either for length or for cost. Crowell ended up not needing as many drawings as they had anticipated, nor the detailed map of their property that Ade had painstakingly created, which was now too expensive to include. Both Helen and Ade were frustrated with this decision as he had worked thirty full days trying to meet the publisher's tight production deadlines.[22]

Next came the galley proofs, the final step in the process before the book went to the printer. Typically, only minor changes are made at this point, as it is expensive to re-set type after extensive changes. Helen's final review identified fifty-five issues with accuracy, word style, or confusing and awkward language, changes that should have been caught earlier in the editing process. She even noted a "correction" made by the copy editor to a section Helen had adapted from an *Audubon* article she had written that had been vetted by the National Audubon Society and reviewed for accuracy by noted Cornell University ornithologist Dr. O. S. Pettingill Jr. In this regard, Helen was no pushover; she had worked for years as a proofreader at the Audit Bureau of Circulations in Chicago, and these errors were no small issue for her. In fact, she scribbled on the letter she received from the production editor "C.E.'s idiocies," indicating her contempt for the copy editor's inconsistent editing.[23]

As the weather turned warmer, the Hoovers had the ability to travel with their recently acquired secondhand car to Grand Marais to go to the bank, purchase groceries, stock up on bird seed and suet, and even have an occasional meal at a restaurant or a soda at Leng's Fountain.[24]

By mid-June 1963 the ordeal of editing and reviewing was finally over. Helen and Tripp finalized the page proofs for the printer and made final selections of Ade's artwork. The book, now titled *The Long-Shadowed Forest*, was off to the printer with a November 8 publication date. Helen was relieved to have it done and hoped its fall arrival would make it popular for the Christmas season.

Despite the intense work to finish the book, there were still the daily tasks of gathering firewood, getting water from the lake, and tending to the chickens. One morning, Helen went out to check on the hens and found Tulip dead, likely from old age. She had been eating normally and had not been injured; she simply expired. Now Bedelia was their sole domestic pet.[25]

With the book finished and being prepped for publication, Defenders of Wildlife, the national conservation organization for which Helen had written the commentary on bow-and-arrow hunting, asked her to write a quarterly "woodland article or report" of about a thousand words for its member publication, *Defenders of Wildlife News Bulletin.* They would pay her seventy-five dollars for each column, and the first one would appear that October. The editor, an acquaintance by mail who had purchased notepaper from the Hoovers, also asked if Helen would be willing to write a "blind" review of her own forthcoming book, as advance reading copies were not yet available and the book would be out by the time the issue was mailed. Helen happily obliged with some modest words of praise for her first effort:

> Selected life-history and related material makes a background for the observations of the author, whose respect for life and whose love of wild things for their own sake never wavers. She accepts man's status as a dependent part of the natural world, not as mysticism, but as simple fact, and entreats us all to respect the earth that mankind may not be absent from its tomorrows.[26]

The second installment of Helen's seasonal series for the *Living Wilderness* appeared in the summer, including an illustration of a pileated woodpecker by Ade. In this essay, Helen takes the reader on a tour of their property, describing the forest as she wanders about the yard:

> I walk through the bushes to a sun-dappled aspen grove, where finches and warblers whisk among the leaves. The violets and strawberries that patterned the earth in May have stopped blooming long ago and are hidden beneath 2-foot dandelion leaves. The grove's bunchberry carpet now bears clusters of half-formed little

green fruits. A breeze from the south crosses the road, which lies at the edge of the patch of aspens, and brings me the damp, generic smell of wetland. From not far away comes a musical bellowing. The moose are in their swamp.[27]

September 1963 brought some bittersweet news from Helen's acquaintance Margaret E. Murie, now an author herself. Crowell had sent an advance galley proof of *The Long-Shadowed Forest* to Murie, hoping she would write a review in the *Living Wilderness* magazine. Murie was grateful for having received it because Olaus—her husband, coauthor, and illustrator—was in the final stages of dying from lung cancer, and she read to him from the galleys, which he particularly enjoyed. She told Helen that the book "will be a real contribution both to naturalists, animal behaviorists, and most of all to all those who love and appreciate the natural world." Murie asked if Helen had read their recent book, *Two in the Far North*, published the year before by Alfred A. Knopf. The biographical novel recounted the Muries' years doing research in frontier Alaska and their efforts at nature preservation there.[28]

Helen was sad to learn of Olaus's illness but heartened that her writing had resonated with someone she respected. While Helen had not read their book, she had seen installments in *Audubon* magazine, acknowledging, "I know that, in pleasing Olaus Murie, I have the proof that I succeeded in getting on paper the things I hoped to convey. And I may hope that I will reach others, some of whom may not see the wild world as I do." Olaus died at the end of October 1963.[29]

With the approaching publication date, Crowell was busy sending advance copies to book editors at newspapers and magazines across the country, as well as influential nature writers, seeking reviews and attention for the book ahead of the holidays. That included media outlets in Minnesota, where Crowell was expecting strong sales due to local interest. Charles McFadden, editor of the Sunday *Minneapolis Tribune Picture* magazine, received an advance review copy and was so taken with it that he assigned a photographer to drive up to Gunflint Lake and do a pictorial spread about the Hoovers.

On October 14, *Tribune* photographer Earl Seubert arrived at the cabin, and Helen showed him around, pointing out areas of their property featured in the book. He also took staged photos of the Hoovers in the log cabin reading and eating dinner, and one with Helen sitting at her typewriter. The story, "She Took to the Woods"—the same title of the book by Louise Dickinson Rich—appeared in the Sunday, November 17, issue of *Picture* magazine. At this point, Helen still hadn't received any copies of the book, so she had no idea how it looked.

Crowell had ordered a print run of five thousand copies, based on bookstore preorders of forty-five hundred. (This was not an unusual quantity for a national book in the nature genre; Sigurd Olson's first book, *The Singing Wilderness*, had an initial printing of the same quantity in 1956.[30]) Helen and Ade had also plugged the book to their mail-order customers, inserting a promotional flyer with their notepaper catalogs. Crowell provided postcards Helen could mail to friends announcing the book's publication.[31]

When Helen finally received copies of *The Long-Shadowed Forest*, she felt the book turned out beautifully. The dust jacket was an abstract green illustration that appeared like a dense forest, with the title in script and Helen's and Ade's names across the cover. It also carried a subtitle, "Changing Seasons in a Northern Wilderness." Ade's pen-and-ink drawings appeared in the margins as planned, and seeing them tucked onto the page brought the book to life. The opening chapter took the reader around the grounds of the cabin, observing nature through each season. The second chapter described the four seasons of weather, followed by chapters about specific plants, trees, insects, creatures of the water, birds, and mammals. Each provided details of what was found in the nearby forest, and Helen mixed facts, observation, and storytelling in an approachable and entertaining way.

As intended, *The Long-Shadowed Forest* was a guidebook for readers with a general knowledge of nature and animals. The writing could be a bit academic in places, but it was sprinkled with enough personal observances that made the text appealing. Helen was no doubt feeling her way as a new book author, and her skills at observation after years of scientific discovery and laboratory work were evident in the vivid descriptions of the plants, animals, and insects found in their yard. She also weaved in some gentle admonitions about people's lack of respect for nature and the need to be more empathetic toward wildlife.

The book also revealed two aspects of Helen's style that would both endear her to readers and confirm to local residents that she "may have been in the woods too long."[32] Helen's storytelling was most effective when she could provide examples describing her interactions with animals of all types. In one vignette she matter-of-factly writes about feeding a small shrew with thinned milk via a spoon. In another she describes nursing an injured jumper mouse back to life by feeding it with a straw and some water, and then nonchalantly holding it in her hand while having a conversation with a neighbor. Most people would consider a mouse something to dispense with, but Helen held no reservations about helping nurse a small creature back to health.

Helen had given nicknames to most of the animals that frequented the yard, and these appeared with her stories about their antics. While some observers would call this eccentric or even beneath someone with her intellect, the practice was not uncommon on the Gunflint Trail, as resort owner Peggy Heston had attached names to the deer that she fed regularly.[33] Plus, doing so personalized the animals and provided readers the opportunity to better relate to them as subjects of her writing.

Another distinctive aspect of Helen's writing—something that was also part of her children's columns in *Humpty Dumpty's* magazine—involved educating readers about the balance of nature and dispelling the myths and prejudices people associated with certain animals. Regarding the latter, at the top of this list was the wolf, which she believed had been falsely maligned in outdoor literature specifically and popular culture generally; she wrote of the wolf's beauty and its importance in maintaining a balance in nature. She scolded previous generations of hunters and trappers for nearly eradicating mammals such as martens and beavers. She also tried to dispel people's fear of bats and snakes by writing about them earnestly and factually. This approach gained her accolades from critics and made her writing relatable to a general audience. She hoped it also engendered an appreciation for the coexistence of humans and nature.

Helen's prose in *The Long-Shadowed Forest* gracefully captured the world that existed around her. She splendidly described the dawn of a summer day on a northern Minnesota lake:

The first light reveals the trees and brush as greenish-gray shapes, like amorphous, primordial predecessors to themselves. Across the lake, mist rises and coils above a marsh, ghostly and smoke-white as the light increases and the green growth loses its form-less mystery. Somewhere a bird chirps, a squirrel sputters into lively argument with itself, gulls pass like shadows overhead, and the eastern sky flushes with pink. The rim of the sun lifts over a hill to send a sparkling path across the lake, and the dawn wind rolls the water gently in bands of rose and powder blue.[34]

Later, Helen provides the reader with a strong picture of the animals she sees. One afternoon, while feeding a chipmunk cracked corn from her hand, she noticed a fisher, a mammal rarely seen in her part of Minnesota. Having seen it in both day and night, she offered this description:

By night the fisher is as fearfully exquisite as a creature out of dreams. Moving about in the cold light of the stars, moon, or aurora borealis, it is a mysterious, fluid part of the half-dark. The frosty hairs that give it daytime fluffiness are invisible and, smooth and sleek and sinuous, it flows and poses, a shadow darker than all other shadows, its eyes like emeralds exploding into flame. It glides in the unearthly beauty that belongs to the untamed land and its children.[35]

The first review of *The Long-Shadowed Forest* was a complimentary para-graph in Gladys Taber's highly influential monthly "Butternut Wisdom" column in *Family Circle* magazine. Taber was herself a prolific author and a trusted domestic advice columnist whose words reached two million readers each month. "This is a book that everyone should own, to read and reread. It opens new vistas of understanding of nature. For Christ-mas giving, it is on my list for special people." Helen wrote to thank her, mentioning she only became aware of the column because her grocer and his family in Grand Marais had driven up the trail to bring the Hoovers copies of the magazine after they spotted the review and were excited by her good fortune.[36]

Helen was anxious to receive reviews, so she subscribed to an author's clipping service, which provided clips of newspaper and magazine articles that mentioned the book. The reviews that came in were uniformly positive, with comparisons to other contemporary nature writers like Peter Farb, Sigurd Olson, and even Rachel Carson.[37] John Barkham of *Saturday Review* wrote that "the author is deeply conscious of the variety and continuity of life—and the awesome might of nature. Small things—such as holding a rock in her hand—inspire her to large thoughts."[38] She was particularly pleased with a review by John Perry, writing in the *Atlantic Naturalist:* "Mrs. Hoover writes so evocatively that one can be caught up in the rhythm of her prose . . . she brings scenes to life not by scattering adjectives but by observing things keenly and sensitively and reporting precisely."[39] Additional reviews appeared in the *Chicago Tribune, Duluth News-Tribune, Minneapolis Star, Minneapolis Tribune, New York Post, St. Paul Dispatch,* and *St. Paul Pioneer Press,* among dozens of others.[40]

Not all reviews were positive. Pieter Fosburgh, writing in *Natural History,* wrote that *The Long-Shadowed Forest* was "a good and readable book . . . but I regret, even resent, the coziness and interpolation, whereby an author undertakes to move into the minds of his natural subjects and speak for them with the voice of authority."[41] Her editor at Crowell was not happy with the review, but Helen didn't mind; she had already written Fosburgh and had received a nice letter in return.[42]

In all of the excitement of the book's publication, Helen received a letter from Alfred Knopf, the esteemed New York publisher. Her summer column in the *Living Wilderness* had caught his eye, and he was writing to congratulate her on it and to inquire whether she and Ade might have a book in them. This started a brief exchange of letters that highlighted a series of missed opportunities. Helen informed him that her first book had just been published. Knopf regretted not knowing she was writing one, as he was Sigurd Olson's publisher, had visited the area in the past, and would have done her book well. Helen replied that she had given thought to reaching out to Olson about his publisher, but Crowell had come calling before she could.[43] Helen was flattered that her writing had caught Knopf's attention and made sure he received a copy of *The Long-Shadowed Forest.* Ever the self-promoter and not wanting to close the door on opportunity, she closed one letter with a subtle tease: "The richness of the North can supply many books, and I hope to be added to your list at some future date."[44]

While no reviewers made the comparison, Helen's book was not unlike *One Day on Beetle Rock,* authored by nature writer Sally Carrighar in 1944 and also published by Knopf. Following seven years of observing animals on Beetle Rock, an outcrop of granite near Sequoia National Park in California, Carrighar tells the story of nine different animals on a single spring day, sharing their interactions and the relationship between prey and predator. Carrighar did not have Hoover's scientific background, but she was a self-taught observer and brought a writer's sensibility to the topic, writing elegantly about animals. She went on to write several other best-selling books and was considered one of the preeminent nature writers from the 1940s to the 1960s.[45]

Helen was anxious to know how her book was selling, so she checked in with her favorite bookseller, Kroch's & Brentano's in Chicago. She learned it was doing well, but reorders were slow to be filled. Columnist Gladys Taber also indicated readers were telling her they were having trouble finding the book. Not knowing much about how book publishing worked, Helen trusted that Crowell was on top of things, but she was concerned nonetheless with the missteps.[46] The publisher ordered a second printing in December, and Helen speculated to a friend that Crowell "was caught with his pants dragging."[47]

As a result of the book's success, readers started writing to Helen. "I am being smothered with fan mail and, goodness, anyone who writes the splendid comments I am getting surely deserves a thoughtful answer as soon as I can send it," she wrote to her friend Hopkins.[48]

The hunting season was another difficult one for Helen; eight of the twelve deer the Hoovers were feeding in their yard were taken by a neighbor, she wrote Alvin Tresselt. "Things like this are hard for me to take." Compounding the stress was the November 22, 1963, assassination of President John F. Kennedy, which led Helen to draw parallels between the assassin and the hunters who had taken their toll.[49]

With the initial success of *The Long-Shadowed Forest,* Crowell was interested in a second book. Helen was considering something about herbivorous mammals of the north woods and their ecological role, taking a local approach to animals in their area that were available for close study.

Ed Tripp liked the idea and shared several nature and animal reference books that could be of help in her writing.[50]

In the meantime, Helen received a follow-up letter from Alfred Knopf, in response to his having received a copy of *The Long-Shadowed Forest*. While he admitted he had not yet read it, he admired Ade's drawings but felt the book designer had crowded the text toward the middle of the book, making it difficult to read. Helen thanked him for his insight. She also used the opportunity to report that Ade had only six weeks to complete the illustrations, that thirty of Ade's pictures were left out due to limitations and plan changes, and that she had problems with the copy editor.[51] Helen's willingness to share some of her frustrations with the publication of her first book may have been a subtle way to convey she was not necessarily committed to her publisher or simply a naïve way of keeping the door open.

Positive reviews continued to arrive. Helen was cheered by a short notice of *The Long-Shadowed Forest* in the Book-of-the-Month Club's February catalog: "A naturalist's naturalist, she writes with a dedication to detail and scientific fact that may put off the too-casual reader, but her book is a rich mine of information for students, and in effect a nature guide of the region."[52]

In April 1964, Helen sent Ed Tripp a tentative chapter listing for the proposed new book, dividing it into two sections to reflect summer and winter. Each chapter would take a close look at a specific mammal, and the order of material would roughly follow when the animals emerged from hibernation in spring; the winter animals would be those that were active during that time of year. She liked this approach as she had not seen it used in any other nature book.[53]

Tripp agreed and liked that Ade could also provide illustrations, as the publisher was happy with how the first book turned out, despite not using as many of Ade's drawings as they had intended. Helen expanded her theme further by telling Tripp that she wanted to explore the natural balance of the environment, and when it changes, how others must adapt. In suggesting this she was explicitly aware of human impact and how it can cause imbalance. She lamented that few people knew much about animals and hoped she could help by writing a decent book. "When you live with animals all around you, you see many things which the natural history books omit, probably because of lack of knowledge." She went on to cite observations of nature she had made by living near the animals she wrote about.[54]

In June, Helen traveled to Chicago to see her old doctor, to have some teeth pulled, and to get fitted for new eyeglasses. She had been startled at how overweight she appeared in the *Minneapolis Tribune Picture* magazine feature in November 1963, but she was also concerned because she had inexplicably lost weight during the winter. Ade knew the hunting season took a physical and mental toll on Helen; she would not eat much during the two-week period, staying up to feed what deer returned to the yard at night, spending days firing a handgun to scare off the deer and hunters who continued to be directed to their property. Despite the stress and weight fluctuation, Helen's checkup turned out to be fine for someone fifty-four years old.[55]

Helen learned that *The Long-Shadowed Forest* was going to be serialized in the spring and summer of 1964 in the London-based magazine *Woman's Journal* in conjunction with publication of the book's British edition. Crowell had negotiated the sale of the British rights for both. Helen was delighted the book would be published there; the English were avid readers of nature books, a fact she learned from her writer friend Dorothy Gardiner.

After the Sunday *Minneapolis Tribune Picture* magazine appeared, the Hoovers became local celebrities and were now being recognized on their trips into town. Helen was taken aback by total strangers offering their congratulations.[56]

Summer brought an endless stream of visitors wanting to meet Helen and Ade and get their autographs. The Hoovers continued to marvel at the fact that people would make the forty-five-mile trek up the Gunflint Trail without giving thought to tell them they were coming, much less dropping in as if this were typical behavior. Under these conditions it was nearly impossible for Helen to get started on the new book.

One day, two fishermen were on the lake in front of the Hoover cabin trying to lure some ducks with bread, perhaps hoping to "catch" some dinner. Helen heard the squawking and walked down to the water, her comments about leaving the ducks alone being ignored. She yelled for Ade to bring the bullwhip, prompting the fishermen to take off quickly.

Ade came down wondering what she was talking about, and when she related her stunt, all he could do was suggest that this would only add to her local reputation as a "crazy woman."[57]

With the approaching deer season, Helen's unease increased. She was troubled by the traffic on the side road and on the lake and "the growing volume of incidents demonstrating man's inhumanity to almost every creature that was unfamiliar to him and many that were familiar."[58] The onset of the deer season had become more of a burden each year as hunters brazenly trespassed on the Hoovers' land and more deer were shot. As hunting wound down near the close of the season, Helen decided to go outside for a walk. As she approached their carport by the side road, a shot rang out. Several hunters moved quickly into the brush to retrieve a deer they had just shot. Hearing the discharge, Ade came out of the cabin calling for Helen, and she ducked down near the car. At that moment a bullet nearly grazed her head, causing a ringing in her ear as it came so close. Ade found Helen huddled in the carport and retrieved the .30 caliber slug from the gravel pile nearby. That night they decided they could no longer risk staying there during deer season.[59]

Helen was not one to "turn and run," but Ade was so angry that she did not put up much of a fight. The Hoovers had also been frustrated with the party-line telephone; they had tried making calls during the deer season, only to find the line blocked by someone whose phone was off the hook. Had there been a real emergency, the phone would have been useless.

Despite these stresses, Helen had the idea for an entirely different book stirring in her head, one about the deer family they had come to love and nurture. She knew those years were special; a starving Peter coming on a cold Christmas Day, Mama and the twins the next summer, and the others that followed over the next several years. In a way, they represented an innocent time living on Gunflint Lake, one that could never be repeated. While the Hoovers had grown attached to the deer family and enjoyed feeding them and learning by watching their behavior, so much had also been lost; Peter would never return, and Pig, Brother, Fuzzy, and Little Buck had been killed by hunters. Only Mama, Pretty, Starface, and several others now remained.

Helen felt strongly she needed to get this story on paper while it was still fresh in her mind. As she noted in a letter, "As I went out this evening to put grain under Peter's tree, I thought of the wonderful return we have received for feeding just one hungry, hurt buck, for without him here and feeling secure, we should not have the others."[60]

Helen Finch, an associate editor at *Woman's Journal* in London, had written to congratulate Helen on the serialization of *The Long-Shadowed Forest* in their magazine and asked if she had other writing they might consider. Helen was flattered by their interest and sent three samples in October, including "Mrs. Mouse's Miracle," a short story she had previously sold to *Nature Magazine*. Finch liked it and accepted it, paying thirty guineas (about eighty-eight dollars in 1964 dollars).[61] Helen also let Finch know she was working on a true story about the deer family, roughly outlining what she had already started to work on. Finch quickly said that it might be perfect for them; Helen was pleased and sent off a rough draft of chapter one and an incomplete outline of the rest of the story.[62]

Whether validated by Finch's enthusiasm for the deer story or feeling obligated to her American publisher, Helen also shared the sample chapter with Ed Tripp and Bob Crowell. They liked what they read and gave it the preliminary green light. In fact, Bob Crowell was so enthused that he flew from New York to visit Helen at Gunflint Lake in October 1964. Helen sent a follow-up note to Tripp, noting, "[Mr. Crowell] likes the first chapter of the deer story, pretty rough but fit for a general impression, so I guess that will be the book. I'd much rather write things of this sort than the half-reference type."[63]

Helen went on to describe specifically how she saw the premise of the book:

> This deer thing is an enlargement, in a way, of your suggestion of drawing portraits in depth of several animals. This will be the portraits of specific deer, drawn in a great deal of detail and depth, along with the things we learned from the deer and about them. You may be surprised that not too much is known about white-tails, except from the production-for-hunting angle. Reason: no one manages to study them as individuals, partly because of lack of interest and partly because it is hard to keep a deer alive

for very long when the guns start up. We've been lucky so far with some of ours.[64]

Helen noted that she would also be reviewing a recent book on deer by Leonard Lee Rue III, *The World of the White-tailed Deer*, which was edited by her old friend John K. Terres, the former editor of *Audubon* magazine. Like Helen, Rue lived in a rural area where he could observe deer in their natural environment.[65]

Given that it was approaching the one-year anniversary of the publication of *The Long-Shadowed Forest*, Crowell was likely happy with anything Helen was interested in writing so long as she could produce a follow-up in short order. Meanwhile, the first royalty check arrived from Crowell, and it was more than Helen expected: $4,296.38. With this windfall, perhaps the years of financial insecurity were now behind them.[66]

The contract for the new deer book arrived in December 1964, and this time Crowell upped the advance, offering $400 on acceptance, with $300 due upon completion of the manuscript the following December. Helen took the opportunity to get in a word about the editing process with Tripp, hoping to avert a replay of the troubles with her first book. "I have high hopes that this will go more smoothly than *Forest*. There is no need for an advisory editor, I don't suppose you are likely to move on in the middle of things [a reference to previous editor Gorton Carruth's departure], and there is no need for an outside copy editor (who has read a book). With such extra cooks out of the broth, so to speak, all should go well."[67]

A surprise appeared on December 24 when the *New York Times* published a review of *The Long-Shadowed Forest* by noted *Times* correspondent and Minnesota native Harrison E. Salisbury. Helen had been somewhat frustrated that Crowell had not been able to secure more national reviews of her book, and now Salisbury, an aficionado of the border lakes region, delivered a ringing endorsement, using excerpts from the book to illustrate Helen's writing. "Mrs. Hoover has written a classic of wilderness life, one to put on the shelf besides Walden and the works of Fabre." He also noted the book had been "virtually unreviewed in New York" the year before and had since sold twenty thousand copies due to word of mouth among conservationists and naturalists. This was high praise coming from a respected writer at the prestigious daily newspaper; the review's visibility and wide distribution would certainly give the book an additional burst of sales.[68]

Helen couldn't resist sharing the *New York Times* clipping with the editor of the *Cook County News-Herald* and sent him a copy. The January 7, 1965, issue of the paper carried a front-page headline: "The Long-Shadowed Forest Gets Excellent New York Review." The accompanying article heavily excerpted the *Times'* review. Clearly the Hoovers were proud of the attention the book was getting, but they also probably wanted to remind local residents they were not necessarily the kooks they had been made out to be.[69]

Helen continued to work on the deer story, but it was not coming together as she wanted. It was important that she perfectly capture this idyllic moment of their time in the north woods. The story not only must tell of how they grew attached to Peter, Mama, and their family of deer and the wonder that relationship provided; it also had to provide a cautionary tale of the changes occurring in the area at the same time. In May 1965, Helen checked in with her editor Ed Tripp. "I have 55,000 words of something about deer, but I can't say how it is. It isn't the book I intended to write—that was a different thing for a special purpose and I couldn't change direction without changing the book. I hope it's OK."[70]

Helen now shifted her attention to organizing a collection of her columns from *Humpty Dumpty's* for Parents' Magazine Press. Management there had seen Harrison Salisbury's review of *The Long-Shadowed Forest* and realized they could latch on to Helen's rising star. Her editor, Alvin Tresselt, came to Gunflint Lake from New York in June so he could finally meet Helen and see the place he had heard so much about. They had developed a close working relationship, and Helen was excited to host him and spend some time together working on the final selections for the book. He was enchanted by the setting with its tall trees, the late summer light, an encounter with a black bear, and even Helen's playing of a Beethoven minuet on her baby grand piano. Tresselt had the run of the summer cabin and later wrote about the experience in a newsletter for subscribers.[71] The selections they chose would be for her first children's book, *Animals at My Doorstep*, which was scheduled for publication the following year.

✳ ✳ ✳

The previous autumn, President Lyndon Johnson signed into law the Wilderness Act of 1964, which set aside 9.1 million acres of federal land as wilderness. In Minnesota, nearly 900,000 acres of land roughly between Ely and east of Gunflint Lake bordering Canada was included in the legislation, along with other areas around the country, primarily in the western United States.[72] A key component of the new law was that it established a national system for defining wilderness in the United States, but a clause in the act allowed for some motor use and logging in the Boundary Waters Canoe Area (BWCA) specifically. This created confusion about exactly how the Wilderness Act would impact Minnesota's canoe country.

U.S. Secretary of Agriculture Orville Freeman—a former Minnesota governor—had oversight of the U.S. Forest Service and was tasked with trying to sort out the situation. Freeman appointed the former commissioner of the Minnesota Department of Conservation when he was governor, George Selke, to head up a review committee that held public hearings to gather information and make recommendations for the management of the BWCA.[73]

The Hoovers had attended one of the hearings in Grand Marais about the Wilderness Act and were supportive of it, even if they were in the minority. While many in the area wanted to keep logging intact, Helen and Ade believed there was enough timber in other areas of Superior National Forest to support logging. They also didn't understand why more people weren't embracing the tourism canoe country would bring.[74]

Plans for restricting access to the BWCA burst onto the national scene in May 1965 when the *New York Times* reported on the divisions between local residents in northeast Minnesota. The story quoted resort owners and conservationists about the pros and cons of restricting access to the area and included comments from both Sigurd Olson and Helen. She noted the forest was a treasure beyond any dollar amount and that the federal plan would be to everyone's advantage in the long run. However, some of the resort owners on the trail took an opposing view. Bud Kratoska, owner of Trout Lake Lodge off the Gunflint Trail, felt the new controls only favored canoeists at the expense of the majority of people who didn't want to canoe.[75]

As for Helen's writing, publisher Bob Crowell followed up hoping to soon have the deer book and illustrations for their 1966 spring list. Despite a contractual deadline of December 1, he was anxious to see an early draft. Helen could not see how this could be accomplished. In a letter, she explained the book had been difficult for her and gained more substance in its writing; she was still struggling to get it down on paper and worked out. Not having extensive knowledge of deer behavior, she was checking with sources to confirm information and therefore could not be rushed. Helen was corresponding with several academic experts about deer behavior, as well as deer author Leonard Rue, fact-checking and verifying other animal behavior she observed, and helping get information for Ade so his illustrations would be accurate.[76] She also noted it seemed odd that the publisher wanted to bring out a book that opens on Christmas, the day Peter arrived, around the Easter holiday.[77]

Adding to her anxiety was that Ade had been ill from shortly after the time Crowell had visited in October through February, again likely from neuralgia. Helen also lost eight days to autograph seekers, and she needed to get three juvenile stories finished, which also weighed on her mind. And another of the deer family, Pretty, had been hit and killed in July by a car on the side road, leaving Helen disillusioned and sad.[78]

Bob Crowell gently persisted in his desire for a look at her progress. Helen sent back a stern letter, arguing she could not get the writing in shape in that time; she had promised only a first draft, not a completed manuscript. She wrote to Ed Tripp that she was "really blocked on the book" and said their efforts to hurry her had thrown her "flat on my face. Now I get violently sick every time I try to get going on the continuity and write the letters that are needed to check certain information." Helen signed off with "I'll write to you or Mr. Crowell when and if. I really can't say anything more definite now."[79]

At the same time, Helen was trying to complete a shorter version of Peter's story for *Woman's Journal* and was corresponding with editor Helen Finch about that manuscript, which they needed by September 1965. The first of three installments would appear in the January 1966 issue, hitting newsstands in England right before Christmas 1965.

It's not entirely clear what Helen's state of mind was at this point. In an undated letter to Tresselt, she confided that she was being pushed too hard for the deer book, which in turn triggered other doubts about the publisher. She believed *The Long-Shadowed Forest* had been rushed; had she not raised objections and done the final editing herself, the book would have gone to press with errors and typos throughout. That was unacceptable to Helen. At the same time, Helen was flattered that *Woman's Journal* in England was publishing part of the deer story. Perhaps she was mindful of what friend Dorothy Gardiner had said about the English being enamored with nature stories.

Given the importance to Helen of the deer book, she reiterated to Tresselt that, to fix inconsistencies and confirm accuracy—goals made difficult by all the interruptions—she had to go back to the beginning to get it straight in her head again. "I'm hooked to the wrong publisher. He [Crowell] wants compilers, not writers. Every time I try to work on the damn ms. [manuscript] I get sick to my stomach, literally."[80]

There was also the matter of Alfred Knopf. Mr. Knopf's personal interest in a book from Helen and Ade, his disappointment that he had not been able to publish her first effort, and his insights about the poor design of *The Long-Shadowed Forest* certainly weighed on her mind. It was also no small consideration that his publishing house was among the most esteemed in the country, a fact not lost on Helen when she read a fiftieth anniversary feature about the publisher and his wife, Blanche, in *Life* magazine that summer. All of this made the situation with Crowell more fraught.[81]

With that in mind, Helen sent a letter to Alfred Knopf reminding him of their previous correspondence and talking in general terms about the deer book and her intent to seek release from Crowell. Helen was not aware that Knopf had suffered a heart attack and was recuperating at home for an extended time. He asked Angus Cameron, a Knopf editor who handled their nature titles, to respond to Helen on his behalf. Cameron wrote back and expressed mild interest in Helen's book, but he also made it clear they would not want to discuss a project until she could assure them that she had no obligation to another publisher.[82]

By October 1965, Helen had sent the final edits of the deer magazine article, titled "A Buck Called Peter," to *Woman's Journal* in London while continuing to make technical refinements to the manuscript that she envisioned as a book. With deadline pressures continuing to weigh on her and doubts about whether Crowell was the right publisher for the book, plus the added interest from Cameron at Knopf, she decided she needed to be released from her contract. She wrote to Bob Crowell, citing interruptions and both her and Ade's inability to prepare the book and illustrations in time for the publisher's spring schedule. Crowell and Ed Tripp tried to convince Helen to set it aside for a while and pick it up later, but she could not be persuaded. She returned the $400 advance— not an easy thing, given the Hoovers' finances—and requested a release from her contract, including the option for a second book. She wanted to be free and clear of Crowell because the relationship was making her physically ill.[83]

While corresponding with Crowell about her release, Helen related some of her apprehensions about the situation in a follow-up letter to Cameron in late November. She noted all the work Ade had put into the illustrations for her first book only to have many of them not used. She also mentioned that she had been asked to do an index and spent seventeen days working on it, only to learn that Crowell had done one without informing her. Cameron was sympathetic, but he did not quite know how to react to Helen's three-page venting.[84]

Angus Cameron was a respected book editor with an intriguing past. He had been editor in chief of Little, Brown and Company in the 1940s and had published well-known writers J. D. Salinger and Lillian Hellman. Cameron's leftist politics caught up with him in the anticommunism backlash of the early 1950s, and he left the publisher when asked to curtail his political activities. To get away from public scrutiny, he moved his family to the Adirondacks and then to Alaska, but soon he returned to start a small publishing house. Cameron landed at Alfred A. Knopf in 1959 after the "red" frenzy had subsided. He went on to edit and oversee nature titles for the publishing house, including works by Sigurd Olson.[85]

Helen continued to pursue a release from her contract with Crowell, and after much persistence in trying to convince her otherwise, Bob Crowell relented in December 1965. While he thought she was perhaps letting the pressure of meeting deadlines get her down, Helen actually wanted to be done with Crowell. She continued to be allured by the interest of Alfred Knopf himself, a publisher known for the quality of the authors he signed. Being in the company of nature writers like Sigurd Olson and Margaret E. Murie would certainly give Helen's writing the gravitas and wider exposure she sought for the book about Peter and his family.

Bedelia, the Hoovers' remaining chicken, died after having reached the age of nearly eleven years. The bird's death was sad for Helen: Bedelia had become a daily fixture in their lives and been a stalwart hen in the early years, providing eggs when they had little other fresh protein to eat. It was difficult for Helen not to cut up leftover food scraps for the chicken as she had done for years. However, taking care of Bedelia was the last thing keeping Helen and Ade tethered to the cabin. They began to think more about the day when they might be able to get away for an extended period without having to worry about asking neighbors to look in on her.[86]

Meanwhile, Cameron had been noncommittal about the deer book; he did not want to become entangled in a dispute between an author under contract with another publisher. As the year came to an end, Helen was concerned she may have been too forthcoming with Cameron about her troubles with Crowell. She had a manuscript of a book that was important to her and Ade but was now without a publisher. "A Buck Called Peter" was about to appear in *Woman's Journal* in England, and she had no idea how it might be received there. And she was growing weary of having to do all of this selling work herself. Helen now understood she needed an agent to get the book manuscript into the right hands, including Cameron's. Helen's credentials had been established; now she needed to take the next step and get serious about her future as a writer.

# 7

# Paradise Lost

### *Gunflint Lake, 1966–1971*


HAVING BEEN RELEASED FROM HER CROWELL CONTRACT in early December 1965, Helen had the month and holidays to put the finishing touches on the manuscript she now titled "A Buck Called Peter." She was finally satisfied with how it turned out, and Ade had finished working on eight pen-and-ink drawings to accompany the text. When the time came to submit the manuscript for publication, it would be understood that the illustrations were part of the offering.

Relieved to be free and clear of Crowell, Helen was still restless about where she could get this homage to Peter published, so in February she wrote to Gladys Taber, the *Family Circle* columnist who had enjoyed *The Long-Shadowed Forest*. Writing from one author to another, Helen admitted she was stuck and needed advice on how to find a literary agent. Gladys recommended that Helen reach out to her own agent, Carol Brandt, at the well-regarded Brandt & Brandt literary agency in New York. "You can tell her too I suggested it, because since I have never done it before, she will pay strict attention. I feel you are too good a writer to erode yourself battling any more." [1]

In March, Helen sent a letter of introduction to Brandt, asking if she would be willing to look at her manuscript for the deer story, and if she liked it, take her on as a client. Brandt was more than happy to read it and was quite impressed. Helen had mentioned her past correspondence with Alfred Knopf, so Brandt sent the manuscript to Knopf for review. Unbeknownst to Helen, Brandt was close friends with Knopf and his wife Blanche, who ran the publishing house together. Brandt wrote Knopf to tell him she had forwarded the manuscript to Angus Cameron for review and reminded him of his previous interest in Helen's work.[2]

Carol Brandt was a respected literary agent, and Brandt & Brandt was considered one of the top firms in the business. Her stable of authors included John Dos Passos, Minnesota native Margaret Culkin Banning, novelist and playwright Thornton Wilder, novelist Marcia Davenport, historian Wallace Stegner, and horror and mystery writer Shirley Jackson, best known for her short story "The Lottery," who had died the previous year.

Helen's now completed manuscript opens on Christmas Day in 1958 with a malnourished buck appearing in their yard after the Hoovers celebrate a holiday meal with their friend, outdoor guide and trapper Ollor Snevets. With his advice and help, Helen and Ade nurse the deer back to health, providing dinner scraps and cedar boughs gathered from the woods for nourishment.

The book follows the life of Peter, the starving deer, from that Christmas Day encounter through early 1962, when he is killed. It is organized by years and describes how the Hoovers began to feed the deer family, including the arrival in the spring of Mama and her twin bucks, Pig and Brother; the birth of Pretty and Fuzzy the following year; and then Little Buck and Starface the next summer. Helen blends the stories about each of the offspring and the personal and physical traits she and Ade recorded, charting their return each year. There is the joy of feeding the deer each winter into spring, their summer departure for the deep forest when nearby activity increases and the does need privacy to have their fawns, and the steps the Hoovers take to try and protect the deer each hunting season. As with *The Long-Shadowed Forest,* Helen wove in stories about other animals in the yard and details about life in the woods. But the focus of the story Helen wanted to tell was on Peter, his family, and the pleasure they brought to the Hoovers over those nearly four years.

Helen chose to end the book by suggesting that Peter knew that wolves were moving in on some of the deer in the yard that winter. Peter goes away and does not return; Helen and Ade go on a walk along their road and discern from the tracks that Peter drove a wolf away from Starface and became a victim of the wolf pack, completing the circle of life in the forest.

The book was important to Helen, and she wanted to remember those years as special. She saw no point in revealing what really happened to Peter as it did nothing to end the story in a positive way for readers. Here she was applying what she learned from A. L. Fierst, the literary agent she had sent her first rough work to: that fictionizing was indeed desirable. The world did not need to know that Peter had been killed and left for dead.[3]

Brandt was delighted with the manuscript. "I cannot tell you how much I love this book," she wrote Helen weeks after receiving it.[4]

Once the manuscript was sent to Knopf, the waiting began. Cameron read the text immediately and liked it; in fact, he recommended it for consideration at the next Knopf editorial meeting. In his pitch to colleagues, Cameron noted the two-year cultivation that had started with Mr. Knopf's initial letter to Helen in 1963 and his own subsequent correspondence with her. "Mrs. Hoover . . . is an excellent nature writer and in this manuscript, combines the account of the deer, Peter, with other general nature writing. Her shortish book should find a solid audience, I think, with the people who buy Knopf nature books."[5]

Cameron found Helen's writing a bit sentimental, noting to colleagues her habit of naming the animals and how the ending of the book demonstrated a level of anthropomorphism, though not in any way more offensive than some other Knopf nature authors. He did suggest that some of the more sentimental passages would need to be revised. Cameron also anticipated Helen could produce other salable books for Knopf, so he clearly believed she had long-term potential for the publishing house.[6]

Knopf offered to publish the book. They proposed an advance of $2,000, with a royalty break of 10 percent on the first five thousand copies sold, 12.5 percent through seventy-five hundred copies, and 15 percent thereafter. The book would retail for $4.95. Ade would receive $500 for his drawings.[7] Helen accepted the offer in a letter to Carl Brandt, Carol's son, who was a partner in the business. Helen thought Ade should have received more for his drawings, but she asked only that they be returned after their use in the production. She also indicated her pleasure at having someone tend to the business details of the contract.[8]

Cameron had only minor suggestions related to sentimentality in the manuscript, which he knew could be easily revised. Knopf decided it would

publish in the fall of 1967, appropriately recognizing that a book opening on Christmas Day needed to come out ahead of the holiday selling
season. There was concern that, given Helen's abrupt break with Crowell,
some carryover language used in *The Long-Shadowed Forest* would need
to be rewritten entirely so as not to run afoul of contractual obligations.
Helen also agreed that some of her more strident language about "outlaw
hunting" should be modified or dropped altogether in keeping with the
tone of the book—and more importantly, for the Hoovers' own safety.
They feared local reaction if residents easily identified some of those she
mentioned in the book.[9]

Now everything started to move quickly. After sending the manuscript to Knopf, Carol Brandt also forwarded it to the Reader's Digest
Book Club for consideration for their condensed books, quarterly vol-
umes that contained four or five best sellers. These collections were popular in the 1960s as an inexpensive way to introduce new readers to a variety of best-selling authors and their books, which were easily promoted
through the magazine's book club. Brandt had a close relationship with
one of its editors and enthusiastically advocated for the book's consideration once Knopf published it.[10]

In a surprise to both Brandt and Knopf, Reader's Digest came back
with an acceptance of the book under one condition: they wanted to
add it to their autumn 1966 selections, necessitating Knopf's publication
at the same time. That meant moving up publication date by a year to
October 1966, only six months away. While not impossible, it was quite
a departure for a publisher to accommodate this type of change to its
publishing schedule. Fortunately, Helen's manuscript only needed minor
edits and revisions, reflecting the "labor of love" she had worked so hard
on the previous two years.[11]

More significantly, the Reader's Digest arrangement came with a
sizable financial windfall. The Hoovers were guaranteed $20,000, with
extra royalties of $2,500 also guaranteed for foreign editions in ten lan-
guages. The fees and royalties were split with the publisher, so Knopf
also had a vested interest in the arrangement. The simultaneous publication by Knopf and Reader's Digest Book Club practically guaranteed a
best seller.[12]

Carol Brandt was vacationing in Europe when the Reader's Digest news came through, and her son Carl placed a call to Helen to let her know. Helen literally sputtered on the phone with excitement at their good fortune. Later, she followed up with a note to Carl, assuring him that, despite her garbled response, she understood what he had called about. Helen was more delighted that Peter and Mama's story would likely be read by millions of people around the world.[13]

These high-level publishing interactions were new to the Hoovers. They confirmed to Helen that she had been right to seek out a knowledgeable agent who could do all the legwork on her behalf. After the contract details, publication date, and book club deal were sorted out, Helen sent Brandt a thank-you note. "I have never told you how happy I am to have you representing me. I don't suppose you and Mr. Brandt [Carl] can know quite what a relief it is to NOT have to struggle with all of these things. It probably is easy—when you know how, as you do."[14]

Brandt, too, was pleased with having Helen as a client. She wrote a note of thanks to Gladys Taber for sending Helen to them, noting that *The Gift of the Deer* (as the book was now called) was "going to be a charming thing, which will, I am convinced, be a modern day, THE YEARLING."[15]

With the Reader's Digest Book Club deal in place and the book's subsequent publication in several languages assured, Brandt went to work on finding foreign publishers to handle *The Gift of the Deer* outside the United States. Manuscript copies were sent to literary agents in Denmark, France, Germany, Italy, Japan, the Netherlands, Norway, Spain, and Sweden for foreign language editions.[16]

When the serialization of "A Buck Called Peter" in *Woman's Journal* ended in March, securing a London publisher was critical for capitalizing on the British public's interest in Helen. Brandt had a close arrangement with an agent in London who started to pitch the book, with noted publisher William Heinemann among those they approached. Staff at Heinemann read it and immediately accepted it. Charles Pick, the managing director, said in a note to Brandt, "this is the very best kind of animal book, free from sentimentality, highly informative and of the caliber of RING OF BRIGHT WATER and Sally Carrighar's books."[17]

The summer was a busy one for the Hoovers. In addition to the usual autograph seekers and unannounced visitors, Helen met with Carol Brandt, who by chance was traveling with her husband on a business trip to Duluth. Brandt was taking advantage of the trip to see both Helen and another of her clients, Margaret Culkin Banning, who summered in Brule, Wisconsin. Banning had grown up in Duluth and was the best-selling author of several novels and an early advocate of women's rights.

On July 14, 1966, Helen traveled by bus from Grand Marais to Duluth, excited to meet Brandt but also worried about her own appearance. On the trip to visit family in Cincinnati in 1957, Helen realized living in the woods without a care about personal appearance had shocked her back to reality when she was out in public. She felt she had looked frumpy, so this time she made every effort to look presentable. Helen later recalled meeting Brandt: "I shall always treasure my first sight of her—tall, slim, elegant, and gracious." The women met for dinner, and Helen immediately knew they would get along both as business associates and as people. That night Duluth was wracked by a strong thunderstorm—something that terrified Helen. Brandt was kept awake by the harbor's foghorn. They had breakfast the next morning before Helen returned to Grand Marais.[18]

Brandt was so charmed by the meeting that she sent a note sharing her impressions with the British literary agent they were using to sell *The Gift of the Deer*. "When Helen Hoover received our check representing the $2000 advance from Knopf, she had exactly $118 plus some odd cents in her book. This is one of the most extraordinary human stories I have ever known, but we have a writer here who is going to do for us perhaps not entirely what Marjorie Rawlings did, but she is going to verge on it."[19] While the dollar amount cited by Brandt in Helen's bank account was an exaggeration, there is no question the Hoovers' finances might still have been shaky, given their expenses: food and heating oil, supplies for the notepaper business, and seeds and corn for their wild animals.

This was the second mention by Brandt of Marjorie Kinnan Rawlings and her book *The Yearling*, a best-selling novel and winner of the Pulitzer Prize for fiction in 1939. Brandt was a story editor at the Metro-Goldwyn-Mayer (MGM) studio in 1946 when the movie of the book was released. Her late husband, Carl Brandt, had been Rawlings's literary agent from 1931 until she died in 1953.[20] *The Yearling* follows a poor farm family in rural Florida that endures hardships trying to make a living after the Civil War. The son raises an orphaned fawn, only to learn the grown deer is eating the family's corn crop, which they rely on. The father forces the son to shoot the deer, providing the boy with a tough coming-of-age lesson. Brandt was hoping the story line of *The Gift of the Deer* might attract a broad readership as *The Yearling* had a generation before. Given that connection, Knopf sent the book to the Walt Disney Productions offices in New York for consideration as a television movie. While there was initial interest from one of their producers, nothing came of it, as the book lacked a dramatic storyline.[21]

Brandt was also shopping *The Gift of the Deer* to movie studios in Hollywood, using an agent there to make inquiries. After Disney passed on the possibility, it was sent to MGM and Paramount for consideration, as well as to family film producer Robert B. Radnitz (who produced *Misty,* based on the popular juvenile book *Misty of Chincoteague*) and animal television producer Ivan Tors of *Flipper* and *Gentle Ben* fame.[22]

With the excitement of the book advance and the Reader's Digest Book Club guarantee, the Hoovers could now afford a new car, which they would need if they intended to travel. Ade went into Grand Marais where he bought a new Ford Mustang for the princely sum of $2,410. Helen thought the car was quite sporty, and there exists 8 mm color film of the Hoovers showing off the car to some of their neighbors.[23]

In August 1966, Helen's seventy-seven-year-old uncle Bruce Gomersall died, requiring her and Ade to travel to Cincinnati to help settle his affairs. They were there for more than a month, also helping the surviving bachelor brother Robert, all of which was a source of frustration for Helen, as *Animals at My Doorstep* was coming out October 1 and *The Gift of the Deer* was being published November 11. In fact, Cameron had to forward the first copy of the finished book to Helen in Cincinnati. Holding the actual book in their hands, the Hoovers were excited at how it turned out.[24]

One could see that *The Gift of the Deer* was indeed the labor of love Helen had hoped to write. The story of Peter, Mama, and their subsequent families was brought to life by Helen's ability to observe animals and write about them in a way that was appealing without being sentimental. She described two of the bucks, Pig and Brother, playing in their yard:

They glided, curved, circled, raced, with first one, then the other leading. They flashed across the yard in front of me, their leaps so long and effortless that their hoofs seemed hardly to skim the ground. They cleared a brush pile as though riding a wave. They flowed like liquid, soared like winged creatures, seemed to hover in mid-leap as their lithe young bodies stretched through the exciting air of spring.[25]

While the book captures the wonder and amazement the Hoovers had for the deer and their constant presence during the fall, winter, and spring, Helen's epilogue put the years of Peter, Mama, and the other deer in elegant perspective:

When Peter came into our yard, we had a choice to make. We could stand by and see for ourselves how a deer starved to death. We could assume that he had no chance of recovery and kill him, in the way called humane. Or we could reach out with the compassion that has the power to lift man above the brute level. We chose the last, and when Ade cut the first cedar branch for Peter, he stirred the air among the branches. This whisper of a breeze turned into a wide-spreading wind, swaying the trees and changing the life of the forest. And it still reaches out and blows back to us, sometimes a raging, violent gale, more often a soft and gentle zephyr.[26]

What made the book so special to Helen was that in the end, the story of Peter was essentially a modern parable, as she closed the book:

If we had not brought Peter back from the edge of death, he would not have led Mama to stay with us. Starface would not have been born. Most of the things—the personal things—I have been writing about would never have happened. And the wind from the branches Ade moved is still blowing. When these deer have gone on the long road that Peter, and so many others, have taken, there will be deer still, following the old trails through the forest, perhaps to come to us for help in another winter of bitter cold and deep snow.

Peter brought them to us, he left them for us, a gift priceless beyond all accounting. What can I say of him?

He was Peter, our buck with the generous heart.[27]

When the Hoovers arrived home from Cincinnati, a reporter from the *Duluth News-Tribune* scheduled a visit so he could write an article about the new book. His subsequent story offered the usual details about living in the woods and feeding deer, but he also coaxed out of Helen how she approached her writing: "I don't take notes and have to arrange sequences in my head. . . . If I lose my concentration, I have to start over from scratch."[28] These comments echoed those she had shared privately with Alvin Tresselt and friends by mail who had asked the same question.

Alice Carlson, the book buyer at Powers department store in Minneapolis, asked Helen if she could arrange media interviews and autograph signings November 16 and 17 as part of a "Hoover Days" promotion at stores in downtown Minneapolis, suburban St. Louis Park, and the Highland Park neighborhood of St. Paul. Helen was loyal to Carlson, who had been an early fan of *The Long-Shadowed Forest*, and the timing was ideal as it got the Hoovers out of the cabin during deer hunting season.[29] The autograph parties were staggered so that Helen and Ade could sign books at each location, celebrating the publication of both *The Gift of the Deer* and *Animals at My Doorstep*. The Hoovers participated in three radio interviews and made one TV appearance. Helen related to Cameron that they "were mobbed and couldn't get away for four hours." While she was pleased with the effort by the department store, she also chided Cameron for not sending review copies to some of the local journalists for which she had previously provided names.[30]

*Animals at My Doorstep* also garnered positive reviews, including one that was particularly endearing to Helen and Ade, written by Henry B. Kane. He was the illustrator of *Cache Lake Country*, the book Helen said partly influenced their decision to move to the north woods. Kane's review appeared in the Sunday *New York Times Book Review* and noted that Helen had written many columns for *Humpty Dumpty's* magazine. "Thirteen have been selected for this book and they are much more than recordings of observations. There are explanations of camouflage, hibernation and other phenomena that will open a child's eyes to the wild world."[31]

When the Hoovers returned to the cabin, they found that hunters had overrun their land and neighboring properties and killed several deer. Helen lamented to Cameron that she had done a lot to promote the area over the years but regretted it now after seeing all of the damage done. She was so furious at the contempt of local residents for those efforts that she signaled she and Ade might not stay. "We will be moving when and if we can find a suitable location." She signed the letter, "Forgive this outburst, but I am both bitter and depressed."[32]

Interestingly, while they were in Cincinnati, Helen purchased a Colt .22-caliber revolver from a local sporting goods store. She had indicated to Cameron that they had been thinking of ways to deter the hunters who trespassed on their property, but she was never specific as to what they were. Ade had a .45 automatic pistol that they had used for protection and to scatter the deer from their yard before hunting season, but the addition of a second gun seemed out of character. According to the gun permit application, the intended purpose was for "target practice." The application also provided Helen's personal details: age fifty-six, height five foot seven inches, weight 225 pounds, brown hair, blue eyes, complexion fair, and face smooth.[33]

Despite Helen's concerns about local media not receiving review copies, the Knopf publicity department knew how to get national press coverage for its books, and *The Gift of the Deer* was no exception. They not only had a long list of newspaper and magazine reviewers all over the country who regularly received Knopf books; they also could support their titles with substantial trade advertising in select national magazines and newspapers. *The Gift of the Deer* was among the books featured in Knopf advertising that holiday.

Nature writer Hal Borland wrote a flattering review in the *New York Times*, although he did offer some minor criticism, noting that Helen "participates emotionally" in the story. He did soften, though, offering that "Hoover fills in the background with a wealth of knowledge and observation, not only about the deer . . . but about the birds, trees, wild flowers, the whole natural background. But the book is primarily about the deer, and

1 | Thomas, Helen, and Hannah
Blackburn, Greenfield, Ohio, 1910s.

2 | Helen Drusilla Blackburn, dressed
formally, late 1910s.

3 | Main Street, Greenfield, Ohio, postcard, 1900s.

4 | Helen as a teenager, 1920s.

5 | A high school portrait of Helen, 1926.

6 | The library of McClain High School, Greenfield, Ohio, 1920s.

7 | A stylish Helen out on the town and Adrian Hoover at a Chicago public beach on Lake Michigan, both from the 1930s.

8 | Gunflint Lodge, postcard, circa 1930.

9 | Automobiles on the Gunflint Trail, 1932.

10 | Adrian Hoover in U.S. Navy uniform, circa 1943.

11 | Helen in the laboratory, 1950s.

12 | Sign listing resorts and campgrounds on the Gunflint Trail, 1939.

13 | Schedule for the Wilderness Express, bus service from Grand Marais to the resorts on the Gunflint Trail, late 1930s.

14 | Alvin Tresselt, editor of *Humpty Dumpty's* magazine, at the Hoovers' cabin in 1965.

15 | Carol Brandt, Helen's literary agent, 1940s.

16 | Donald "Angus" Cameron, Helen's editor at Knopf, 1960s.

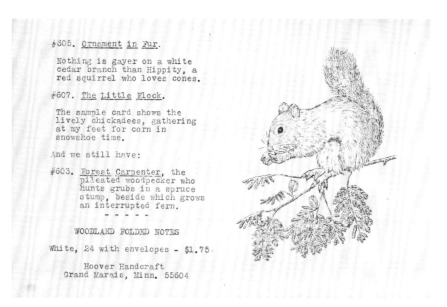

#605. Ornament in Fur.

Nothing is gayer on a white cedar branch than Hippity, a red squirrel who loves cones.

#607. The Little Flock.

The sample card shows the lively chickadees, gathering at my feet for corn in snowshoe time.

And we still have:

#603. Forest Carpenter, the pileated woodpecker who hunts grubs in a spruce stump, beside which grows an interrupted fern.
- - - - -

WOODLAND FOLDED NOTES

White, 24 with envelopes - $1.75

Hoover Handcraft
Grand Marais, Minn. 55604

17 | Page from catalog sent to customers of Hoover Handcraft, Helen and Ade's business.

18 | Humphreys department store and Jackson's Café, early landmarks in Grand Marais, 1950s.

19 | Downtown Grand Marais, Minnesota, 1950s.

20 | Ade Hoover at his makeshift drawing table
in the log cabin, 1963.

21 | Helen and Ade outside the summer house, 1963.

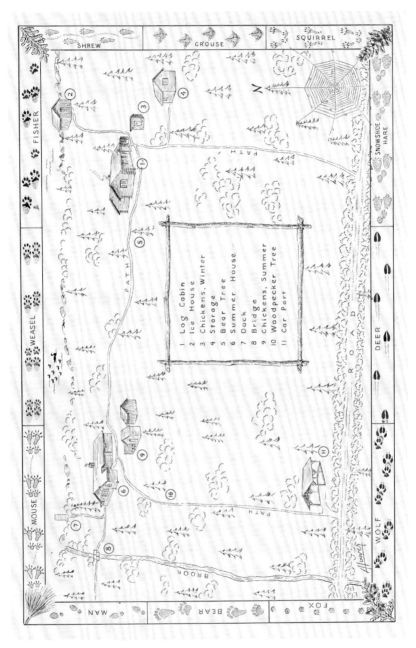

Border labels (clockwise from top left): SHREW, GROUSE, SQUIRREL, SNOWSHOE HARE, DEER, WOLF, FOX, BEAR, MAN, MOUSE, WEASEL, FISHER

N (compass)

PATH

PATH

ROAD

BROOK

1  Log Cabin
2  Ice House
3  Chickens, Winter
4  Storage
5  Bear Tree
6  Summer House
7  Dock
8  Bridge
9  Chickens, Summer
10 Woodpecker Tree
11 Car Port

22 | Ade's hand-drawn map of the Gunflint Lake property,
published in *A Place in the Woods*.

23 | Helen plays her baby grand piano, 1963.

24 | Helen's crowded writing desk, 1963. Note the gas lamps
above her desk and the full bookshelves.

25 | Ade and Helen in front of the summer house
fireplace, 1963.

26 | The Hoovers read under the watchful eye of Mona Lisa, 1963.
Helen is absorbed in Ian Fleming's *Thunderball*.

27 | Two photographs of Peter, "the buck with the generous heart." The first was taken in January 1959, just days after the Hoovers began feeding him; the second was from the following winter, before he shed his antlers.

28 | Two of Ade's original drawings for *The Gift of the Deer.*

29 | Helen feeds wildlife at the Gunflint Lake property, 1963.

30 | Resort owner Peggy Heston, 1970s.

31 | Helen and Ade outside the log cabin in the garden, 1966.

32 | The Hoovers' log cabin in the 1970s.

33 | Her place in the woods, 1963.

that is its lasting virtue." He ended by saying "I can name on the fingers of one hand the wild-animal stories that fulfill the ideal—true, credible, warm and unsentimental. 'Gift of the Deer' stands close besides those few."[34]

While most people would have been thrilled by such a positive notice in the Sunday *New York Times Book Review* section, Helen believed that her old acquaintance Harrison E. Salisbury, who had not received an advance copy and had written positively of *The Long-Shadowed Forest*, would have done better by it. Borland was both influential and a Connecticut neighbor of Cameron, but Helen conceded that "it is a lot to expect a NY publicity department to accept the fact that some female in the boondocks knows who will give the best review in the TIMES."[35] Cameron had a different issue with Salisbury; his reporting from the war in Vietnam was getting him in trouble with the U.S. government, and he didn't need a controversial correspondent writing a review of Helen's first book for Knopf. Having been in the spotlight himself during the McCarthy era of the 1950s, Cameron knew not to court trouble.

Other reviewers provided positive notices. Writing in the *Chicago Tribune*, Ethel Jacobson said, "it is the story of a haunting friendship, and of a company of deer as few are privileged to know them." Victor H. Cahalane, a well-known retired biologist for the U.S. Forest Service, observed in *Defenders of Wildlife News:* "Every page is a pleasure to read. Some paragraphs can only be described as lyrical." The *Chicago Sunday American* ranked the book in its top ten for the year and called it "The best 'outdoor' book of the year, by far."[36]

Some reviews hinted at the anthropomorphism that Cameron was concerned about when initially recommending the book for publication. Helen was sensitive to these remarks and as a scientist took these critiques personally. The Borland review particularly vexed her, as she felt his review was more about her than the book. He had certainly praised her work but inferred she may be too close to her subject. John Perry, who had written a flattering review of *The Long-Shadowed Forest* in the *Atlantic Naturalist*, had misunderstood her description of Peter being scared by a nearby fire to which the deer had alerted the Hoovers. Ever the scientist, she was compelled to write to both to offer some explanation on how she arrived at her observations.[37]

Anthropomorphism is an issue many nature writers are confronted with, particularly when observing animals in the wild. The challenge is that the writer often ascribes human traits or emotions to animals, thereby asserting that an animal's behavior can be expressed in human terms. While Helen was criticized by some reviewers for naming her animals, this was not so much a case of anthropomorphism as it reflected how Helen distinguished the different animals in her writing. But in some passages of *The Gift of the Deer*, particularly at the end where she suggests that Peter somehow drew the wolf away from one of the younger deer it was pursuing, she was speculating about Peter's intentions and injecting emotion into the story for dramatic effect. While it may have helped provide the reader with a plausible—and less tragic—ending, it was not something she observed firsthand, and she therefore opened herself to criticism. Still, much of the narrative was based on her actual observations of the deer and their interactions with each other and did not resort to fictionizing their activity for the sake of the story.

Heading into the holidays, book sales for *The Gift of the Deer* were strong. Sales in the first month were around seven thousand, and Knopf ordered a second printing right before Christmas. Helen kept close tabs on how it was doing by checking with her favorite bookstores in Chicago and with shops in Grand Marais, as well as reports from friends.[38]

Gladys Taber and Margaret Culkin Banning shared their accolades, endorsements that were personally rewarding to Helen. "Your book is lovely. I am lost in admiration. How you do write! And the sensitive feeling for the wild creatures is an inspiration," gushed Taber.[39] "You have written a quite extraordinary book—weaving beautiful description, a human and personal story and a study of the habits of deer together. I am proud that it was written of my part of the country and in my part of the country," wrote Banning.[40]

Helen also penned a note to Alfred Knopf to thank him again for reading her magazine article in 1963, an action that had set everything on its path.[41]

Following the Twin Cities publicity tour and the end of the hunting season, the Hoovers could take a break and not worry about deadlines or notepaper orders. After returning to the cabin, they took in a Christmas Day movie at the Shore Theatre in Grand Marais: a double feature of *Bambi* and *Tarzan the Ape Man*.[42]

By the end of the year, they had placed the last classified ad in *Audubon* magazine for their notepaper business, no longer needing the income from that endeavor. The long, hard pull was over, but not without new challenges.

✳ ✳ ✳

After the holidays, Angus Cameron asked Helen what she had in mind for her next book, careful not to push too hard but also knowing that her readers would soon be wanting more from her. Helen said she was thinking of their early days on Gunflint Lake, when it was quiet and undeveloped and they had to adapt to living in their new environment. There would be lots about the animals, which were plentiful then. She knew from fan mail that her readers wanted stories on animals.[43]

*The Gift of the Deer* continued to do very well into the new year, selling 16,279 copies through mid-March of 1967. Helen was thrilled because Peter's story and this time in their lives on Gunflint Lake was an important milestone. When they bought the log cabin in 1948, Ade noted the clock was ticking; it would only be a matter of time before roads and modern conveniences intruded on their tranquil spot. The years of Peter's first appearance and of feeding and observing his family were part of that special time for the Hoovers.[44]

Helen also learned around this time that *Animals at My Doorstep,* her collection of stories from *Humpty Dumpty's* magazine, had just passed fifty thousand in sales. As she noted to Cameron, she didn't earn much from those juvenile book club sales, but they were good advertising for her adult books.[45]

Helen had a complicated relationship with Cameron. She respected him as an editor but thought he lacked an understanding of the business side of publishing. Helen was concerned when *The Gift of the Deer* sold out quickly in the Twin Cities after the book-signing parties, believing that Knopf had not sent enough books to the local market. She was surprised that he was slow to share with the Knopf publicity people her relationships with Gladys Taber at *Family Circle* and Harrison E. Salisbury at the *New York Times,* two influential writers whose mentions of the book would have garnered many more sales. Helen also sensed a bit of the

conservation world's "good old boy network" when Hal Borland seemed
to get first crack at all the nature titles from Knopf. While Cameron believed Borland wrote a good review of *The Gift of the Deer*, Helen thought
his focus was more directed at her motives for writing the book than at
the actual content. As she commented to her agent: "Borland is the type
to take a magnifying glass and count the florets on a spray of goldenrod;
I see captured sunshine, nectar for the insects, even the flaw in everything
in the form of hay fever. He would never understand me."[46]

Cameron was well regarded as an editor of nature titles, and Knopf
had a sizable share of that market. He was excellent at the care and feeding of his authors, as evidenced by his correspondence with Helen, where
he gently inquired about the progress she was making. He sent her Knopf
books she might be interested in and shared details of his own outdoor
adventures, particularly excursions to Maine, New Brunswick, and the
Adirondacks, where he had lived with his family for several years. Cameron was an active outdoorsman who enjoyed fishing and hunting but was
careful in his letters with Helen about the latter. Interestingly, she seemed
not to quibble with him as a hunter despite their moral differences on
the topic, possibly for a couple of reasons. First, he was a well-educated
New York editor whom she could engage with on an intellectual level
in their discussions about hunting. Second, she might have perceived
him to be entirely different from the types of hunters she encountered
in the Gunflint area. While Cameron kept his distance on the topic, he
always registered concern about the Hoovers' welfare when it was hunting season in Minnesota and agreed with Helen's anger at the behavior of
irresponsible hunters.[47]

In the spring of 1967, after living more than a dozen years on Gunflint Lake, the Hoovers were finally able to take a much-needed vacation.
With a new car, money in the bank, no more chickens to care for, and
family matters in Cincinnati settled, they left on May 1 for several weeks.
Their travels took them to parts of the Southwest, taking in a variety of
locations and exploring places that might be suitable as a new home, as
Helen believed the years of living in the woods would soon be behind
them. The trip was satisfying, and Helen stayed in touch with Cameron
and Brandt from the road. While a complete itinerary does not exist, it
appears they went through the Rocky Mountains to the national parks in

Utah and then south to Tucson and Sedona, Arizona, even visiting places as far-flung as Waco, Texas, where Helen sent Cameron a paper place mat from a restaurant called the Black Angus. They also spent time in Taos, New Mexico, as they were interested in Pueblo culture and the artist community there. The Hoovers returned to Minnesota in late June, and Helen indicated to Cameron she would be starting on the new book.[48]

As was to be expected following the success of *The Gift of the Deer*, the Hoovers were swarmed by drop-ins and autograph seekers. At the end of the summer, Helen tallied up the number of visitors: 189 visits, with groups ranging from three to five people, the largest being eleven. She informed Cameron that the visits weren't the result of publicity so much as people wanting to buy the book, which was sold out in the shops in town. "People are simply crazy about the book. They aren't conservation people, most of them. They are people like me who love and respect the wild animals for what they are."[49] Helen was a bit more somber with her children's book editor Alvin Tresselt, noting the increased number of visitors and year-round traffic: "If I can't have either privacy or animals to study, that is the end of the road as far as this place."[50]

Due to the interruptions, Helen told Cameron she would not be getting to the new book until after Labor Day. In the meantime, a check for $3,500 came from Carol Brandt, payment for a damsel-in-distress story Helen had written in twenty-seven days while Knopf was considering the manuscript for *The Gift of the Deer* the previous year. Helen had sent it to Brandt on a lark, thinking it might make an interesting mystery her agent could sell as a paperback, but instead Brandt tried first to interest Knopf and then shopped it to several women's magazines before paperback publishers. Knopf had Helen under contract, so Brandt reasoned they should look at it first; Helen never thought it was something a major publisher would even consider. Not surprisingly, Knopf passed on it. Brandt eventually found a home for the manuscript with the Chicago Tribune–New York News Syndicate for newspaper serialization and syndication. The story, "Is He the Man for Me?," would run in thirty-five installments the following spring in the *New York Daily News* under the pseudonym Jennifer Price, a name that Helen had used as the narrator of her draft manuscript "A Little Place in the Woods."[51]

Anticipating that post–Labor Day would be better for writing, Helen hoped to dig in on the new book but was thwarted when the landowner immediately to their east started building an access road into his property. Bulldozers started knocking over trees just two hundred feet from the Hoovers' door; the noise impeded Helen's efforts to concentrate and write.[52] The construction left Helen disheartened, but she told her agent that they would manage and move on, "although I did think we were settled here for years to come." Helen was still sentimental about their cabin but was enough of a realist to know their property could no longer provide the sanctuary they needed.[53]

To lighten their mood, Helen and Ade went to see the Ringling Bros. Circus in Duluth, something she had not done since they lived in Chicago in the 1940s. It was the first time in fifteen years the circus had visited the port city. The Hoovers looked forward to indulging themselves on popcorn and peanuts.[54]

Helen had a speaking engagement in Minneapolis in December 1967, and since the Hoovers needed to vacate for the deer hunting season, they left in early November for a motel in suburban Minneapolis. They moved again to the downtown North Star Inn in early December where she spoke to the Minnesota Ornithologists Union and promoted her second children's book, *Great Wolf and the Good Woodsman*.[55] She had written this short tale on Christmas Day in 1956, and it had appeared in *Humpty Dumpty's* magazine two years later. Her editor Alvin Tresselt and Parents' Magazine Press thought it would make an excellent children's book and hired noted book illustrator Charles Mikolaycak to do the artwork. Helen was thrilled that it had finally been published, as she felt all along that it had commercial appeal and had tried shopping it to several publishers herself after the story appeared in the magazine. In a review of children's books for the holidays that December, the *New York Times* looked upon it favorably, noting "Mrs. Hoover's fine narrative is sparing in the use of sentiment."[56] Helen's old friend Gladys Taber was also a fan, writing to Parents' Magazine Press that "Great Wolf is a classic that will appeal equally to adults and children and I would like to see it in every home. Mrs. Hoover brings magic to the reader."[57]

On New Year's Day 1968, back at Gunflint Lake, Helen turned her attention to getting the book about their early years started. She had a framework and most of the material already done in the form of the manuscript "A Little Place in the Woods," the book she had started writing off and on from 1956 to 1958. While she had focused on her magazine writing during that time to build a portfolio of work and earn money, the early manuscript included details of their quest for old-growth forest: trips to Wisconsin and Michigan's Upper Peninsula and how they discovered Minnesota's North Shore and eventually Gunflint Lake. It sketches out meeting Justine and Bill Kerfoot of Gunflint Lodge on their first trip, learning about the Walt Yocum cabin being for sale, and then purchasing it and fixing it up. She covers making the decision to buy the second cabin five years later and gives background on how they eventually decided to leave their jobs. The manuscript also includes anecdotes about adapting to their new environment by cutting firewood and buying winter clothing; the car accident their first winter; the help of neighbors and resort owners such as Myrl and Peggy Heston, who offered advice and tips for getting settled; and the attendant challenges of adapting to a northern winter and figuring out how to make a living.[58]

Helen started reworking the manuscript, inserting recent animal stories written for nature magazines, making composite characters out of their neighbors, and expanding on the challenges they faced. She also added material about how they were perceived by local residents and described some of the less savory activities of hunters and fishermen who came onto their property. Helen also modified some of the more unfiltered dialogue in the early manuscript—for example, Ade admitting they had bought a "dog" when surveying the extent of the damage to the foundation of the log cabin that first year. She also eliminated some parts of the story that were fiction, such as the chapter that included a mental hospital escapee who dies in a lodge fire.[59]

In January 1968, *Minneapolis Tribune* outdoors columnist Jim Kimball came to the cabin for a visit. He had wanted to write about the Hoovers, and he was familiar with Helen's first book; he had provided some comments on the manuscript back when he was with the Minnesota Department of Conservation. His column provided the backstory of their move from Chicago and the hardships they endured during those early years, living on "potatoes, spaghetti, pancakes, sugar syrup, powdered eggs and occasional hamburger." But Helen also noted that the hard circumstances allowed them to get acquainted with nature, seeing the animals up close and learning about them.[60] While Helen appreciated the attention from an old acquaintance, the subsequent article invariably meant more fans would be seeking them out in the summer.

Helen spent the balance of the winter tightening up the manuscript. In April she wrote to Cameron that the rough draft was nearly done and about eighty thousand words, making it longer than *The Gift of the Deer*. She noted having fun with her animals, inserting stories like "Mrs. Mouse's Miracle" (the *Nature Magazine* story about an injured mouse Helen returned to health so it could nurse its young), which she believed was a strong metaphor for triumph over adversity. There were also pickups from other magazine pieces, such as "Walter the Weasel," the ermine she fed by hand that had been the subject of an *Audubon* feature, and "Gregory," the groundhog that lived under their shed. And there were the chickens they had raised from chicks—Bedelia, Crown Prince, and Tulip—and the efforts that went into protecting them from predators and the cold of winter. Helen also indicated she was going to be "unorthodox" by including a section that noted "in so many words that nobody <u>knows</u> about anthropomorphism and teleology; one only believes because you can't cross the barrier of non-communication."[61]

Cameron was astounded to hear the rough draft was nearly finished and pleased to learn about the material on anthropomorphism, believing it would make a good foreword to the book. Helen shared a piece she wrote on the topic that would be appearing as her "Wilderness Chat" column in the June 1968 issue of *Defenders of Wildlife News*. Cameron was enthusiastic about her take on this vexing issue and believed it would be a great way to answer some critics of her writing in *The Gift of the Deer*.[62]

In the book's foreword, Helen broaches the topic of anthropomorphism by acknowledging that she and Ade have human limitations that prevent them from having a deep understanding of the living creatures that live around them:

> Those limitations are very real because there is as yet no way to communicate more than superficially with other species, or to understand their mental processes. Thus, we cannot *know* how an animal thinks or why he behaves as he does. We can only believe, and such beliefs range all the way from the conviction that

animals are capable of abstract thought to that which sees them as mere puppets, jerking about on the strings of instinct. I cannot accept either of these ideas, again within my limitations of human thinking: the first because abstractions are almost always thought about in words or mathematical symbols, which animals do not use; the second from my own observations during the past dozen years.[63]

Another popular nature writer of the era, Sally Carrighar, also wrote books based on personal observation of animals in their environment, most notably *One Day on Beetle Rock* in 1944, followed by *One Day at Teton Marsh* in 1947.[64] Carrighar's work was also criticized for relying on anthropomorphism, but spending two years in college studying biology and having done extensive research in the field provided her with an impetus to engage in the debate. In 1965, Carrighar wrote *Wild Heritage* in defense of the emerging science of ethology, the study of behavior in animals. In it she explores behaviors humans share with animals, such as parenting, sex, aggressiveness, and play. Carrighar's book attracted attention because to some critics its discussion of ethology bordered on anthropomorphism, but her clear argument and extensive scientific bibliography demonstrated her scholarship on this area of study.[65] There is no record of communication between Helen and Carrighar, but Helen was certainly aware of the author; her British publisher had favorably compared Helen's writing to Carrighar's work.

By May the drop-in visits at the cabin had already started, so the Hoovers decamped from Gunflint Lake seeking quiet and solitude to finish their work on the book uninterrupted. They headed west and found a reasonable motel in Laramie, Wyoming. They liked the proprietor, Edna Moxley, and knew they would be left alone. As a bonus, it was a pleasant luxury to have electricity and a shower.[66]

Moxley recalled that Helen had asked her not to tell anyone they were in town, insisting if people knew there would not be a moment's peace. While Helen's celebrity was certainly not developed this far west, she was taking no chances. Ade set up his easel while Helen worked on revisions to the manuscript. Ade came by the motel office each day to have coffee and then took some to Helen after she woke up. The Hoovers spent a month in Laramie, making good progress on the text and illustrations.[67]

Ade's drawings for the new book put the animals front and center. In the few illustrations that included Helen, Ade, or both, the humans were clearly placed in the background, "which is really where people belong in our kind of life and forest," Helen wrote Cameron. An illustrated map—originally drawn for use as endpapers for *The Long-Shadowed Forest*—would be placed at the front of the book to orient readers to their property.[68]

The Hoovers then left Laramie for points farther west, including a visit with Margaret E. Murie, author of *Two in the Far North*, in Moose, Wyoming, and a quick trip through Yellowstone National Park and the Grand Tetons. They were back at the cabin by the end of June. In early August, Helen sent the finished manuscript to Brandt, who shared it with Cameron. Helen wanted the submission out of the way; Alvin Tresselt, her *Humpty Dumpty's* editor, was coming to visit so they could edit the manuscript of *Animals Near and Far*, her second collection of stories from the magazine.[69]

After Cameron and Brandt reviewed the new work—what Helen flippantly titled "Bears in the Basement," after an incident in which a bear trapped under the log cabin during a storm started clawing at the trap-door while Helen was there alone—both were enthusiastic and delighted. Brandt wrote Helen to say, "we are both waltzing with joy, pleasure and everything you can name about the manuscript. We think it is beautiful. It is a wonderful love story. It is moving, sensitive, delicate—everything it should be."[70] Cameron was equally effusive and even a bit grand: "I feel that you have balanced the narrative elements of acclimatization to that new life with the evocation of the scene in a beautifully artistic blend."[71]

Indeed, Helen could strike such a balance. Consider this excerpt from the manuscript, in which she turns the simple observation of an animal outside her cabin window into a vivid description of one of the creatures of the wild:

In early evening Ade made whispering sounds from the work-room. Outside, paws on the bench, intent on chewing a bacon rind fastened flat to the bench top with roofing nails, was one of the most beautiful animals I have ever seen. He had the long, lithe body, the short legs, the inquisitive pointed face of the weasel family, and he was at least three feet long from nose to tail tip. He was so dark a brown he looked black where shadow touched his long-haired glossy fur. His nose and feet might have been swathed in black velvet. A sparse layer of long, white-tipped hairs over his head and upper back gave him a frosted look. He was very like a large mink and even had a small white throat patch, somewhat smaller than the mink's chin patch. He sat up and looked in the window at us without alarm, but made many trips to the corners of the cabin, looking cautiously around the log ends to assure himself that no danger was approaching unseen. And when he did this, his bushy, tapering tail and sinuous body flowed as one, glossy as black river water against the snow, and his haunches rippled with leashed power. This was a fisher, reserved hunter of deep woods, brought to our clearing by hunger.[72]

Her writing also had the ability to connect nature with their own arrival in the woods, as this passage illustrates:

On March fifteenth the crows arrived to flap above the cabin and complain noisily from tree tops whenever we went outside. Then the wild geese passed over in their high, trailing wedges, their shrill cries coming down to us like bugles blown far away, stirring an ancient restlessness from days when men moved from hunting ground to hunting ground with no barriers except those of mountains and waters and canyons they could not cross. Ade and I felt a special kinship with the geese and with those nomads of long ago because we, too, had moved from one hunting ground to another and, different though our methods of hunting might be, our ultimate aims were the same.[73]

\* \* \*

In September 1968 the Hoovers headed to New Mexico. They had rented a nine-room furnished house in Ranchos de Taos, a place where Helen and Ade hoped to get some much-needed rest. Helen knew from their visit the previous year that writers and artists would blend in and not be recognized in this part of New Mexico.[74]

Before leaving, Helen shipped Ade's drawings to New York and engaged further with Cameron on a title for the new book. He did not like the "facetious overtones" of "Bears in the Basement," which did not do the book justice. His initial idea was "Retreat to the Wilds" or "Retreat to the Wilderness," but then he didn't care for "retreat." Cameron had also wanted to use "cabin" or "wilderness" in the title, going so far as to suggest "The Gift of the Wilderness" to give it a "family resemblance" to her previous book. Helen thought using "wilderness" was a stretch given that their location was never truly that. Also, people used the shorthand "Gift" when asking her about *The Gift of the Deer*, and she didn't want there to be confusion. After kicking around several more ideas, they settled on *A Place in the Woods*, which was not far from what she had originally titled the early manuscript.[75]

Cameron also shared the good news that Reader's Digest wanted its book club to publish a condensed version of her new book the following June. They offered a $25,000 guarantee—$5,000 more than what they had paid for *The Gift of the Deer*. Cameron was happy, and the Hoovers were thrilled.[76]

Helen went to work on revisions to the manuscript while they were in Ranchos de Taos and was amenable to the changes Cameron and Brandt thought were necessary, particularly related to the car accident. At first Cameron thought the story extraneous, but Helen argued it was critical given that Ade lost the art contract that would have assured their income. Without the resources for a new car, and with no other transportation, the accident forced the Hoovers to reconsider their circumstances and be creative about how they would make a living. The scene stayed in with some minor changes.[77] The actual car accident and the lawsuit the other driver filed a year later were sanitized in the book so that it looked more like a misunderstanding than a malicious attempt to shake down the Hoovers for damages. It was another example of Helen softening actual events so as not to reveal personal identities and invite trouble. In fact, Knopf's outside legal counsel ended up vetting this section carefully for exactly that reason.[78]

Helen finished the manuscript just in time. Her last surviving uncle was in failing health and needed to have a guardian appointed, requiring yet another extended visit to Cincinnati. The Hoovers drove there at the end of November only to be confronted with a scene out of a gothic horror novel. The housekeeper had been stealing from the elderly uncle and doing little to keep the house clean while at the same time encouraging him to name her as his executor. He was frail and in failing health. Once the Hoovers settled in and could attend to matters, Ade contracted the Hong Kong flu, which was spreading across the country that winter.[79]

Helen's uncle Robert, the last of her mother's siblings, died a few days before Christmas 1968. Following the funeral, Helen also became sick with the flu. She and Ade were both stuck in a hotel in downtown Cincinnati, having to deal with settling the estate, selling a house, and trying to get well before they could return to New Mexico. At the same time, Helen was trying to review galley proofs sent from Knopf to keep the new book on schedule for a June publication date. The Hoovers didn't leave Cincinnati until the end of February, arriving back at Ranchos de Taos in early March.[80]

While in Ohio, the Hoovers took a side trip to Helen's hometown of Greenfield in late January, having dinner with some of her childhood friends. She arranged for the local paper to do an interview with the famous "first daughter," who was now fifty-nine years old. It ran on the front page with a photo of her and Ade. Helen again showed her talent for self-promotion.[81]

While laid up in Cincinnati, Helen had time to contemplate what she would write next. She was quickly coming to realize that another book about the north woods was going to be tough, and she signaled this to her agent. "Our area is being overrun with tourists in winter and that puts a plug in the wild animal work. We are also getting a bit old for the hard labor at −30°. I think I'll have to work out some kind of transition to the sun country, and try to show people that it's the same wild earth, wherever it is still wild."[82]

In March 1969, Helen received word from Knopf that Reader's Digest had sent its final accounting for the inclusion of *The Gift of the Deer* in its "Best Sellers from Reader's Digest" edition, a sampler of their most popular condensed titles which had sold nearly three million copies, providing a royalty payment of $29,768. Cameron's comment the previous fall that the arrangement "could amount to something more than peanuts" was certainly the case. As with her other Reader's Digest royalties, they were split fifty-fifty with Knopf.[83]

By mid-April 1969, the Hoovers were back at Gunflint Lake. Brandt wrote to Helen, worried about her health following the lingering flu and a persistent cough, which Helen attributed to her smoking. The motherly scolding from Brandt triggered Helen to write a couple of reflective and expansive letters where she shared more about her past than she had with anyone. Helen related being "slandered" by someone at International Harvester in 1949. This was likely the incident where she had submitted a lab photo to a trade magazine without clearing it with her supervisor. That led to a bout of pneumonia and a near nervous collapse, followed by an operation Ade had from which he did not properly recover. He was in the hospital for two months, and then her mother, Hannah, collapsed with heart issues. By the time both were home, Helen had a miscarriage, went into shock, and began stuttering off and on for the next three years. "I went right on working, even did my best at the time, but all of it took something out of the old gal," she recalled rather nonchalantly.[84] Helen also shared more details about those tough years, which she did not include in *A Place in the Woods*. She told Brandt that from 1956 to 1960 they "more or less lived on starch and sugar, went in rags, burned old clothes to keep warm when Ade wasn't able to cut wood, and thought heaven was a pound of hamburger." Helen admitted the high-carbohydrate diet turned her muscle to blubber.[85]

The Hoovers' attention turned to getting ready for the publication of *A Place in the Woods* on June 23, 1969, with a book signing at the Glass Block department store in Duluth before heading again to Powers department store and press interviews in Minneapolis and St. Paul. Knopf also arranged an interview with NBC-TV's *Today* show for July 3, so the Hoovers traveled by train from Minneapolis to New York. The ten-minute interview with host Joe Garagiola gave the book nationwide visibility. Cohost Hugh Downs was intrigued enough that he asked several questions as well. The appearance generated a considerable amount of fan mail.[86]

While in New York Helen and Ade were able to meet Angus Cameron in person for the first time, calling on him at the Knopf offices after the television interview. The meeting left a lasting impression on Cameron, as he wrote to Helen afterward. The encounter was "something I have been looking forward to a long time, personally and professionally." They also discussed what she might be interested in doing for the next book; from Helen's allusions during their meeting, Cameron inferred a working title might be "The Search for Your Place," an extension of her previous two books for Knopf. While she had hinted at wanting to do a book about the Southwest, Cameron was clearly looking for another north woods title.[87]

Helen's reply to Cameron about their first meeting was glowing. If she still had concerns about his business acumen, as she had previously expressed to Brandt, she didn't voice them. "I had the usual misgivings that come when you are going to meet your formerly unseen editor, but they vanished like smoke. From all our letters I doubted that we would be incompatible, but it can happen, and how awful for future work. Instead I find an old buddy behind a desk. Marvelous, I think."[88] She also offered some additional thoughts on the books she had written. "When I work, and for a long time before, I simply cut out everything that lies outside my immediate environment. You'll notice all of my books so far have dealt with the days before 1961, when the outside began to creep in and distract me. I'm by nature a loner and by that method I must work."[89]

Helen continued to consider ideas for the next book, possibly something similar to *The Long-Shadowed Forest,* but in a western location, or something else about animals, like *The Gift of the Deer,* depending on where she and Ade ended up. "One thing I know: I must have animals, special ones." Helen was not necessarily thinking of a north woods book, but one where she could explore a different place with new animals and the privacy to observe them.[90]

Reviews for *A Place in the Woods* were very positive, and the "back-to-the-land" theme of their first fifteen months in the woods captured the imagination of people everywhere who dream of leaving the city for an idyllic life away from it all. In a sense, it was an updated version of Louise Dickinson Rich's *We Took to the Woods,* but with its own charms and challenges. Will Muller, writing in the *Detroit News,* declared, "Mrs. Hoover has written a tale of warmth and beauty born in bleakness and loneliness. There's no self pity in the whole book, only great understanding of the worth of the simple things which make life attractive and endurable."[91] A *Chicago Tribune* review seemed to capture the zeitgeist of the times:

> Helen Hoover and her husband are two of civilization's antibodies. In their mid-forties, both with good jobs in Chicago if there is any such thing, they discovered what they really wanted from life was rapidly passing them by and would soon be irretrievably lost unless they did something to decivilize themselves. So in a gamble that will variously horrify, dazzle, and inspire readers, they put most of their funds into a few acres of land and a log cabin deep in the forests of northern Minnesota. Here they have lived for 15 years, communing more with animals and birds than with humans.[92]

Nature writer Hal Borland again wrote a perplexing review, this time in *Natural History* magazine. He gave the book a positive notice, saying that "to the general reader the trials and tribulations of the newcomer in the country will be the reward, though a good many country folk may wonder why they didn't find quicker or easier solutions."[93] He took issue with Helen's foreword on anthropomorphism and suggested that "she seems still to be smarting about some things that were said about *The Gift of the Deer.* She has been at this nature-watching, nature-writing business less than fifteen years. Perhaps in another ten or fifteen years she will have mellowed a bit and be less defensive."[94]

Helen queried Cameron as to why Borland always seemed to focus on her rather than what she wrote, assuring her editor that she had a thick skin and did not take his remarks personally. Besides, she was more interested in what the readers thought, "because they are the ones who buy the books."[95] Cameron's response was that Borland's review was "a very good one. If I didn't know either the author or the book, but did know the reviewer, I certainly would go right out and pick it up."[96]

Before the Hoovers left for New Mexico in August, Helen responded to Anne Walentas, the new editor of *Humpty Dumpty's* magazine, to apologize for not writing any "Nature Story" columns in the past year and explain that she was no longer doing magazine pieces except for her quarterly column in *Defenders of Wildlife News*. Helen felt badly, but the press of fans and autograph seekers, travel, family issues, and the just completed book and publicity tour had left her exhausted. Besides, her former editor, Alvin Tresselt, had been moving up the ladder at Parents' Magazine Press, and it was not the same as when she started out writing for him. And without living at the cabin full-time, it was difficult to write about animals. It seemed that yet another page in their north woods life had turned.[97]

Although Helen was no longer actively seeking magazine assignments, her stature as a successful nature writer was providing opportunities to review books, offering comments that publishers could use in promoting new titles. Not only did Knopf call on her, but other publishers reached out as well. One notable book that Helen was enthusiastic about was *The Winter of the Fisher* by a Canadian author, Cameron Langford. The book follows one year in the life of a fisher, an animal the book's editor knew Helen was familiar with. Helen noted the book "is a special reading experience. The fisher's savagery in defense, his careful taking of food from a human hand, his intelligence, his exuberant play in the snow, are all as real as the fishers I used to know. The wild and beautiful North-Woods setting, with its chains of life, is as real as living there."[98]

✳ ✳ ✳

Once settled in Ranchos de Taos, Helen had to contend with the flood of fan mail that was arriving as a result of the *Today* show appearance. Based on the mail she was receiving, Helen thought that perhaps half the country had watched. She was hearing from friends and coworkers she had not heard from in years.[99]

While sorting and answering letters, Helen was also reaching out to the U.S. Department of the Interior about the possibility of setting up a base camp somewhere in or around Canyonlands National Park in Utah, which had been established in 1964. The Hoovers had visited the area on their earlier trip west, and Helen had been suggesting to Cameron that this could be the location of their next book.[100] As Helen noted later, she needed to live in a place for an extended time so she could get into the rhythms of the environment and observe its animals and plants firsthand.

The Hoovers explored the possibility in several visits with local National Park Service managers. Helen was certainly trading on her success as a writer in hopes of securing some preferential treatment, but the Park Service personnel were cautious and concerned about setting a precedent for others who might also claim some sort of long-term "research" project to camp in the wild. While she remained enthusiastic with Cameron that something was going to happen, it appears from later correspondence with the Park Service that they were wary of her request and dragged their feet in making a commitment. The plans eventually evaporated.[101]

Helen still thought a book about the Southwest was possible when she learned that a friend they met on their first visit to Arizona in 1967 might be interested in renting his house to the Hoovers the next year. She was intrigued; the friend had twenty-seven acres of desert populated with quail, rattlesnakes, and javelinas, and he had been feeding and watering the wildlife for years. She knew it would be expensive to rent, but the location and time they would have there could give her the outdoor material she needed for a book.[102]

Reviewers of Helen's books had always pointed to her lack of sentimentality, a quality validated by an article in the *Wilson Library Bulletin* in October 1969. Richard G. Lillard, a professor at California State College, Los Angeles, surveyed the field of nature and conservation writing at the time. He specifically called out Hoover and Borland, and editors like Cameron, who were "determined to avoid personifying, anthropomorphizing and sentimentalizing animals and other phenomena such as trees or winds. Like good scientists they don't want to be accused of falsely assigning a conscious purpose to natural events."[103] Ironically, it was Borland who alerted Helen to the article. Perhaps their shared mention in the piece, along with their mutual friend Cameron, eased some doubts Borland had of Hoover's writing abilities.[104]

After *A Place in the Woods* was published, Helen noticed that younger readers were more philosophical about her writing. They posed questions about man and nature and questioned whether the two could coexist at all. One of these writers was a college student, Gary C. Brown, and his comments about the state of the world inspired Helen to include some of his thoughts in her next book. People were also curious at how the Hoovers managed to endure in the woods. Helen's philosophy was apparent in both her personal responses and what she shared in a later book: they did not think of themselves as any better than the plants or animals in their immediate vicinity, and they tried to leave as little trace on the earth as possible.[105]

Young people like Brown stimulated Helen's thinking, and she often exchanged letters with them, feeling useful in sharing her observations about nature as well as offering life advice when asked. Brown corresponded with Helen for several years, and he even visited the Hoovers twice in Ranchos de Taos. He found her engaging and enjoyed their conversations; she was curious and intellectual, interested in what the youth of the day were thinking.[106]

To another fan who asked how they were able to adjust to the hardships of their early years, Helen shared her recollections of the difficulties of the Depression. "Real poverty is hunger and cold, rags and dirt, terror and the hair-trigger temper that comes from low blood sugar that comes from an inadequate diet. . . . Ade and I had six years of it up here in the woods before we got ourselves in a position to buy eggs and bacon, so to speak, and even now we sometimes look at each other and wonder how we stood it."[107]

✳ ✳ ✳

To help publicize Helen's latest book for the holiday selling season, Knopf had arranged for the Dayton's department store chain in Minneapolis to mail two hundred thousand enclosures promoting *A Place in the Woods* with its November credit card billing cycle. The promotion demonstrated Knopf's clout as a publisher and its acknowledgment of a strong Minnesota author in its stable of nature writers.[108]

*A Place in the Woods* received a boost in the United Kingdom when *My Weekly,* a popular women's magazine, serialized the book in seven consecutive issues the following spring. This would coincide with the British publication of *A Place in the Woods,* providing valuable publicity for the book.[109]

In December 1969, Helen told Cameron she hoped to have something new started after the first of the year. She lamented that she had had endless interruptions—not from autograph seekers dropping in but from friends and fans by mail who had seen her on the *Today* show. Regardless of where Helen resided, that ingrained sensibility of responding to every kindness continued to have a hold on her and worked her into a dither. In correspondence to friends, she lamented the "flood of mail" that always needed tending. Throughout Helen's papers, there are lists on the back of letters or scraps of paper with the names of people she needed to write to. These numbered anywhere from a dozen to two dozen, whether business, personal friends, or selected fans.[110]

Given how Helen's method of book writing required her to concentrate and form the flow of the story in her head, interruptions would inevitably cause her to start over. This led to restricting visitors and calls, which also meant that mail could pile up for weeks. When Helen found a suitable break in time, she sorted and organized the mail and prioritized her responses. This cycle of attending to her mail between periods of writing kept her forever behind in her correspondence, likely causing her anxiety about finding time to write while also exhausting her.

In early 1970, Helen announced to Cameron that they were now formally living in New Mexico, having officially changed residences. One of the first things Helen noted was that income taxes were one-fifth what they were in Minnesota. They had decided to sell the summer cabin, which they had no use for now.[111]

Helen's second collection of stories from *Humpty Dumpty's* magazine, *Animals Near and Far,* was finally published, having been delayed due to the schedule of the illustrator, Symeon Shimin, who had also illustrated *Animals at My Doorstep.* The thirteen animal stories chosen for this book were those that might be found while taking a vacation around the country: a polar bear in Alaska, a manatee in Florida, and a bison in the Rocky Mountains, among others.[112]

In March, Helen had the stirrings of the next book in her head. She continued to entertain the idea of doing something similar to her north woods books, but elsewhere:

I have a stack of file folders stuffed with notes, parts of letters, what-not, relating to all our years in Minnesota. I'm not sure whether I have one book or two—depends on the amount of usable material and how I tie things together. This will develop in due time—I hope. The thing breaks naturally into quiet early years and following years of change. Whether I can still get a story line or not is still a question, but I'll have something fit to publish, I think. The tough part will be making people see why we are pulling out without destroying the illusion they have of us sitting peacefully among a throng of animals. I'm hoping to do that by having us end up sitting peacefully in some other quiet place with another throng of animals.[113]

Helen was again not well in the spring, feeling listless and lacking motivation. She was still kicking around the ideas for her last woods book and whether it would turn out to be one or two. She also noted to a friend, the science fiction author Andre Norton, that she was regretting the upcoming trip to Gunflint Lake. "All work there and such a sense of loss," she wrote in April.[114]

The Hoovers remained in Ranchos through early summer 1970, returning to Gunflint Lake in July to assess their belongings and determine what would be moved to New Mexico and what would stay at the log cabin, which would now be a vacation spot and no longer a home. The Hoovers had not spent much time at the cabin in three years, so they returned to a jumble of musty books, papers, and other belongings. Mice had burrowed into blankets, and some candy bars left behind had been eaten, the wrappers scattered over the counter. In a letter to Cameron, Helen let him know of their return and observed that the whole place looked rather haunted. Squirrels and birds returned once the Hoovers started feeding them again, and Helen noted that one squirrel remembered them and scratched on the screen door in the evening looking for graham crackers as it had done years before.[115]

Helen indicated that she would likely start writing again that winter. She needed to find additional source material, as she hadn't had the time to keep a diary or record of their activities after their first few years. She asked Alvin Tresselt for copies of all the letters she wrote to him

starting in 1956, which were copied and shipped to her. Helen had told
Carol Brandt early on that Tresselt was like a brother she never had, and
their correspondence was a combination of business, current events, and
descriptions of day-to-day living. Helen read the correspondence, cutting up the letters and using paragraphs that she found appealing and
well written to insert into file folders organized by year. Sometimes this
would include a comment about deer hunting that was well articulated, a
humorous observation about one of "their" animals, or the usual weather
details noting temperatures, rain, and snowfall.

Helen did the same with her friend-by-mail Winnie Hopkins, re-
membering that she had kept all of Helen's correspondence. These
letters—often long and newsy—would help Helen remember events
that occurred, fill in dates, and provide additional anecdotal material that
might fit in as she developed the manuscript.

Although the book was to be more or less a chronological retelling of
the years 1956 to 1971, Helen struggled to find a storyline that would carry
through to keep it interesting. She finally found it among the papers and
other accumulated notes and ephemera they had cleaned out of the cabin
as they prepared to move items to New Mexico. In the back of a drawer,
Helen discovered an old "to-do" list of projects that Ade had started,
dating from 1953, the year they purchased the summer cabin. The list had
been ambitious, and of course everything on it had taken much longer to
accomplish, but Helen thought this would provide an interesting framework to organize the chapters.[116]

As she had originally suggested to Cameron, the book would be in
two sections: the first part would focus on the "innocent years," roughly
starting in 1956 following the fire of the workhouse where *A Place in the
Woods* had left off, and going through hunting season in 1961, when several
of their beloved deer were shot. The second part, "the years of change,"
would cover 1961 to 1971, when she found success as a writer coupled with
increased development, more visitors, road traffic, and growing numbers
of hunters who threatened their privacy and ability to safely feed and observe the animals.[117] Helen did offer a caution to Cameron: "Hope I don't
disappoint everyone with the next book. It bothers me because I know
that so many people just don't want to believe that things change."[118]

As the Hoovers settled into a rented three-room casita in Ranchos de Taos, Helen started in earnest on the new manuscript. She spent the winter working on it, culling her files, letters, and magazine pieces for additional content that would help tell the story of their years living in the woods. She continued to read the Tresselt and Hopkins correspondence for details and key dates. By the spring of 1971, she told Cameron that she had a very rough draft of the book and was setting it aside for a while. They were on their way back to Gunflint Lake to move items to New Mexico they had stored the previous year.

Helen shared the rough draft with her agent Carol Brandt, who was able to negotiate a contract with Knopf—her best one yet: a $15,000 advance, with $7,500 at signing and $7,500 upon delivery of manuscript and illustrations from Ade. Brandt also secured a 15 percent royalty and an April 1972 deadline, giving Helen the much-needed time to get the work into shape. She signed the contract on May 14. Helen wrote to Norton that she was amazed Knopf bought a manuscript sight unseen.[119]

Brandt's initial reaction to the work was that it was "moving and fascinating. It is as always exquisitely written with the extraordinary bringing to the reader the outdoor world and nature as well as the animals." She offered some suggestions to tone down Helen's editorializing about the environment and to avoid writing in "hindsight," which Brandt felt spoiled the suspense for the reader.[120] Helen replied that she would need to "bury myself to check the continuity," particularly as she was drawing on many sources for the year-by-year structure and was concerned that careful readers of her previous books would notice something out of place. She also cautioned Brandt that "this isn't supposed to be a conservation book, in the main, but the story of how we worked to get ourselves set without harming our surroundings, and then found ourselves crowded out."[121]

The Hoovers traveled north to Gunflint Lake to meet the movers, who would take items to New Mexico. It would be a brief trip because everything had been packed the previous year and held over because of a trucker's strike. Despite arriving in a car with New Mexico license plates, Helen and Ade assured neighbors and long-standing friends like the Hestons that they would be back, keeping the cabin as their vacation retreat, which had been their original intent when they bought it in 1948.

In letters to Norton during this time, Helen regularly lamented that she was sad remembering the old days. "I think my listlessness, which I did not have in earlier years, is due to my ever-present feeling of regret at the things that took away our Eden. I have to push myself past it all the time up there and the longer I stay, the more unhappy I get."[122]

By the end of summer 1971, Helen had landed on an idyllic ending to the book with a powerful and evocative epilogue. Once she saw it on the printed page, she might not have wanted to return to a place for which she had written such an elegant elegy.

After the Hoovers returned to New Mexico, Helen met with Brandt once again, this time in Santa Fe. Brandt and her husband traveled there in August for the opera, and Helen and Brandt spent time together catching up. Brandt was curious about what might be next; Helen had made it clear another woods book was not possible because they no longer lived there, and it would be difficult to write about animals without being around them.

Helen's agent continued to encourage her and Ade to travel to Europe. Given Brandt's success in publishing circles and her husband's high-profile legal career, they traveled extensively and stayed at the finest hotels across the continent. Brandt was partial to Switzerland, and she did all she could to entice the Hoovers to travel there, going so far as to gather brochures and other travel information. Brandt thought Helen could take on a book about Switzerland and located several hotels that might serve as a base camp if Helen and Ade were to pursue such a project. Brandt even suggested an options contract for such a book, which would give Knopf right of first refusal.[123] While the subject matter might have appeared as a stretch to Helen's fan base, Brandt understood this was the last north woods book; given Helen's depression about writing it, she was likely pushing her toward something different for the next project.

Helen worked on the woods manuscript steadily throughout the rest of the year, taking some time off for Christmas and then continuing to edit and rearrange passages. As she reread letters and samples of her articles and children's writing, she must have had a sense of melancholy about all that had been lost since those early years. The narrative presented an interesting conundrum: the years when the Hoovers had the most privacy and enjoyed the birds, deer, and other animals were the times they endured the most hardship. They barely subsisted during those early winters—sometimes hardly able to feed themselves—but at the same time, they insisted on buying corn, seeds, and graham crackers for the wildlife. Helen's eventual success paralleled the increased development on the Gunflint Trail and changes in their immediate vicinity. By the mid-1960s, due to Helen's successful first book, magazine writing, and their notepaper business, the Hoovers were much better off financially and could enjoy some conveniences. Regardless, progress all around them and Helen's increased celebrity had spoiled the refuge they had created.

Spending time rearranging the manuscript, Helen noted a certain behavior among her fans that came into perspective, an observation she shared with her author friend Norton:

> The odd thing about the changes up north, and this will apply to the book, too, is that people who are coming there for the first time won't have the least idea of what I'm talking about. They hear, they read, they see—but they do not seem to perceive. And I doubt I can do anything about this because they basically do not want the wild beauty that they think they want. They buy virgin land, then set about clearing, bringing in power, putting in a cesspool instead of another kind of toilet that does not require all that disturbance of the land, planting exotic plants instead of encouraging the wild ones, etc. They <u>think</u> they want wilderness, when they only want urban domestic comforts in a place somewhat remote from a city. They'd flee like a shot if the phone was cut off or the road could be returned to its earlier rough and 20-miles-per-hour condition. I can't make them see it, because they don't want to see. They look around our wild setting, which truly is unchanged, as though they were visiting a "backward" nation![124]

Helen's correspondence with Norton was occurring more frequently, and each shared progress on their respective projects. Norton always seemed to have two or three books going at once, invariably with multiple publishers. Helen was amazed that she could keep all of the manuscripts straight in her mind. She reported that her agent had provided good feedback on the book in progress and that she was on the third reworking of the manuscript, which now had grown to 508 triple-spaced pages.[125]

When not exchanging updates on their work, the talk turned to what books they were reading, the antics of Norton's cats, what Ade was getting at the grocery store for their meals, the scourge of needing to reply to letters, and the usual complaints about taxes. The Hoovers paid quarterly estimates, and with the unpredictability of royalty checks from Knopf and Reader's Digest, Helen was always concerned about staying current on what she owed to the government.

As Helen continued to work on the manuscript in Ranchos de Taos, she was able to focus her attention on it without interruptions, filling in areas she missed in earlier versions. She checked her work against her previous books, always concerned that readers might find an event or story she referenced out of place. The Hoovers had a quiet Christmas, enjoying the solitude of the New Mexico high desert. Had they been on Gunflint Lake, now with its year-round resort visitors, Helen's ability to concentrate would have been an entirely different story.

# 8

# Free to Roam

## *Florida and New Mexico, 1972–1977*

AT THE HOOVERS' RENTED ADOBE HOME in Ranchos de Taos, the land-lady had dogs and fed some of the stray cats in the neighborhood. Ade and Helen enjoyed the various cats that were regular visitors. One day a smaller cat showed up and was being bullied by the others, so Helen and Ade decided it needed to be brought inside and protected. Exhibiting some of the traits that she showed while living on Gunflint Lake, Helen took to caring for the Burmese cat, which quickly took a liking to Ade. After several weeks of care and feeding, the Hoovers now had a new do-mesticated pet: Sheba.[1]

By February 1972, Helen had reworked the manuscript and got it to a place where she was ready to share it once again with her agent, Carol Brandt. The rough draft was about 120,000 words, a considerable amount over what Angus Cameron was expecting, but Helen felt it needed to be that long to effectively tell the story of how she and Ade adapted to their surroundings and the reasons that eventually drove them from Gunflint Lake.[2]

Upon initial reading, Brandt thought there was too much about the answering of fan mail and too much about Helen the writer. "Authors are not necessarily interesting characters to a great many people," Brandt offered gently. "They are to literary agents, but we're a peculiar breed."[3] Still, Brandt believed it was good enough to submit, understanding that Cameron would want to make edits for length.

Cameron was eager for the manuscript and read it at once. Overall, he liked it, but thought it was repetitive in places. He agreed with Brandt's assessment about the material on Helen's challenges with publishers and writing. He was also concerned that there was a lot about how the Hoovers were treated by locals on the Gunflint Trail, which was likely more than readers would care to know. He suggested some sections where she could consider making edits, but "found it hard to mark places for they are all so well written and so evocative."[4] Cameron also focused on cuts for physical length, and therefore of cost and cover price, but he also believed in good editorial reasons for proposing cuts. Having noted that, he was quick to assuage any fears his comments might elicit in his writer. "I want to say again that I think you are a very, very good writer. Your ability to evoke the natural scene, to add your own insight to heighten that of your reader, is quite fine and the best of it is that you do it every time."[5] Cameron was the editor, but he sensed it would be better to suggest changes Helen could make rather than doing it himself.

Helen grudgingly accepted the feedback and went to work making cuts. In the process, she had several follow-up telephone calls with Cameron to go over parts she felt were essential. She had never had to edit as much as she was being asked to do now; Helen had always written to a specific word count, more familiar to her as a magazine writer. She had resisted previous efforts to edit her other books—certainly her first, *The Long-Shadowed Forest*, which was a constant battle with a copy editor who knew little of the subject, and then particularly with *The Gift of the Deer*, for which she had felt very protective. As far as editors went, Cameron had mostly left her manuscripts alone, except for the occasional passage that he deemed was too sentimental, but now he wanted to pare the text down to about 105,000 words, telling Helen that they needed to keep the book at its $6.95 price.[6]

Brandt sensed frustration and some depression on Helen's part. She encouraged her client not to cut to a specific number of words but do it either by line editing or taking out brief stories. Perhaps echoing what Cameron was thinking, she reminded Helen it would be better for her to make the cuts than have him do them, which she would like much less.[7]

In the meantime, after Brandt received the manuscript, she shared parts of it with Kenneth Wilson at Reader's Digest, who was also eager to see Helen's next book. By the end of April, Brandt was able to share with Helen that Reader's Digest again wanted one of her books for its condensed book club. This time they were willing to pay more, offering $30,000. Helen received the news via telegram and was ecstatic.[8]

Now Helen and Cameron worked on coming up with a new title for the book. She had been calling it "The Years in the *Woods*" before deciding "The Years in the *Forest*" sounded better. Cameron thought "*of* the Forest" better reflected the sweep of the book, and so they decided it would be *The Years of the Forest*.[9]

Helen continued to tweak the manuscript but grew weary of the editing. She had taken Brandt's advice to remove lines, rewrite parts, and eliminate entire sections. Helen was getting worried about how the book would read in the end and spent time making additional edits to accommodate her publisher. As was her habit, she read sections to Ade out loud, wanting to make sure she had events in the right sequence and maintain a cadence that her readers expected. By mid-May, Helen was done with the final edits and sent the manuscript off to Knopf. She was relieved to finally have it off her desk. Now all she could do was wait for the edited copy to review.

In a letter to Andre Norton, Helen shared her frustration about the editing. She indicated she wished she could have had the time to rework the whole manuscript rather than simply make cuts to reach Cameron's desired word count. Helen felt the manuscript was

> warped in two ways: it does not now show the changes in our activities as brought about by the changes in our circumstances in connection with the successful writing because almost every reference to activities not connected with the woods is gone; most of the general and cumulative actions that finally drove us out are cut. This makes the book into what I believe he [Cameron] thinks of as a nature book—I thought of it as a study of our changing lives against a wild background—and tends to whitewash the crowds of tourists and throw much too heavy emphasis on a few incidents, mostly involving locals.[10]

Throughout the text, Helen had scattered examples of the changes coming to the Gunflint area. Following Peter's death in 1962, she noted some of the lodges and resorts were staying open all year, creating more activity and traffic on their side road, which led to one of their other deer being hit and killed by a car. She noted the shooting of a bear at a nearby resort by one of its guests; she was sickened by the event, but the perpetrator was treated as some sort of hero. Similar anecdotes and stories that signaled the changes they endured were critical in explaining how life had changed the longer they stayed at Gunflint Lake. Helen was also concerned about how these incidents would be perceived and was not happy having distortions come out under her name. "I did want my northern swan song to tell the truth, if it did nothing else. But there's nothing I can do about it, except tell the editor what I think a bit later."[11]

The Hoovers had decided that with their extended travels away from Gunflint Lake and their sadness over all the changes, it was time to sell the summer house and they finally put it up for sale. It sold in June for $10,000 on a contract-for-deed, with $2,000 down, which brought in additional income.[12] This fit their plan to simplify their Minnesota real-estate holdings and therefore cut their property taxes significantly. The log cabin would now serve as it did in the beginning—as a vacation retreat.[13]

By July 1972, Brandt had not heard from Helen in some time. Growing concerned, she dropped a letter inquiring how she was doing. "Actually, the last time we did talk, you seemed to me to be not only feeling tired and not too well, but were depressed, too. Are things any better?"[14] Not getting an immediate response, Brandt wrote again and encouraged Helen to take some time off and noted she would push Cameron to get everything wrapped up. They would see each other in August when Brandt and her husband were again at the Santa Fe Opera.[15] The Hoovers shared they were pleased with the cabin sale. Helen was able to get her bearings back now that the long effort of completing the book was over.

As the summer of 1972 went by, Helen was increasingly frustrated by Cameron and his colleagues at Knopf. No one seemed to know when she was going to get the final galley proofs for review, and Cameron's assistant was pestering Helen about permissions and other minutiae. She indicated to several Knopf staff editors that work on the final manuscript was taking on the quality of a "recurrent nightmare" and she was anxious to know a publication date.[16]

Brandt ran interference with Cameron, which seemed to solve some of the stress Helen was feeling.[17] Still, Helen was resigned to the fact that the book as edited was not what she had planned to write. She had several calls with Cameron in November about their differences over the final manuscript and followed up with a letter. "You looked for a nature book because that's what I'm expected to write," and she reflected on how she had originally viewed the idea for the book:

> Two people, having found the place they had dreamed of, worked against great odds to establish themselves there. Then changes, evolving from their success, from an increase in the area's population, and from growing lawlessness, forced them to seek another place for their work. During their first years there, they were almost ostracized, and from this came not only great difficulty but also much beauty and the seeds of their success. During the latter years, they were subjected not only to incidental nuisances but to a certain amount of direct persecution. It is in the reasons for the ostracism and the details of the later problems that you and I did not communicate, and I see weakness in motivation and much chance for misunderstanding by certain local people and even some outsiders.[18]

Helen went on to elaborate that she omitted some of the crueler incidents from the book because of possible retribution among people who would be able to identify those who were involved. She felt the final, edited version made their reasons for leaving seem only minor when they were in fact significant. In the end, however, Helen didn't think the readers would care, much less want to read about anything that was not positive and appealing.

Helen also wrote Brandt about her calls and letter to Cameron, lest he raise any alarms with her agent about the final edits. Helen relayed the substance of their conversations while also sharing some of the unpleasant episodes that occurred over the years but had been toned down in the book. "Something had to be done to make him [Cameron] understand that I was not making a lot out of little things, but had been playing down the ugliness because there would have been no point in horrifying the readers."[19]

Regardless of Helen's own misgivings about the work, Cameron and

Brandt were on the same page about the finished manuscript. As Brandt put it in a letter to Helen, "Angus and I stand as one however against you in saying that you have written a very good book and one that will be successful."[20]

By December 1972 Helen had finished reviewing the galley proofs, finding some omissions and continuity issues that were easily rectified. Despite having the editing and proofing done, she was still feeling depressed and run down. Brandt was concerned enough that she wished Helen could have a relaxing Christmas, once again encouraging her to get out of the country. For whatever reason, Helen was reticent to go on an extended trip overseas, although in letters to Brandt, Norton, and others she often talked enthusiastically about visiting Switzerland. It may have been their age: Helen and Ade were both sixty-one. She was averse to flying, but that did not stop Brandt from suggesting she and Ade make the crossing to Europe via ocean liner. The Hoovers may have given thought to overseas travel, as they had gotten passports the previous August.[21]

While the book was in production, Knopf was ramping up its plans for publicity. By this time Helen's heart was not in it; she now found it difficult to even make small talk with people who imagined the Hoovers still lived in the woods, happily feeding their animals as they had done through all of her books. The autograph sessions became an extension of the fan mail and drop-ins who came to the cabin, and Helen had had enough of that. Cameron told her that other authors in the area—which likely included Sigurd Olson—had reported random visits from fans and autograph seekers as well, so she was not alone in this regard. While she knew there would be disappointed fans who hoped to find them at Gunflint Lake, she also felt she had done more than her share to accommodate them over the years.[22]

Helen's spirits brightened in the new year when Cameron shared the book jacket copy he had written for the forthcoming release:

> Good times and hard times, good neighbors and bad neighbors, the strains engendered by conflicting views—and passions— about the use of the environment: Mrs. Hoover shares her experience without stint. But above all—over, under, and all around her straightforward and practical approach to life in the wilderness—

there is, as always, the sensitive and moving awareness of nature (especially of the animals with whom she and her husband shared the forest, often helping them through starving winters) that is the special quality of her writing and her life.[23]

Helen was happy with his description of the book and said she could not have written it as well.[24] The Hoovers were further pleased when the actual books arrived. They were impressed with the excellence of design and presentation, something she had always admired of Knopf books. Helen loved the cover jacket with its reddish-brown color, to her reminiscent of the iron ore of northern Minnesota and therefore a very appropriate touch. And the glossy finish of the jacket made Ade's small animal illustrations pop.[25]

Cameron wrote to Helen that the new book had also been accepted by two book clubs that would be paying nice advances. The Book-of-the-Month Club was offering $3,000, and the Christian Herald Family Book Shelf was paying $4,000 for a December distribution. It appeared Cameron was hoping this early interest in a title still months away from publication would reassure Helen that it was indeed a good book.[26]

Despite her weariness about publicity and more attention from fans, Helen did acquiesce to her old friend Alice Carlson at the Powers department store and agreed to a round of interviews and book signings in the Twin Cities later in the year. Carlson had been an early supporter of the Hoovers and plugged hard for her books, and Helen felt a debt of gratitude for all she had done for them over the years.

While Helen may have been tired of *The Years of the Forest* and the long struggle to pull it together, her fans were looking forward to another woods volume filled with animal stories and anecdotes in the warm and comforting writing style Helen was known for. While she delivered on that promise, there was also a wistful feel to this book, from its organization into "the innocent years" and "the years of change" to the growing sense of loss that permeates the later chapters.

Helen's earlier books, while each different, had an underlying optimism about them. *The Long-Shadowed Forest* offered readers a friendly, guidebook approach to the northern woods, with keen observations of nature and entertaining animal stories. *The Gift of the Deer* was a tender and engaging story that provided insight into how two people could help a deer survive the harsh winter and then engage with a deer family over several years. *A Place in the Woods* captured the Hoovers' early years of struggle but also the joy of achieving success on their own, far from the urban jobs that had previously defined them. Taken together, these were mostly positive, upbeat books that left the reader enchanted with the Hoovers and a desire to know more about the life they had created in the woods. But the idyll Helen and Ade created could not last forever, and *The Years of the Forest* aimed to bring the reader along on this journey of change, and ultimately for the Hoovers, the betrayal of a dream.

So rather than sharing only more of the folksy and upbeat anecdotal stories about adapting to life in the woods that had enlivened *A Place in the Woods,* there is an edge to the narrative in *The Years of the Forest.* The book includes unpleasant incidents with locals who refer to the Hoovers as "kooks" while taking advantage of their lack of woods experience; run-ins with hunters trespassing on their land, and then the shooting of many of the deer they were feeding. Helen writes of the callousness of people's cruelty to animals and lack of concern for conservation, particularly among those who lived in the woods. This comes into clear focus in the chapter "1964" when Helen reflects on the deer that were gone:

> Ice bells tinkled on the shore; needles trickled from a tree with a faint rustling. An owl hooted in a cedar, then flew as silent as mist. I looked at the tree that was Peter's tree, and remembered that he would not stand under it again, that Pig and Brother would not come back to this place where they had been reared by Mama and Peter, that Fuzzy was gone, and Little Buck. I was filled with pain as I realized that Ade and I would never have truer friends, and that Mama and Pretty and Starface were somewhere in the forest that was now unsafe for them. When they were gone we could have no more friends like them because of the approach of civilization and its influx of humans, who did not understand either the forest or its children, and many of whom would not trouble to learn.[27]

It was these losses, and the hope that her writing might help future generations bring forward a kinder world, that were the inspiration for *The Gift of the Deer.*

> Gregory, Peter, Pig, Brother, all the others we would see no more, were still part of the forest but as individuals they were lost, except in my thoughts and love—and in Ade's. And when we went they would, in a sense, die with us. I would not accept the going of so much beauty and gentleness from the world. I wanted others to know them and perhaps keep them in their minds and hearts as time left me behind, and I could do something about this. My next book would be the story of Peter and our special deer.[28]

✳ ✳ ✳

*The Years of the Forest* was published on April 25, 1973. Of all Helen's books, it took the longest amount of time from conception to publication: nearly three years. She had not published a book in nearly four years. Reviews were very good, and despite Helen's misgivings about the final product, she was pleased with the publicity, particularly the positive notices in the *New York Times* and the *Minneapolis Tribune.*[29]

Gerald Carson, a historian, wrote the review for the *Times* that was for the most part complimentary. He noted Helen was a "compassionate observer of the fauna that surrounded her and a sensitive and poetic chronicler of what she saw and felt." Carson did quibble with her assigning animals names, finding it beneath her since she accurately portrayed them as the "wonderful and mysterious creatures they are." He speculated that perhaps her writing for the juvenile market might have relaxed her principles.[30] But beyond those minor criticisms, Carson understood the major theme of the book: that the wilderness that had attracted the Hoovers was eventually violated by the arrival of the "bulldozer, power line, the telephone cable, the hunter with the whiskey flask and the nerve-wracking snowmobile." He concludes by noting the book was written in Taos, "where the memory of the good years could be recollected in tranquility and shaped into this wistful, appealing and very personal account of paradise lost."[31]

The *Minneapolis Tribune*'s Anne Cawley Boardman found *The Years of the Forest* "a compelling combination of wilderness adventure and misadventure," noting how the Hoovers created a sanctuary for their wild animals but never tamed them, adding to the excitement. She recognized the drama built throughout the book as Helen describes the advancing "civilization" of roads, autos, boats, and hunters. The book "provides a comforting and happy reading experience. Warm and unsentimental it stands in a class by itself."[32]

Hope Sawyer Buyukmihci, founder of New Jersey's Unexpected Wildlife Refuge and author of *Hour of the Beaver*, wrote a review for the *Philadelphia Inquirer*: "laced with humor and sparkling with philosophy, Mrs. Hoover's story entertains while it teaches."[33] And Helen was particularly cheered by the brief review in *Publishers Weekly*, which deftly captured what she had hoped the reader would take away. "This is essentially a happy book by a sensitive writer and contented woman whose feeling for nature and wild animals—and dismay at the encroachments of civilization—are evident on every page."[34]

But the notice in *Kirkus Reviews* may have been the most spot-on, noting Helen's memoir "is overcast with the sadness of farewell to the wilderness as they knew it and she recalls the telltale signs of encroaching change, weighted with portent. . . . Mrs. Hoover, who can and does wave a rifle at cloddish intruders, is a spunky woodswoman with a fiery sense of human and animal territoriality and it is this wood-chip on the shoulder which prevents sentimentality from seeping in."[35]

After the book's publication in April, the Hoovers left Ranchos de Taos for Florida to spend time with Norton, the science fiction writer. Norton had first written Helen after *The Long-Shadowed Forest* was published in 1963, asking what else she had authored. From there a close relationship by mail began. Only a few of Norton's letters to Helen survive, but Helen's correspondence with Norton provides a view of Helen as an author sharing news, gossip, and professional observations with a peer. Starting around 1969 and covering most of the next decade, the letters offer a compelling look into Helen's interests and viewpoints, especially during the writing of *The Years of the Forest* and her subsequent efforts to find new topics. On this trip, Helen would be meeting Norton in person for the first time. She was also looking forward to the warm, humid air of Florida, hoping it would cure some of the stiffness that resulted from the dry air of New Mexico and the accumulated ailments that she attributed to the hard years living on Gunflint Lake.

Norton was a successful and versatile author, known primarily for writing science fiction and fantasy but also a writer of historical fiction and adventure stories. Helen and Norton were kindred spirits in many respects. Both were from Ohio, Norton having grown up in Cleveland. They also were aspiring writers in their early years, and both had those wishes dashed by the Depression. Norton first worked as a librarian in Cleveland and then started as a writer of adventure stories for juveniles, switching to science fiction in the early 1950s when the genre caught on. A woman science fiction writer was uncommon then, but she developed a strong fan base and became a best-selling author, likely because she used the masculine-sounding pseudonym "Andre" for her first name; her given name was Mary Alice.[36]

Norton had a home near Orlando, and sensing Helen's health issues and exhaustion after the long editing process for *The Years of the Forest*, invited the Hoovers to spend an extended period with her. They were able to bring their cat, Sheba, eliminating the concern Helen had about leaving their pet in the care of others. Norton had recently emerged from her own health challenges and wanted companionship; friends who had cared for her had recently left, and she was eager for new house guests. She provided the Hoovers with a one-room apartment, which they used as their base while exploring other parts of Florida.[37]

As part of their Florida travels, Helen had Cameron pull strings with Kenneth Wilson, the Reader's Digest editor who adored her books. Wilson had sent the National Aeronautics and Space Administration a request for the Hoovers to be the magazine's special envoys for the launch of the Skylab 3 mission from the Kennedy Space Center on July 28, 1973. Ade and Helen were thrilled with the VIP treatment they received, as both were enthusiasts of the space program.[38]

Later that summer, the New Mexico Press Women honored Helen with their Zia Award, given annually to a woman writer or journalist with strong ties to the state. Regina Cooke, the *Taos News* editor, had authored several stories about the Hoovers once they moved to the area and had nominated Helen for writing *The Years of the Forest*. No doubt Helen had cultivated the relationship once she had arrived in New Mexico, despite her stated wish that they be left alone in a place teeming with artists. Helen was unable to attend the ceremony as she was in Florida, but she was flattered by the recognition and made a point of sharing the news with Cameron.[39]

Brandt kept Helen apprised of how the book was selling and hoped its success overseas would be good news. She wrote to Helen in Florida to tell her that the Reader's Digest Foreign Books in Australia, Denmark, Holland, Germany, Italy, and Sweden had exercised their options for publication rights to *The Years of the Forest*. "Perhaps this will add one more drop of forgiveness by you to that book?"[40]

In fall 1973 Helen heard from Grand Marais friends that it was rumored they had moved away from Gunflint Lake permanently—and, more shocking, that Ade had died.[41] This gossip was, to a degree, a continuation of the pettiness they experienced while living there. Given that the Hoovers had been away for several years, it was not surprising the rumor had started. Still, Helen was perturbed enough that she penned a letter to the editor of the *Cook County News-Herald* in Grand Marais, noting they had just finished three years of work on *The Years of the Forest* and were about to take a lengthy vacation. She noted they had sold their summer house but not the log cabin, and she signed off, "will you please, by publishing this, help us clear up this misconception?" In reality, the Hoovers were no longer living there at all and had not been back to the winter cabin in more than two years, but Helen was not about to let local meddlers have the final word.[42]

In early October the Hoovers made a quick trip back to the Twin Cities for the book signings and interviews Helen had promised to do at the Powers department store. Book buyer Alice Carlson did not disappoint: there were interviews with both the *St. Paul Pioneer Press* and the *Minneapolis Tribune* along with several television and radio appearances. Helen and Ade booked signings at all three Powers stores as they had done in the past, promoted via prominent advertisements in the local newspapers.[43]

The Hoovers returned to Andre Norton's home and stayed through the end of October 1973. They then moved to an oceanside resort in Marathon in the Florida Keys and stayed through May 1974. After that they returned to Norton's. Helen and Ade loved the Florida Keys, and they settled in for a long stay, taking side trips up and down the islands. Helen likely enjoyed the time away from deadlines and future books as she had little correspondence with friends during this time and had shared a forwarding address with only a few people who would need to reach her. She later commented to friends that she and Ade should have figured out a way to put down roots in Florida, as the climate was preferable to the dry weather of New Mexico.

Spending time with Norton and her circle of author friends likely got the group talking about writing and relationships with their publishers. Helen, still unhappy with the edits to *The Years of the Forest*, crabbed to her agent that her friends were having trouble finding the book in stores and that some journalist friends had not even received review copies. Helen claimed twenty-five reviewers had not been sent advance copies and thirty bookstores didn't have it in stock. Brandt asked Cameron for an update; he in turn asked for a list of reviewers Helen said had been slighted. He was less forgiving about bookstores, which he said typically blame the publisher when books are out of stock. At this point, *The Years of the Forest* had sold more than eighteen thousand copies, which Cameron believed was quite good, considering the book was different from her previous two Knopf bestsellers.[44]

During their final months in Florida, Helen had been kicking around ideas for a possible book, something light and fun like she had done back in 1966 when she quickly wrote a damsel-in-distress story that her agent sold as a newspaper serial. She had an idea for a gothic murder mystery, which she wrote quickly on the road before returning to Ranchos de Taos. Helen set it aside and would look at it when they were settled back home; she planned to send it to Brandt in the new year.

Lingering aspirations for a book about the Southwest had not come together. The Canyonlands idea had fallen through; the Hoovers were simply not going to get the sort of accommodation they were seeking with the U.S. Forest Service to establish themselves in a remote location and do the observational work necessary for a book. The area around Ranchos de Taos didn't provide the privacy they needed to blend into their surroundings and observe the animals; plus, they were renting a house, so they couldn't put down the permanent roots required for the intensive research. Besides, Helen found that New Mexico did not provide the stimulation of four seasons that the northern forest setting had. "There's no point in writing pages and pages about the country around here since this kind of earth doesn't change much."[45] One also must wonder if the success of her four adult nature books and her three juvenile works had left Helen lacking motivation. She was now sixty-four years old and certainly not in need of income; her books continued to sell well, and the foreign editions of both her Knopf books and the Reader's Digest Condensed Books were still popular and providing steady royalties. She seemed to enjoy her life of travel, corresponding with friends, reading books, and watching late-night movies and television programs. She liked network shows such as *Mannix, Cannon,* and *McCloud,* the last being even more exciting as it was partially shot on location in Taos. She and Ade were finally able to relax from the hard years of living in the north woods and their earlier professional careers.

Despite Helen's feelings that New Mexico lacked subject matter, a different Minnesota nature writer had found the place stimulating enough that he wrote a book about it in 1972. Calvin Rutstrum was a popular outdoorsman who authored several "how-to" books in the 1950s and 1960s about wilderness canoeing, winter camping, and cabin building, as well as reflective essays on nature. He and his wife had come under the spell of the Pecos Canyon region in the northeast part of the state. *Greenhorns in the Southwest* captured the beauty of the landscape, its adobe structures, Mexican cuisine, and Pueblo culture. Having spent years paddling through Minnesota and Canada, Rutstrum was equally charmed by the Southwest and cast an observant eye on its sharply different environment. It's interesting to speculate how Helen would have approached her new environment had she the desire to pursue it.[46]

Once back in Ranchos de Taos, the Hoovers quickly became cat aficionados, as their landlord still had several cats and fed the neighborhood stray cats, which Ade and Helen were coming to enjoy. The time spent with Norton's cats certainly made an impression, and they continued to keep Sheba inside, who was now Ade's favorite. Helen liked cats for their independence and curiosity; she had never cared for dogs, as she believed they were too noisy, dirty, and subservient.[47] Besides, she had nothing but problems with neighbor dogs and their owners on Gunflint Lake.

In early 1975, after letting the gothic murder mystery sit over the holidays, Helen sent the manuscript to Brandt for consideration. Titled "The House of the Tarnished Shield," the story was about a young woman, Eileen, who returns home to Cincinnati to attend the funeral of her great-grandmother. The house where the character's aunt and two uncles live closely resembles the house where Helen's aunt Helen and uncles Bruce and Robert Gomersall lived. In typical gothic fashion, there are strange happenings at the house, and Eileen soon learns the family patriarch who built it had placed stipulations on both the inheritance of the house and the sizable trust for operating it. Unbeknownst to Eileen, she is in line to inherit the house, much to the chagrin of her older relatives. A romance with a local architect, the sudden death of an elderly aunt, an increasing fear and mistrust of her relatives, and several mysterious attempts on Eileen's life all build toward a suspenseful finish. In the end, one of the uncles, who had faked being blind for decades, tries to kill Eileen, but falls off the roof following a harrowing chase through the attic.[48]

The story's detailed descriptions of the old house, the furniture, and the day-to-day activities of the aunt and uncles were definitely drawn from the visit Helen made to see her relatives in 1957 and subsequent visits to care for ailing uncles. When unable to do the writing she had hoped to on that first trip, she explored the old house and kept notes of her discoveries, thinking the material might be useful for a future story.[49]

After renting in New Mexico for several years, the Hoovers decided to buy a home so they could put down roots and not have so many of their belongings in storage. They purchased a large adobe house in Ranchos for about $45,000 and moved into it in May 1975. They bought the home from abstract expressionist painter Lawrence Calcagno.[50] Helen noted in a letter to Norton that it was "a real home for the first time in our lives. The cabin was not, in the modern sense, a 'real home,' but a place that is utterly special for its own reasons."[51]

Brandt liked the gothic novel and hoped Knopf would consider it for the young adult market. Regardless of its sales potential, Brandt was more excited that Helen had started writing again. Helen casually mentioned that she had the spark of an idea for yet another book that would be about adapting to changes in lifestyle as a result of different places of residence. She said she had floated the concept with Cameron the year before but had gotten no reply.[52] Brandt and Cameron connected and talked about the lifestyle idea. Helen's agent reported back: "we are both absolutely mad with enthusiasm" for the project.[53]

Helen began setting down her ideas about how she would approach the book and sent a tight outline to Brandt. She wanted to look at the differences in locale and then at lesser changes relating to financial status, education, personal interests, and character differences. The first part would be about small-town living, with parents, relatives, and friends who provide support. It would be followed by a section about life in a large city as she had experienced in Chicago, having friends, neighbors, and co-workers to interact with. The last section would be about the years living in the woods, where the Hoovers needed to rely on each other to make a living and survive.

As Brandt often did, she shared Helen's idea for a book about lifestyles with Kenneth Wilson at Reader's Digest, who was always a good sounding board. Given the success of the condensed versions of her previous three books, Wilson was eager to know what she would do next and was intrigued. "Coming from any other author we would be put to it to know how to react, unless the idea had been further fleshed out. In Mrs. Hoover's case we know that she will bring all of her wonderful qualities—her highly developed common touch and her vivid anecdotal style—to the task, and will no doubt transfer the germ of the idea into a thoughtful, entertaining and rewarding book."[54] Wilson's response only inspired more enthusiasm from Brandt, who forwarded his letter to Helen. "I enclose the original in the very, very urgent hope and, indeed belief, that you and the typewriter will shortly become friends again. Also, that Ade will start thinking of illustrations." She signed off the letter with a postscript: "If you should decide that you want a Knopf contract, I will then send a copy of this [Ken's] letter to Angus." Brandt was doing her best to cajole Helen into writing again.[55]

In a letter to Norton, Helen declared that this book would not be "a nature thing," elaborating that "it will deal with the adaptations to change in life style. Too many people can't think of living any other way than they do at the moment and can't understand learning ways beyond those they have known for years."[56]

Brandt kept encouraging Helen to sign a contract for the book, and by virtue of her success with Knopf, receive a nice advance to get started. But Helen was reluctant to commit until she had a better idea of what she was going to write. As with her previous efforts, it had to come together in her mind first before she could start to write.[57] Brandt suggested the book should be roughly autobiographical and start in 1929, when Helen and her mother moved to Chicago. She felt the 1930s could provide rich material, suggested skipping much of the war and 1940s, and then explore their time in the woods during the 1950s and 1960s from a different angle. Likely Brandt was trying to get some aspect of the north woods back into one of her books, the more to bring her readers along for a different take on this part of their life. She also encouraged Helen to feature Ade more prominently in the chronology.[58]

Helen set aside further work on the book to focus on unpacking after the move to their new home. She spent a good part of the summer organizing the thousands of books, hundreds of records, and (of course) getting the baby grand piano tuned and set in place. The house needed minor repairs, which kept Ade busy, and finding workers to help him provided a steady stream of people coming and going. Helen started making curtains and organizing closets as they got settled. They also entertained several visitors, likely pleasant diversions from the chores at hand.

After some consideration, Knopf weighed in on the gothic murder mystery, choosing to pass on the book. Cameron had thought it a possibility for the young reader market, but their editor in charge of those titles felt it was better suited to the adult market.[59] Helen was not put out by the rejection; she never envisioned it as a book that would interest the highbrow publisher. Now she contemplated shopping it on her own to a less discriminating press, but she couldn't muster much enthusiasm given all that was going on getting settled in their new home.[60]

Helen confided to Norton that her idea for a book on lifestyle changes might be hard to pull off, given her carefully cultivated image as a gentle writer of nature books. "I have the feeling that the brittle, cynical me of earlier years, and so carefully hidden in the woods books, may deal a death blow to people who like the other censored me. I mean a death blow to sales to these silly and sentimental souls who make up a large percentage of my readership. I might try the thing, but it will be as flip and indifferent as I was and still am to many things. I can't possibly make myself into a saint forever."[61]

Alongside the house, the Hoovers had a patio that Ade had improved. It became apparent that it might serve better as a place to keep the growing number of stray cats and kittens that were appearing. The cats gathered there, and Helen put out food and water for them, assigning the names and enjoying their antics and comings and goings. On one level it was not entirely different from their yard on Gunflint Lake where they fed the forest animals seeds, corn, and suet.

Jim Kimball, the outdoors columnist for the *Minneapolis Tribune*, visited the Hoovers in New Mexico in early 1976. Helen had known Kimball since the early 1960s, when he was the deputy commissioner for game and fish at the Minnesota Department of Conservation and had been a resource for her first book. After leaving the department to join the newspaper, he wrote a column about the Hoovers in 1968 following the success of *The Gift of the Deer*. Now, during Kimball's New Mexico visit, Helen shared her apprehension about whether her readers would accept her writing about something other than the north woods. She cast the lifestyle angle as something her publisher thought readers would be interested in, a timely story about people challenging social norms and lifestyles. The publisher believed Helen was ideally suited to write about her drastic lifestyle changes, given her forced move to Chicago with her mother, her years working in metallurgy, and then the Hoovers' move to Gunflint Lake, followed by nearly fifteen years adapting to living in the forest.

Kimball wrote about his visit with Helen in a March 1976 newspaper column. It relays Helen's suggestion that the characteristics that let her succeed in Chicago also gave her the stamina to persevere in the woods. But she wondered: Would readers want to know this side of her story? Or would they be happier with the prevailing image of her? Kimball captured these thoughts, asking his readers to share their opinion and offering Helen's P.O. box address so they could write to her directly. Helen soon regretted that accommodation; she received more than three hundred letters, and as usual she was compelled to reply to nearly everyone.[62]

Among the many files of correspondence in Helen's papers, only a few contain fan letters, but she kept nearly all of those she received from the Kimball column. Most were handwritten cards from readers or scrawled notes from students ripped from spiral-bound notebooks. The verdict was overwhelming: she should write the book of her early years.[63] Many believed she was well suited to write the story her publisher wanted and were curious to know about her life before Gunflint Lake. Some also said they would read anything she wrote. "You seem like an old, dear friend," one reader commented. "Go ahead and write <u>anything</u> you desire—we know it will be excellent." Even 1970s self-help guru Jesse Lair weighed in from his ranch in Montana. "I would enjoy hearing your personal story . . . even more, I think you and all of us would benefit from an honest telling of your story. There is a real shortage of that and that's why some books have been so successful."[64]

A few had doubts. A woman from Paynesville, Minnesota, opined that "many might like this. However on thinking it over it just might destroy the image I have of you. I'm completely satisfied now." But such people were in the minority.

Helen had routinely confided to her editor, agent, and close friends that she was not necessarily the nice, pleasing nature writer her readers thought she was. In her books she toned down some of her stronger opinions about the environment and hunting while still making the points she wanted to, albeit in a softer way. An old journalist friend from Chicago, Donald Zochert, challenged Helen on that self-assessment. "You also have, it seems to me, entirely unjustified quivers and quakes that the real Helen Hoover is something different than the Helen Hoover of the books. I read you just as clear as can be in your books, and that is really your virtue: honest about yourself and your life. I note no difference in your letters."[65]

Another respondent struck a nerve close to Helen's own life. "I, for one, certainly want to find out more about your background, specifically how you acquired the strength to turn your back on a steady salary and the conveniences in life for a log cabin and virtually no money whatsoever.

Most of your readers, including myself, are living corporation-governed lives closely paralleling your pre-wilderness days. The type of book you are considering would be valuable to us."

Helen marked one letter "keep for reference." A woman from Maynard, Minnesota, encouraged her to write the book, as it would be eagerly awaited. She quoted newspaper columnist Ann Landers: "The same fire that melts butter is also used to forge steel. Altho I have never met you, you seem like a friend. As in our relationship with friends—I'd love to know more about you." The analogy about forging steel was not lost on a former metallurgist.

Writing to friend Peg Miller, Helen struggled to reconcile her urban self with her forest persona. "To me, the odd thing is that I was exactly the same in Chicago as in the woods, but the woods books were edited to make me a sort of 'St. Helen of the Forest.' Who will believe that I wouldn't kill an insect in Chicago either?"[66]

Whether the reader letters sowed doubts about what to do next or provided a path forward is unclear. For the balance of the year and into 1977, Helen continued to contemplate writing such a book, but she was unable to find an approach that suited her.

Cameron was curious about Helen's progress and dropped her a note to check in. The more she communicated with him about the lifestyle book, the more intrigued he became. She must have shared possible anecdotes, as he referred to some of the adventures she and Ade had during their courtship in 1930s Chicago. "If you write this kind of book, it aught to be written in a kind of free association. You can't write about two (or three) lifestyles without giving a full picture of what each lifestyle is like . . . I see no reason at all why you won't be even more interesting to your fans who read the first book if they see their favorite author in rich contrast. That's the whole fun of it."[67]

Helen continued to correspond with a wide circle of friends, some she knew only by mail from the Hoovers' notecard business days. There were old Chicago work colleagues and Greenfield high school friends, neighbors from Gunflint Lake, and authors such as Andre Norton and Gladys Taber. The closest of the Gunflint Lake friends was resort owner Peggy Heston, who sold Helen's books at their resort store and requested that Helen sign adhesive labels that she could then affix to the books' title pages as autographs. Helen would replenish the stock of labels regularly, and Heston could sell these genuinely autographed books to guests.

Aside from the typical news updates about their travels and how Helen's books were selling, one consistent message in Helen's letters to Heston was the various reasons they were unable to come back to the cabin for a visit. They were either traveling or too busy to make the trip while at the same time insisting they would return to retrieve some irreplaceable sentimental items still in the cabin. One of those was a portrait that Hannah had painted of Thomas in 1891, something that moved with them from Chicago to Gunflint Lake. While Helen fretted about not being able to get back for some of these items, she also did not arrange for them to be sent to her.[68] After selling the summer house and making a point of keeping the log cabin as their vacation place, the Hoovers were still reluctant to return.

Helen worried about the Minnesota property and wrote to her friend Peg Miller about it. "Repairs—the fire menace—and the paradise we had there went with the coming of men. I really don't think I like this world very much," she lamented.[69]

An editor at Parents' Magazine Press shared with Helen that *Great Wolf and the Good Woodsman* received a Brooklyn Art Books for Children citation from the Brooklyn Museum and the Brooklyn Library, an award that recognizes both the author and the illustrator. The book had been out for nearly a decade, and books currently available were eligible for the award. Helen mentioned to friend Andre Norton that she might try another children's book if she could get the same illustrator.[70]

The Hoovers divided their time with leisure pursuits. Ade puttered around the house, making improvements and building bookcases. He worked on plastic models and electronics projects, building radios and repairing their record player. He still used the telescope Helen had purchased for him after *The Gift of the Deer* was published. And he doted on their black cat Sheba. They took driving trips around Taos, taking the Mustang up mountain passes and navigating side roads that took them back into the beautiful scenery surrounding the area. They both enjoyed their garden, despite the lack of rain and the cold nights at their elevation in Taos. Helen loved to freeze fresh vegetables so they could enjoy them all winter and made note to friends of the money she saved by doing this.

She continued to read voraciously during these years and enjoyed reread-
ing old gothic and romance novels. She still fed stray cats that showed
up in their yard, unable to resist helping them. Sending Christmas cards
was an annual endeavor; she began addressing envelopes by late October
and (depending on the year) would send more than two hundred cards
to friends and fans.

Despite these everyday distractions, Helen continued to kick around
the idea for the lifestyle book, trying to land on a narrative that would
meet the premise of what she proposed to her agent. It still needed to
come together in her head, but she couldn't find the energy to get started.
But that was the least of her worries—a more pressing issue would soon
occupy her time.

# 9

# Looking for a New Hook

## *Laramie, 1977–1986*

AT RANCHOS DE TAOS, where the Hoovers fed stray cats at their rented home, local authorities were not pleased with the community's growing cat population. In 1977, the city passed an ordinance requiring collars on all cats, including those kept indoors. This ultimately forced the Hoovers to make a decision.[1] Their cat colony had grown considerably, with many of the stray cats having kittens. The patio had turned into an oasis for the cats, and with the Hoovers feeding them, the animals had no reason to go elsewhere for food.

Helen was so indignant with the ordinance that she wrote to friends that she and Ade were being forced out of their home in violation of the Fourth Amendment, which protects people against unreasonable searches and seizures. Some local residents were similarly outraged about the ordinance and tried protesting its adoption, but to no avail.[2] Helen told Gunflint Lake friend Peggy Heston they would leave New Mexico immediately and find a new house, looking first in Laramie, Wyoming.[3]

Choosing Laramie was somewhat spontaneous. Feeling the need to quickly find a new place to live, Helen reached out to her friend Edna Moxley, owner of the motel they stayed at in Laramie in 1968 when the Hoovers were finishing *A Place in the Woods*. The Moxleys had stayed in touch with the Hoovers and visited them in Ranchos de Taos a few years earlier.[4] Moxley recalled that Helen chartered a small plane and flew to Laramie, staying at the motel and hiring a real estate broker to help her find a house. Helen found one and some land on the south side of town and purchased it in October 1977. The Hoovers moved to Laramie, with fifteen cats at this point, some pregnant. Helen told friend

Andre Norton that movers arranged to haul their car, and she found a man to move the cats.[5]

Arriving hastily, Helen sized up their new location fairly quickly, as she related in a New Year's Eve letter to Angus Cameron. "Laramie is varied. I detect an odor of snobbishness and stiffness among some of the university people—the older ones; a narrowness in attitude toward things and people who are different."[6] Helen had also shared her frustration about their new location with her friend Gladys Taber. Taber wrote to Helen, "I am so grieved that you hate Laramie—I bet I would too. I would never uproot successfully to such an alien climate and/or people." Trying to strike an empathetic note, she added, "somehow your life in the North Woods fulfilled you—I wish now that the Taos house is sold you could move somewhere back north or East."[7]

Despite the challenges of Laramie, ideas started to stir in Helen's mind that pulled together a variety of things. In a sort of free association letter to Cameron, she mentioned nostalgic "souvenirs" as a way to organize the proposed lifestyle-change book, referencing items from their Gunflint Lake days that she had recently unpacked. Helen also acknowledged that she needed to include animals and talked about her "cat house critters" and her observations of their family life as a way to meet that reader obligation. "I'll drag the woods in, of course, but I've really had enough of the 'simple life.' The beauty we once knew in our isolation is gone and now is a nostalgic memory, 20 years behind us."[8]

As the Hoovers settled into their new home in Laramie, Helen became ill. She was sick in bed with asthma for several weeks from January to February 1978, requiring her to take oxygen. By March they understood the house had been an impulsive purchase and they needed to find a home with one-level living, another indication Helen's health was not good.[9]

By May, Helen was telling close friends the sudden move to Laramie had been a mistake. "I freely admit that coming here was the worst & most expensive error of my life," she wrote to Norton. Helen elaborated that she was so shocked by their needing to leave Taos that she had acted impulsively. She should instead have called a friend who was relocating to Arizona and figured out a way to move there, as the climate would have been better for them.[10]

Helen's health continued to be an issue. She came down with the flu and pneumonia, which took several months to recover from. Then she tore a knee tendon, slowing her down yet again. Despite these challenges and the unhappiness with Laramie, however, the move must have been inspiring on one level: while on the mend, Helen started to write again, this time a variation of her children's book *Great Wolf and the Good Woodsman*.

Called the "The Princess and the Woodsman," the story was another fairy tale, although a darker one. Set a hundred years earlier, the protagonist, Princess Anne-Elizabeth, was the adoring daughter of her father, who is prince of the country. As she plays in the garden with her beloved pet deer Sasha, her father's assistant Peter comes to take her to see him. The prince tells the princess she will be going away to visit her grandmother, which is also where her mother is staying. The princess quickly understands that all is not well in the kingdom as some men are coming to visit her father. Before she can be sent away, the men kill Peter and take her father prisoner. The princess hides from these bad people; a woodsman who is a friend of Peter and her father watches from the shadows and takes the princess away from danger, hiding her in his cabin in the forest for some time. She trusts the woodsman and does as she is told. The princess and Sasha stay with him until he can get them safely across the border to be reunited with her mother and grandmother. The fate of her father is not revealed.[11]

The story could be read to have allegorical as well as nostalgic aspects. The princess could be a young Helen, who adored her father. He had indulged her with pets when she was young, so the fact the princess had a pet deer could be a nod to both her youth and to her beloved buck Peter from *The Gift of the Deer*. The woodsman might be a composite of her husband Ade and the guide and woodsman Ollor Snevets, who helped the Hoovers in their early years on the Gunflint Trail. Once it's safe, the woodsman takes the princess over the mountain and out of the country to be reunited with her mother. The eventual happy ending is brief: there is only the anticipation of a reunion with her mother, not one that actually occurs in the story. This might refer to Helen's desire that there could have been a happier ending to her relationship with her own mother—or that there might be one to come in the afterlife.

The source for the idea of the tale has a curious backstory. It came from either a fan or an acquaintance by mail of Russian heritage who told Helen stories of her privileged mother's upbringing at the end of the Czarist era. Her mother had a pet gazelle and was related to the Romanov family. These details sparked an idea, and Helen asked if she could use parts for a children's story. The friend obliged, and Helen shared the story with her to read.[12]

Helen sent the draft to Carol Brandt's colleague Charles Schlessiger, who was taking over Brandt's clients as she moved toward retirement. He immediately took a liking to it and suggested minor changes, which Helen quickly made. Schlessiger had ideas about children's publishing houses that might be a fit, hoping to capitalize on Helen's success both in the adult and juvenile markets. He was no doubt aware that this would be the first new writing from Helen in five years and understood it might be of interest to her regular readers. He began by sending the manuscript to publisher E. P. Dutton for review.[13]

Helen and Cameron continued to correspond, and even five years after *The Years of the Forest* had come out, she still lamented all the edits to the manuscript. Cameron couldn't resist responding: "I know you hated the cuts to *Years* but still can't agree with you that the cutting 'slashed the book to nothing.' I still think it was a damned good book."[14]

Helen kept up on local news and happenings among the Gunflint Lake neighbors in letters to friends there. She closely followed the battle to establish the Boundary Waters Canoe Area (BWCA) Wilderness in 1978. The BWCA Wilderness Act was the result of several lawsuits that had been filed since the amendments about logging and motor use in the Boundary Waters were added to the Wilderness Act of 1964. The issue came to a head in 1977 with public hearings in St. Paul and Ely about whether logging and motorized recreation should continue to be allowed. In 1978, after compromises on competing bills in the U.S. House, agreement was reached to add more land to the Boundary Waters, ban all logging and mining, and set more restrictions on motor use. After passage in Congress, President Jimmy Carter signed the act into law in October.

Helen tried to keep up with the news, but coverage in Laramie was scant, so she relied on correspondence with Peggy Heston and others to keep her on top of developments. In these letters to Heston, Helen increasingly leaned on her friend to keep tabs on the cabin and asked her to take care of various maintenance chores, such as fixing foundation cracks or clearing windfalls from storms. Helen even enlisted Heston's help in trying to sell the old Chevy that Snevets had given them in 1963, sending the title by mail and directing her to where the keys were in the cabin, but no one was interested in buying it.[15]

In addition to the requests for help, these short notes to Heston were full of nostalgia for the quiet years on Gunflint Lake. Milestone dates would suddenly trigger reasons to drop Heston a note, such as Helen and Ade's fortieth wedding anniversary in May 1977, or the thirtieth anniversary of their first summer at Gunflint Lake in 1978. Helen shared memories of local residents who had helped over the years. She discussed Charlie Boostrom, the former resort owner and area handyman, who had fixed the cabin foundation in those early years. She wrote about Eve and Russell Blankenburg, who sold them land after they bought the cabin, as well as firewood their first year living there. Helen's letters hold other sentimental recollections of those times. She continued to drop hints that they would return, but the reality was that neither she nor Ade were healthy enough to attempt a long trip back to Minnesota. Unsaid in these letters was Helen's lingering sadness over those difficult later years, which likely thwarted her will to visit the cabin.

Helen's earlier books continued to sell. In February 1979 she was surprised by a letter from Schlessiger informing her of a proposal by Reader's Digest Japan to condense *A Place in the Woods*, paying a $2,000 advance and a two-cent royalty for each book sold. She was amazed they were willing to make this offer ten years after the book was published.[16]

Schlessiger still had not received any interest in "The Princess and the Woodsman" from the juvenile publishers he had queried. As a last resort he sent it off to Parents' Magazine Press, which had published Helen's earlier juvenile titles, including *Great Wolf and the Good Woodsman*. Helen had originally nixed sending the story to them; she was discouraged with her former publisher because their royalty paid so little and her old friend Alvin Tresselt had moved on, leaving few people there that she knew. In May Schlessiger heard back: because of organizational changes, Parents' Magazine Press was no longer doing this type of book. Schlessiger tried to soften the blow by telling Helen the juvenile market was in a bad state given cutbacks in library funding.[17]

Despite the lack of interest in her children's book, Helen was think-ing about something else. She confided to Schlessiger that simmering in her mind was an idea for a book about cats. Helen's growing family of cats obviously influenced this thinking, as she had ample time to observe their behavior and interact with them. She was also a fan of cartoon artist B. Kliban, whose 1975 book about cats had become an unlikely best seller, kicking off a craze that placed his cat cartoons on cards, coffee mugs, tote bags, and calendars. Helen may have been calculating a broader interest in cats she could capitalize on. Even her author friend Gladys Taber encour-aged her to write about cats, starting with when they acquired Sheba.[18]

The Hoovers found a more suitable place to live in June 1979. They moved five miles north of Laramie to open prairie, on five acres of land with few neighbors. Helen was delighted: they had ten rooms and two fireplaces, and she noted to Peggy Heston the cost of wood was fifty dol-lars for a cord, delivered and stacked, and only fifteen dollars for slab wood. As always, the cost of things was engrained in Helen's psyche. Getting a deal, whether it was firewood, groceries, fresh produce, or something else, brought joy to someone who weathered not only Chicago during the Depression but also the north woods when they hardly had any money for food.[19] To shelter their growing family of cats, the Hoovers built a structure that could house them all, which now numbered more than thirty. The 30 × 40-foot "cattery" cost $15,000 to build, which was quite an investment.[20]

Orville Gilmore and his wife, the couple who had purchased the Hoovers' summer cabin in 1972, were traveling to Laramie to visit their daughter and offered to bring the Hoovers any items from their cabin. They took a load of books, two of Ade's hats, some of his navy memen-tos, and some sketches. In a letter later to a Gunflint neighbor, Gilmore remembered the cat structure was overflowing with animals and "smelled like a zoo."[21]

During this time Helen was informed by Ohio University that they planned to honor her in fall 1979 as one of a dozen alumni Medal of Merit recipients. Interestingly, Helen was the only honoree who was not a graduate. She was recognized for her work in the field of literature as a "renowned ecology and wildlife writer" and author of several works on nature. Although unable to attend the ceremony, this recognition from a place that meant so much to her in her formative years inspired Helen to write a moving tribute of her time at the school.[22]

Helen and Ade were happier with the new surroundings, which was a relief for both. The house had ample room, and the one-level arrangement made it easier for both to get around. A long driveway stretched from the main road, and in the winter, Ade parked the car at the end and used a snowmobile to ferry back and forth to the house. With this new environment and a sense of nostalgia, Helen was ready to write again.

While Helen had landed on the idea for a book about changes in lifestyle that she had proposed several years earlier and had excited both Cameron and Brandt, she could not muster up much enthusiasm in the intervening years. Whether it was moving into a new house in New Mexico, the interruption of fleeing Taos for Laramie, or the subsequent illnesses that kept Helen unsettled during this time is not known. She continued to receive occasional inquiries from her agent and editor asking how she might be coming along with the idea, but her responses were always evasive and noncommittal.

In 1979 Helen finally started working on a manuscript that roughly covered the years 1929 to 1954. Whether this was an updated version of the "lifestyle-ambience" story she had attempted before or something entirely different is unclear; a detailed outline and other notes are all that exist. Perhaps the outpouring of fan mail from the Jim Kimball column in 1976 had swayed her to revisit her life's story before the Gunflint years. Regardless, this version, encouraged by her agent Brandt, covers those years in Chicago when she first came to the city in search of work, her courtship with Ade, the hardscrabble years of office work, the interruption of World War II, and the postwar years when both of their careers began to advance.

There is ample narrative of Helen's mother being a constant burden, from the time her father died and they left Greenfield to their early years in Chicago with Helen barely making enough for them to live on during the Depression. There are adventures about her courtship with Ade and the places they visited but not much about their domestic life once they married, other than their annual summer trips seeking land or a cabin in the northern forest. The manuscript provides little sense of what they did for fun while Helen, Ade, and Hannah lived together in the city. More interestingly, there is nothing about the writing she attempted in 1938 while employed at the Audit Bureau, something one would expect to be included in a manuscript written by a successful author. Perhaps Helen was still smarting from the criticisms by Cameron and Brandt that led to her cutting material from *The Years of the Forest* about her challenges working with magazine and book editors. Or perhaps she simply did not think those early attempts at writing were worth mentioning.

By the spring of 1980 and seventy years old, Helen had written about thirty thousand words covering the move from Greenfield and their early years in Chicago. She was not sure her agent would like it, but she was enthusiastic about it in letters to friends.[23] Helen also noted she wanted to do two more books. One was likely the cat book she was supposedly working on; the other was the evolving lifestyle book.[24]

Brandt quickly read what Helen sent. She thought it was going to be a good book but suggested that Helen could cut some of the details. Brandt loved the Chicago stories and voiced her belief that as Helen began writing faster she would gain momentum and self-edit less, thereby getting the best material on the page. She also concurred with Helen on the difficulties a mother can pose but suggested she ease up on the complaints about their difficult relationship.[25] Inspired by her agent's comments, Helen kept working, adding more about the postwar years in metallurgy and the challenges she encountered at International Harvester.

Brandt had been ill during this time, so her son and business partner Carl Brandt kept up communication with Helen. He read the pages she had sent to Carol "with interest and some admiration—and even some horror, particularly when presented with certain aspects of your mother. I can only admire the fortitude and the loving kindness with which you went through all that."[26] He continued to urge Helen to send more when she was ready, noting "there is a great deal of interest these days in books by and about women who took their own lives in their own hands, and it seems to me that much of your book fits that."[27]

In early 1980, after years of telling friends that they would return to Gunflint Lake, the Hoovers finally sold the log cabin to a neighbor who had inquired about it. It had been eight years since they had been there, and that was only a brief visit to get a few things out of storage and arrange for the movers to send their belongings to New Mexico. Helen had told a friend that they would likely sell in the next year, admitting that they had hung on to it so long largely for sentimental reasons.[28] Given all the signals the Hoovers had sent about never selling, some neighbors seemed miffed about this sudden decision. Helen's response was that the new owners had been the first to make known their interest when she and Ade were ready to sell. She was annoyed that any decision they made continued to draw the scrutiny of the Gunflint neighbors.

The new owners packed up the Hoovers' few personal items as neither one was able to travel back to Minnesota for the sale. Helen's health prevented it, and she needed to tend to the growing cat colony. Ade's reason for not being able to travel is unclear, as previously Helen had suggested he would make the trip. Likely, Ade's age and health were catching up with him, too. Upon receiving some old desks and chests, the Hoovers discovered that many items were missing: address books, clothes, and even an old Saks Fifth Avenue robe Helen had brought from Chicago. They mused about why seemingly random items of little value were taken. It was another disappointing chapter to the end of their Gunflint years.[29]

Helen's first book, *The Long-Shadowed Forest*, had gone out of print as the original publisher, Thomas Y. Crowell, was sold to another publishing house. Helen had always been frustrated that Crowell had not done more to reprint it or allow another publisher to do so. In late 1978, an inquiry came (through her book-buyer friend Alice Carlson) from New York publisher Bonanza Books showing interest in a possible hardcover reprint of *The Long-Shadowed Forest*.[30] Brandt started to look at publishers who might reissue the title in both hardcover and paperback and received interest from W. W. Norton, a respected independent publishing house. To Helen's delight, they released both versions in the summer of 1980, paying a $500 advance. By the fall, the book was already in a second printing, selling nearly four thousand copies in paper and several hundred in hardcover. Norton editor James L. Mairs noted, "while this doesn't make it a bestseller, it certainly is proof that there is a solid market for your very good book."[31]

Helen had also pestered her agent about getting Knopf to issue paperback versions of the three books she published with them. They had resisted this, claiming their nature books published in hardcover did not sell well in paperback. After persistent pressure from Brandt, Knopf

reluctantly sought bids from other trade publishers that might be interested. Houghton Mifflin stepped forward and paid a $2,500 advance.
They proved to be an ideal choice, as the publisher was well known for the
nature writers it handled, including Roger Tory Peterson, Rachel Carson,
and John Muir. The plan was to start with *The Gift of the Deer* in 1981; if
that was successful, they would consider paperback versions of *A Place in
the Woods* and *The Years of the Forest.*[32]

These developments with W. W. Norton and Houghton Mifflin gave
Helen a great deal of satisfaction. It was not about the money; she had
always believed her books had a wider audience, which affordable paperback versions could deliver. She felt vindicated that the books had
found publishers and a new market for her work.[33] Magazine publishers
also demonstrated their interest. In June, *McCall's* magazine requested
permission to reproduce the first chapter of *The Gift of the Deer* for their
December 1981 holiday issue. Helen was pleased by interest in her deer
story, fifteen years after the book was published. *McCall's* paid $500 for
the rights, and it appeared alongside a fictional story by Isaac Bashevis
Singer about a deer appearing at Hanukkah. *Orion Nature Review* paid
seventy-five dollars for the chapter "Mama and Her Twins" for its September 1981 issue.[34]

Helen continued to work on the book about the early years, but it
became more of a memoir than a book that would truly explore lifestyle
changes. By the summer of 1981 she had about two-thirds of the book
finished and sent it to her agent to review. If Brandt liked it, she would
then finish the last part.[35]

Carol Brandt, now back at full strength, and her colleague Charles
Schlessiger, both read the partial manuscript. Neither one was impressed.
"I find this manuscript curiously brittle and somewhat monotonous and
dull—disappointing indeed," Brandt stated in a letter to Helen. She observed that in Helen's woods books "there is a motion, feeling, struggle,
growth, failure, heartbreak, love—everything. All of these should be here
and they are not."[36] Brandt provided a detailed critique of the manuscript, picking apart Helen's focus on her mother's cruelties, the dearth of
insight into Ade and their life (aside from their courting years and their
choice not to have children), and other incidents she highlighted during
her years in metallurgy. She closed the letter by suggesting Helen might

want to "simmer down" before calling or writing, as Brandt knew the candid feedback would come as a disappointment.[37]

Brandt also shared the manuscript with Cameron at Knopf. It eventually landed on the desk of his colleague Bobbie Bristol, who was increasingly handling Cameron's authors as he, too, was moving toward retirement. Bristol read it in one sitting and agreed that it was not Helen's best effort. Bristol wrote to Helen, telling her it lacked the focus of her other books and would not reach the audience she was trying to find. She offered ideas for improving the manuscript, suggesting Helen focus on either the relationship with her mother or her career as a metallurgist. Bristol clearly felt a simple chronological accounting of the years from Ohio to the north woods was not unique and lacked broad appeal.[38]

Helen made notations on the letter from Brandt, more for her benefit than to challenge her agent's critique. It appears this feedback from both her agent and Bristol ended Helen's attempts at finishing the "lifestyle-ambience" book she had been working on for several years. She was resigned to the fact that the book was not commercially viable, but she was also not that upset about the lack of enthusiasm for her effort. As she wrote to a friend, she had found the writing hard because she did not like remembering. "My way is to look to today & leave the past behind."[39]

Even though no one asked her to complete the manuscript, there are handwritten pages that finish the book, bringing the story up to when the Hoovers find a cabin on Gunflint Lake.[40] Whether these were completed while her agent had the first two-thirds of the book in hand is not known. Perhaps Helen was compelled to finish it by bringing her story of the early years to where *A Place in the Woods* begins, essentially completing her life story for some future consideration. The last page ends with Helen's handwritten ending: "We discover virgin timber on the fairytale North Shore."[41]

\* \* \*

Helen was cognizant that the growing cat colony in Laramie was becoming a challenge to manage, and she needed to determine a future home for the cats. She reached out to Living Free Animal Sanctuary, a cat and dog refuge in Mountain Center, California. Living Free had been established in 1980 as one of the first privately funded no-kill sanctuaries in the country. Helen had likely read about their efforts and believed it would be ideal for the cats. She talked with Living Free about taking the cats at some future date and discussed how they might transport the animals to California. She even enlisted some of her friends to make charitable donations to Living Free to demonstrate her interest and help develop funds to offset the moving cost.[42]

The Hoovers' health continued to decline. Both were seventy-three years old. Ade had been diagnosed with emphysema, and Helen thought it was getting worse. She encouraged him to take the prescribed oxygen, but he was forgetful about doing so. She continued to blame her own ailments on the hard years of heavy lifting and poor diet when they lived in the north woods. She also had a cataract in one eye but felt she was not ready for an operation. Everything likely took a physical toll—an inactive lifestyle coupled with existing ailments, the stressful move from Taos, a second move after reaching Laramie, and all with several dozen cats.[43]

In 1983, Helen approached Ohio University about donating some of her papers, scrapbooks, and first editions of her books. She was aware of her legacy, as she had donated some of her children's book manuscripts and related papers to the Kerlan Collection of children's literature at the University of Minnesota in 1968 after they asked for materials from the writing of *Animals at My Doorstep*.[44]

According to several local people from Laramie who knew the Hoovers, once they moved to their final house outside town, they rarely left home except to occasionally take a meal in town with one of their lawyers or their friends the Moxleys. Helen was also overweight, with one acquaintance referring to her as "a very large lady—I guess you would say obese." Helen did not leave the house the last year of her life, except to visit the doctor.[45]

In a brief note to her accountant, Helen claimed she was still try-ing to complete the cat book, but blamed the mess of mail on her desk from getting it done. To the end, Helen was still under the pressure of too much correspondence that needed attention. No doubt her cataracts and other health issues also made it difficult to work on her writing.[46] Not much correspondence exists from the last years of her life. Most of the letters are personal, such as Christmas cards, but these are mostly holiday postcards with a brief greeting—not the long, newsy letters she was known for previously.

In late June 1984, Helen became ill with peritonitis. She was transferred from Laramie to a hospital in Fort Collins, Colorado, where she died on June 30. She was seventy-four years old. Her remains were cremated on July 2. Helen's passing shocked Ade. He was distraught as he tried to sort out the cat colony, Helen's accumulated papers, the thousands of books they owned, and the fact he would now be living alone in rural Laramie.[47]

The *New York Times* observed Helen's death with a short news obituary that ran on July 7, noting her work as both a nature writer and a metallurgist. It appeared on page fourteen of the paper's national edition; its placement was likely the work of her publisher Knopf or agent Carol Brandt. Helen would have been pleased that her death was recognized in such an important newspaper. Other media outlets picked up the notice and ran short mentions.[48]

For all of the news coverage Helen had garnered over the years in the *Cook County News-Herald* in Grand Marais, there was only a brief mention of her passing in the newspaper, in Justine Kerfoot's weekly "On the Gunflint Trail" column, which erroneously noted the Hoovers lived in Boulder, Colorado. One local reader sent an anonymous letter to the newspaper the following week scolding it for not doing more to honor a former local talent who had done so much for the area. Helen would have enjoyed that, since she had indeed done much during her time to put Gunflint Lake, the Trail, and Grand Marais on the map for nature lovers.[49]

Ade was overwhelmed with cards and letters of condolence from friends wide and far, as well as from fans who had read the obituary in the *New York Times* and other newspapers. He was always uncomfortable with correspondence, and his handwriting was poor despite his ability to illustrate his artwork with beautiful penmanship. He wrote brief notes to several close friends, including Peggy Heston, the resort owner at Gunflint Lake. "It's the memories we all have that are locked in time that can neither be expanded nor erased," he penned only a few days after Helen's death.[50]

Carol Brandt sent Ade a brief letter, noting sadness over the "loss of a remarkable, fine, unique and talented woman. I know how very much you will miss her, and I will, too."[51] Brandt herself was not well. She died later that year on October 25 at age eighty, leaving the agency to her son and business partner, Carl, who had shared in many of Helen's literary successes.[52] Angus Cameron learned of Helen's death from his colleague Bobbie Bristol and wrote Ade with his condolences "and at the same time to say goodbye, as it were, to a very able and creative lady. I enjoyed our years of editorial contact and was always proud of Helen's achievements."[53] Richard Reilly, Helen's friend from the James S. Copley Library, was at a loss, writing, "she loved, appreciated and respected nature and helped the rest of us to feel as she did. We have all lost a great friend."[54] Ade also received a letter from Sister Noemi Weygant, a Benedictine nun at the St. Scholastica Priory in Duluth who was an internationally known nature photographer and author of books featuring her poems and photographs. Like many people, Sister Noemi was attracted to Helen's sensitive writing, and they developed a friendship by mail. Her condolence letter to Ade noted, "I am very glad that she had you, one who seemingly had always understood and appreciated her, because I always felt she had [been] most dreadfully hurt by life. To be as sensitive and brilliant as she was is indeed a cross."[55]

Although there is no complete record of it, Helen's ashes were said to have been spread over a river in New Mexico, per her wishes, after her death. It is not known who did this final act, or if it happened at all; Ade would have needed help doing it.[56]

Ade was understandably lonely without Helen. Their friend Andre Norton was worried about him having to deal with the cats, Helen's papers, all of the books, and the antique furniture that had followed them from Chicago thirty years prior. He felt adrift without any clear guidelines, and Helen likely kept details to herself about how these matters should be handled. Wisely, Norton recommended that Helen's papers be gifted to a college library and told Ade to find someone he could trust to help with this task.[57]

At seventy-four years old, Ade was not in good health. Norton, worried about him being so far out of town, suggested that he might find a retirement home helpful.[58] Fortunately, a young neighbor couple looked after him, providing meals and companionship as he grieved.[59]

Helen's substantial book collection was donated to the Albany

County Public Library in Laramie. As for the cats, Helen had been handling those arrangements with Living Free in California, so Ade was not certain what to do. He made inquiries with them about removing the cats, but they gave him a story that was different from what Norton remembered Helen telling her. The arrangement was to send a plane and veterinarian to take the cats once a shelter on their grounds was completed. Norton asked Ade if there was a contract and suggested getting their lawyer involved.[60] At considerable expense Ade moved the more than sixty cats they had accumulated to Living Free, but he kept his favorite, their first cat, Sheba. Norton and Helen's friend Richard Reilly made substantial donations to the animal sanctuary.[61]

Norton and Ade likely had telephone calls, something she had done with Helen frequently in their later years. She continued to be concerned for Ade, particularly that first Christmas after Helen's death, and was frustrated she could not do more to console him. "To have such a close and warm relationship broken so abruptly is simply tearing out part of one's life and one does not feel whole," she wrote. "I do wish you had some friend near you on whom you could depend and with whom you could talk."[62]

Ade sent a photograph of him and Helen to friends he had received cards from that first Christmas after she died. Many wrote back, grateful for the memento. Very little is known about Ade's remaining time in Laramie. He was not much of a letter writer; his communication with friends was likely by telephone and an occasional handwritten card. He died at Ivinson Memorial Hospital in Laramie on April 1, 1986, twenty-two months after Helen's death. He was buried three days later at Fort Logan National Cemetery in Denver, Colorado, and had a military funeral at his request.[63]

The Hoovers had planned for the day when they would die, and Ade left a last will and testament. There were no known immediate relatives. The original drawings from *The Gift of the Deer, A Place in the Woods,* and *The Years of the Forest* were donated to the Copley Library in La Jolla, California, where Helen's friend Richard Reilly was the curator. She had previously donated her original typed manuscript for *The Long-Shadowed Forest.*[64] The bulk of the Hoovers' estate was left to Ohio University to establish the Helen Hoover Memorial Endowed Scholarship to provide student scholarships in the fields of chemistry, computer science, electrical engineering, and journalism. The copyrights to Helen's works were given to the literary agency Brandt & Brandt, which assigned them to Ohio University so the scholarship program would benefit from future royalties.[65] Ohio University also was to receive her literary and personal papers, photographs, and other materials. By arrangement with the University of Minnesota Duluth, the papers were transferred there, likely to be closer to where Helen did most of her writing.[66]

Helen's wish that her books be available in paperback was later fulfilled when the University of Minnesota Press began in 1998 to republish her four books as part of the Fesler–Lampert Minnesota Heritage Book series, which also included writings by Sigurd Olson and Calvin Rutstrum, authors who portrayed the uniqueness of the northern lake country. The Press later added *Great Wolf and the Good Woodsman* in 2005, with new illustrations by Grand Marais artist Betsy Bowen.

Helen's writing made a clear impression on her readers. Well after her death, fans would still visit Gunflint Lake, hoping to get a glimpse of that special place so beautifully described in her books. Residents of the area called these visitors "pilgrims": they were often older people who had read her books when they were younger, or they were new readers who found them equally as enchanting as the generations before and felt compelled to find this place in the woods for themselves.[67]

✳ ✳ ✳

Helen had said she wanted to lead three lives: one in a bucolic small town, where she grew up; another in an urban environment, where her mind would be challenged by work; and finally one in a place of peace and solitude, where she could write. She accomplished all of these and so much more, in the process carving out her own unique niche among nature writers. She had the ability to connect with her readers in a natural way, and her books were best sellers in the genre. Reader's Digest would not have purchased the rights to three of her books if she did not have this special appeal. In a sense, her books captured the spirit of the nascent 1960s environmental movement that was stirred by Rachel Carson, which led to a broader desire for a "back-to-the land" sensibility fed by a society yearning to be more connected to nature and removed from the challenges of modern life.

Helen's professional life as a metallurgist always had its challenges, especially as a woman working in a field dominated by men. One can imagine how odd it must have been in the 1950s endeavoring to fix a disc harrow problem that had vexed a large agricultural implement company for decades—a problem eventually solved by Helen, a woman, self-trained and without a college degree, who achieved a patent for her discovery. That alone would have been the pinnacle of most careers.

But for Helen, it was not. The dream of that young girl in Greenfield, Ohio, to live where she wanted and not be bothered while she read and wrote about what she saw, came true. As she said so eloquently in the last paragraph of her final book, *The Years of the Forest:* "I knew that I had found what all men seek—my place in the world of my time."[68]

# Epilogue

## *The Long Road*

AFTER YEARS OF LOOKING for the ideal north woods cabin—the place in the boreal forest with the tall pines that were so important to Helen and Ade—they finally found it. As Ade had said when they purchased the old log cabin on Gunflint Lake, they would be able to enjoy it only for so long before growth and development encroached on them, and he was right. The Hoovers owned that spot for more than thirty years and, as Helen wrote, they were able to enjoy it for only less than half of that time. After departing in 1971, they never returned to Minnesota, choosing to spend their later years on other pursuits in climates less harsh. Still, the remembrance of this special place in the woods was never far from Helen's mind.

It took Helen a long time to come to terms with what she and Ade had created and experienced together. To her, the biggest accomplishment was the fact that the two of them were able to defy the odds of leaving a comfortable urban life where both had well-paying jobs and carve out a living in a way that was completely opposite to their previous lives. They lacked all modern comforts on Gunflint Lake: no electricity, except for occasional use from a generator; some central heat, though early on they were mostly reliant on wood stoves; no running water; and no inside toilet until the very end. Further, for a life in the woods, there was no way to provide for their food other than from purchased groceries and the few eggs their hens produced. They did not hunt or fish, and they refrained from accepting wild game from their neighbors.

Then there was the success that Helen achieved through her writing, capped off by her story of Peter, "The Buck with the Generous Heart," which was the working title of *The Gift of the Deer*. This story, perhaps too sentimental by today's standards but apropos for the mid-1960s, defined the reason they moved north to the woods in the first place: to become part of their environment and not to impose on it. Being able to coexist with so many animals, in a quiet and private location, and learn by observing their activities and interactions with other species was most rewarding for Helen. To tell that story through the deer family was indeed her gift to the world of nature writing.

In retrospect, the success of *The Gift of the Deer* seems almost preordained by the breaks that came Helen's way: the respected publisher, the ideal editor, and the nurturing agent followed by the commitment of Reader's Digest, which brought the book to an audience of millions, larger than she ever imagined, not only in America but around the world. Perhaps after that success nothing else would ever measure up; the rest were just the spoils of being a beloved writer.

The epilogue to *The Years of the Forest,* which was written on one of the Hoovers' final visits to the cabin in 1971, places a coda on their Gunflint Lake years and puts that special time into perspective. Helen reflects on where they had traveled, seeking another special place in Florida or New Mexico yet not having found a permanent location to put down roots since leaving for the first vacation in 1967. As they approach the cabin from the Gunflint Trail after years away, they observe a widened side road and more driveways and power-line poles, all examples of the accelerated development in the area. This only depresses Helen further. After arriving, as they make their way to the cabin to open it up and get settled, a deer appears near the door. It is soon evident to Helen that it is Starface, Peter's last son—she recognizes the marking on his forehead that gave him his name.

Helen is consoled that deer still come to eat and rest in their yard despite there not being anyone at the house to feed them. She now understands the meaning of place and what it means to her after all this time, gathering her reflections in a deeply observant postscript of their years in the forest:

> I knew at that moment that this was still, and always would be, our place, too. No amount of surrounding changes would take it away, because such a place is more than a piece of earth, and its

environment may be anything from the tallest trees to the highest towers. It is where you find the fulfillment of your deepest needs, and you find it only once, if you are lucky enough to find it at all. But once you find it, you never leave it entirely and you never lose it, because it has become a part of you. During all our wanderings it had been with me while I was looking for it in mountains and deserts and plains. From this time on it would be both here and with me wherever I might be, as long as I should live.

# Acknowledgments

WRITING A BOOK is often considered a solitary endeavor, with an author forming the contents and words through thoughts and then committing them to paper (or, more accurately, pixel). Writing a biography is hardly a singular effort: it requires the willingness and enthusiasm of dozens of people, far and wide, to provide information and insights that contribute to the finished work.

This book begins with a copy of *A Place in the Woods*, a gift from close friends wishing my wife and me luck in our search for a cabin. While the book was not the talisman we hoped, it inspired me to explore Helen's writing. I obsessively read all of her books, and then, wanting to know more, I ventured to the Minnesota Historical Society for help. There was a short, unpublished biography in its collection, written in 1990. One thing led to another, and soon I located the daughter of Florence Hart Carr, the author of that biography, who shared her mother's research notes with me. Then I went to the University of Minnesota Duluth, where Helen and Ade's personal papers are held. Next, I met people on Gunflint Lake who remembered or knew about the Hoovers and shared their stories. I wrote an article for *Minnesota History*, which was published in 2014. I thought that was the end of my time with Helen, but there was much more to her story than a magazine article could justify.

Kristian Tvedten, my editor at the University of Minnesota Press, called me just before the Covid-19 pandemic to ask if I was writing a biography of Helen. I had been attempting to do so between work and other activities, but I had made little progress. After outlining my thoughts for a book, we had a deal to tell Helen's story.

Fortunately, my curiosity was well suited for this project, as trying to piece together a person's life from all of the fragments they leave behind can be challenging and frustrating. I started to think of Helen and Ade's

205

life story as one large jigsaw puzzle—with lots of missing pieces. Even though there would be holes in the completed puzzle, I knew there would be enough to see a fairly complete picture. I needed many others to help me find pieces of the puzzle, and I am indebted to them for their interest and goodwill.

At the Minnesota Historical Society, one of the state's underrated treasures, I give my gratitude to Anne Kaplan, former *Minnesota History* editor, who agreed Helen's story needed to be told. Many others in various departments of the Minnesota Historical Society provided help or encouragement over the years, and my thanks go to Patrick Coleman, Jennifer Jones, Josh Leventhal, Pam McClanahan, Jennifer McElroy, Debbie Miller, Jennifer Pogatchnik, John Rahm, Brian Szott, Jennifer Wagner, Kent Whitworth, and Lori Williamson. Many others at the Gale Family Library in the Weyerhaeuser reading room and the Hubbs microfilm room helped retrieve boxes, loaded microfilm, and offered paths to other sources. You will not find more passionate and engaging research partners than at MNHS, and I thank them for their enthusiastic support.

Special thanks to Pam Schoon for sharing her mother's research about Helen. I was amazed at the effort Florence devoted to her biography of Helen, especially since all of her research was undertaken before the internet even existed. She talked with many people who are no longer living, and this information proved invaluable. Although I never met Florence, her fingerprints are all over this book, and I thank her for being among the first to recognize Helen's talents as both a nature writer and a scientist.

The staff at the special collections and archives of the Kathryn A. Martin Library at the University of Minnesota Duluth, where Helen and Adrian Hoover's papers are located, are among the biggest champions of this project. Beginning with Tom Ambrosi, who passed me to the legendary longtime archivist Patricia Maus, and her successor, the ever-engaging and always enthusiastic Aimee Brown, they endured my endless requests for documents, accommodated my two dozen visits over the past fifteen years, and offered ideas and assistance when I ran into roadblocks. Archive colleagues Shana Aue, Percy Calderwood, Laura Vavrosky, and others on staff also offered their help. Student intern Julian Carrero was very patient fulfilling written requests for document copies.

I also owe Matt Rosendahl, library director, heartfelt thanks for his on-going interest in my work.

Early on I spoke with many individuals in and around Gunflint Lake who knew the Hoovers personally, corresponded with them, or were knowledgeable about their time there. Pat Zankman, then head of the Cook County Historical Society in Grand Marais, pointed me to John Henricksson, one of the great raconteurs of the Gunflint Trail. John wrote several books about the area and was very helpful in sharing insights about the Hoovers and their legacy. He had once considered writing a book about the Hoovers and generously shared with me his early research. John and his wife, Julie—both, sadly, no longer with us—were gracious hosts on several visits to their cabin. I shall always cherish his encouragement and support of my efforts.

John introduced me to Sharlene LeTourneau, daughter of resort owner Peggy Heston, and her son Greg Gecas, current owner with his wife, Barb, of Heston's Lodge. Both provided recollections of Helen and shared valuable observations about Gunflint Lake during the time the Hoovers lived there. Sharlene was patient with my seemingly endless requests for additional information about events and neighbors who lived on Gunflint Lake from the 1950s to the 1970s. She, too, shared John's enthusiasm for this project and provided copies of the letters Helen wrote to her mother, which were important in understanding Helen's state of mind after leaving the Gunflint area.

I then met the current owners of the original Hoover "winter" cabin, Les and Liz Edinger. At first they were somewhat guarded toward yet another "pilgrim" making inquiries, but once they understood I was serious about telling Helen's story, they became supportive friends and shared with me personal correspondence and their recollections. I thank them for their trust in me and appreciate the kindness and encouragement they have offered during all of these years. I am also grateful to Ardie and Carol Byers and my visit with them at the Hoover "summer" cabin; they gave me a tour before it was razed. It was indeed as charming a place as Helen described in her books.

Betsy Bowen, artist extraordinaire, chatted with me in her Grand Marais studio and remembered meeting Helen when she was a young girl. I thank Brian Larsen, editor, and Jean Marie Modl of the *Cook*

*County News-Herald* for allowing me to spend time reviewing back issues of the newspaper. Dennis Waldrop at the Cook County Historical Society provided information about Grand Marais in the 1950s and 1960s. Kathy Kundel at the Grand Marais Library helped verify information, and Mary Black at the Cook County Courthouse provided clarification of Hoover property parcels on Gunflint Lake.

At Ohio University, Bill Kimok gave helpful information on the scholarships offered in Helen's name. Lorraine Wochna at the Ohio University Libraries expertly navigated the archives of the student newspaper *The Green and White* for insight into Helen's activities there. The Ohio University Foundation holds the copyrights to Helen's published works, and I thank its president, Lyn Redington, and legal counsel, Robert J. Gall, for extending permission to reprint Helen's papers and personal correspondence.

Among the most impressive research libraries in the country is the Harry Ransom Center at the University of Texas at Austin, where the archives of Alfred A. Knopf, Inc., Helen's primary publisher, are located. During the pandemic, the staff there was most helpful in scanning letters and documents from Alfred Knopf, Angus Cameron, and others within the company. Many research associates and librarians worked on my requests, including Patricia Fox, Maggie Mitts, Courtney Welu, Richard Workman, and especially Kristen Wilson, who went above and beyond in tracking down documents. Thanks as well to Cathy Henderson for providing reprint permissions. For additional information about Angus Cameron, I was fortunate to connect with Jonathan Coleman, who had planned to write a biography of the esteemed editor, and Bobbie Bristol, Cameron's assistant at Alfred A. Knopf. There is an excellent Cameron oral history at the Columbia Center for Oral History at the Columbia University Libraries. And I owe thanks to his son Kevin for providing the photograph of his father.

Due to a series of publishing industry consolidations, information about Thomas Y. Crowell, publisher of Helen's first book, was harder to come by. I thank Tzofit Goldfarb, senior director of archives at Harper-Collins, a successor company, for her sleuthing, and Melissa Murphy at the Baker Library Bloomberg Center at the Harvard Business School for information on its limited Crowell holdings. Nora Ramsey at the Special

Collections Research Center at Syracuse University also provided information from its Crowell collection.

Similarly, not much material exists from *Humpty Dumpty's* publisher Parents' Magazine Press. Also a victim of corporate consolidation, it was eventually bought by the Saturday Evening Post Company, and through ownership changes no archives were retained. I thank Cris Piquinela at Curtis Licensing for her help trying to track down archival material. I was able to exchange emails with Alvin Tresselt's daughter, India, who had fond recollections of her father's work with Helen. India and her sister appear in many of the letters exchanged between Helen and her father.

Andre Norton's papers are at the Special Collections Research Center at Syracuse University, and staff there were very helpful in pulling several hundred of Helen's letters to Andre. My gratitude to Julia Chambers, Julia Dudley, Jeanne Kambara, Amy McDonald, Grace Wagner, and Nicole Westerdahl. I also thank Jay P. Watts, webmaster of the official Andre Norton website, for his help in connecting me with Jeremy Brett at the Cushing Memorial Library and Archives, Texas A&M University, where additional Norton papers are located. Don Boozer at the Cleveland Public Library also helped with the Norton collection there. I'm also in debt to Sue Stewart, of the Andre Norton estate, for help finding information.

Mary Ellen Budney, Matthew Rowe, and Adrienne Sharpe assisted in providing correspondence from the Hal and Barbara Dodge Borland papers at the Yale Collection of American Literature, Beinecke Rare Book and Manuscript Library.

Jane Parr, archivist at the Howard Gotlieb Archival Research Center at Boston University, provided letters from the Gladys Taber Collection.

At publisher Houghton Harcourt, archivist Susan Steinway provided information about predecessor company Houghton Mifflin's later plans to reprint some of Helen's books.

To learn more about Helen's friend by mail Winnifred Hopkins of Milton, Delaware, I was able to find a relative through Melinda Huff of the Milton Historical Society. I spoke with Winnie's niece Pat Crabb, who helped fill in details on the life of this loyal friend. Thanks as well to Don and Judy Fisher of Milton for their recollections.

Arthur Morrissey shed some light on his relatives who sold the "summer" cabin to the Hoovers.

I tracked down several other people who corresponded with Helen and Ade and provided letters and reminiscences that helped inform me about Helen's personality. Gary C. Brown had a robust correspondence with Helen and shared letters she wrote to him, plus he related impressions of his visit with her in Ranchos de Taos. Gloria Palmer was another friend by mail who graciously shared her interactions with Helen.

Christopher Geherin, archivist at the Center for Southwest Research at the University of New Mexico, was helpful with its photography collection.

At the University of Minnesota Libraries in Minneapolis, I am grateful to the Kerlan Collection for allowing access to papers related to Helen's children's books that she donated in 1968. Thanks also to Caitlin Marineau in the Children's Literature Research Collections for help in tracking down juvenile periodicals.

Special thanks to Sister Luce Marie at the St. Scholastica Monastery in Duluth for checking the papers of Sister Noemi Weygant, a longtime professor at the College of St. Scholastica who was recognized for her nature photography and corresponded with Helen.

When I needed copies of obscure periodicals, several libraries helped in tracking them down. In need of a magazine story in the British Library in London during the pandemic, a former colleague living there helped find the document and convinced the staff there to expedite a copy. Thank you, Bev Bratland Hampton, and Christina Campbell and Lisa Kenny at the British Library. Millie Mather and Melissa Lonie at the DC Thomson Archives in Dundee, Scotland, verified another serialization of Helen's work there. Alee Schmierer of the Wilson Library at the University of Minnesota and Beth Standiford at the University of Wisconsin Libraries located hard-to-find nature periodicals. Librarians at the Hennepin County Library assisted with requests when I hit a dead end.

For help in locating Helen's writing for the juvenile religious magazine market, I thank Liz Marston at the Elgin History Museum in Illinois. She connected me with a number of people affiliated with the David C. Cook Publishing organization, past and present: Bruce Cook, Greg Cook, Cathy Herholdt, and Caroline Nelson. Others who helped track down copies of articles from other children's magazines include Marge Sauls, de Grummond Children's Literature Collection, the

University of Southern Mississippi; and Emily Banas, Wheaton College Archives and Special Collections.

The Internet Archive and the website Newspapers.com were invaluable in providing access to old periodicals and newspapers that were difficult to obtain otherwise.

Other authors and writer friends took an active interest in this project and gave me advice, feedback, and ideas about how to approach the book, and I am indebted to them for taking the time to hear me prattle on about Helen. Gratitude to Annette Atkins, Curt Brown, Dr. William Green, Larry Haeg, Lorna Landvik, Mark Neuzil, Betsy Nolan, and James Eli Shiffer. Professional and personal acquaintances who offered encouragement along the way include Suzanne Estelle-Holmer, Margaret Ann Hennen, Sue Lee, and Dawn and Mark McGinty. A very special thanks to dear friends Kris and Mitch Avery for making that introduction to *A Place in the Woods.*

At the University of Minnesota Press, I am grateful to my editor Kristian Tvedten for making that initial call and his ongoing support and patience while I conducted research and wrote the manuscript. His knowledge of the history of the region, and of nature writing in particular, is inspiring, and our conversations helped shape the final work. It has been a true collaboration and I could not be more pleased that the University of Minnesota Press believed it important to publish Helen's biography.

Once the copy editing and proofing was completed, the rest of the Press team kicked into action. Managing editor Laura Westlund and assistant production manager and art director Rachel Moeller expertly guided the project from pixel to printed page. The marketing team of Shelby Connelly, Maggie Sattler, and Heather Skinner did the heavy lifting of getting the word out about the book. To each I am grateful for their enthusiasm and support.

Until you have the opportunity to write a book, you do not appreciate the many others who help bring the project to conclusion. Thank you to early readers Sue Leaf and Kim Todd for their insightful feedback. Rob Hill, copy editor, corrected my dangling modifiers, lapses from active to passive voice, and defiance of the serial comma. A talented editor makes the author's work shine without losing his voice, and I am grateful for his sensitive handling of my writing. My thanks also to Martha Douglas for diligent proofreading.

To any people I have missed, my regrets and grateful appreciation.

Careful readers of Helen's books may notice discrepancies with some of the events noted here. As I conducted my research, and particularly in my extensive reading of her correspondence, I found dates and events that happened at different times from how they appear in her books. I used accurate dates and events in this biography.

Finally, profound gratitude to my wife, Kim, who has been my biggest booster, confidant, draft reader, and all-around good sport for allowing the Hoovers to occupy so much of my life these past fifteen-plus years. Your unwavering support allowed me to finish the puzzle.

# Published Writings of
# Helen Hoover

## Books

*The Long-Shadowed Forest.* New York: Thomas Y. Crowell, 1963.
*The Gift of the Deer.* New York: Alfred A. Knopf, 1966.
*Animals at My Doorstep.* New York: Parents' Magazine Press, 1966.
*Great Wolf and the Good Woodsman.* New York: Parents' Magazine Press, 1967.
*A Place in the Woods.* New York: Alfred A. Knopf, 1969.
*Animals Near and Far.* New York: Parents' Magazine Press, 1970.
*The Years of the Forest.* New York: Alfred A. Knopf, 1973.

## Reader's Digest Condensed Books

*The Gift of the Deer.* Reader's Digest Condensed Books, volume 4, 1966.
*The Gift of the Deer.* Best Sellers from Reader's Digest Condensed Books, 1968.
*A Place in the Woods.* Reader's Digest Condensed Books, Summer 1969.
*A Place in the Woods.* Best Sellers from Reader's Digest Condensed Books, 1971.
*The Years of the Forest.* Reader's Digest Condensed Books, volume 3, 1973.

## Magazine Columns

"Humpty Dumpty's Nature Story," monthly column for *Humpty Dumpty's* magazine, 1959–72 (a total of 123 columns).
"Wilderness Chat," column for *Defenders of Wildlife News*, 1963–72 (a total of 30 columns).

## Magazine Articles

"Weasels Are Wonderful!," *Audubon*, November–December 1957.

"Life among the Shrews, the Littlest Hunters," *Frontiers,* December 1957.

"The Ermine—a Weasel with the Coat of Kings, Princes and Their Kin," *Frontiers,* February 1958.

"Mrs. Mouse's Miracle," *Nature Magazine,* August–September 1958.

"The Moose," *Audubon,* September–October 1958.

"The Lynx: Recluse of the North," *Frontiers,* October 1958.

"Snow Country Thanksgiving," *Gourmet,* November 1958.

"A Christmas Tree for Mr. Bear," *Children's Activities,* December 1958.

"Great Wolf and the Good Woodsman," *Humpty Dumpty's,* December 1958.

"Wilderness Animal—the Fisher," *Audubon,* January–February 1959.

"Wilderness Trail: Spring," *Living Wilderness,* Spring 1959.

"Color of the Night—a Woman of the Wilds Feeds and Observes Her Flying Squirrels," *Frontiers,* April 1959.

"Metallurgical Research Develops Improved Products through Heat Treating," *Metal Treating,* March–April 1959.

"Getting Acquainted with Wild Things," *Nature Magazine,* May 1959.

"Shrews, the Smallest Mammals," *Canadian Audubon,* September–October 1959.

"Our Garden in the Wilderness," *Organic Gardening and Farming,* November 1959.

"The Weasels in My Yard," *Canadian Audubon,* November–December 1959.

"Forest Friends," *Naturalist,* December 1959.

"Wolves and Conservation," *Frontiers,* February 1960.

"Fresh Dug Carrots at Snow-melting Time!," *Organic Gardening and Farming,* February 1960.

"Canteen for Forest Dwellers," *Audubon,* March–April 1960.

"Walter, the Adaptable Weasel," *American Mercury,* June 1960.

"The Flying Mammals," *Audubon,* July–August 1960.

"A Junco Story: Mr. and Mrs. Twit," *Frontiers,* February 1961.

"March: The Fifth Season," *Sunday Digest,* March 5, 1961.

"Twinkle and the Flood," *Humpty Dumpty's,* March 1961.

"Manners—On Meeting a Black Bear," *Frontiers,* June 1961.

"Spring Comes to the Wilderness," Sunday Digest, June 18, 1961.

"Wizard of the Wilderness," *Audubon,* November–December 1961.

"With My Bow and Arrow. . . . ," *Defenders of Wildlife News,* 1962.

"I Go to the Forest for Rest," *Sunday Digest,* April 8, 1962.

"Open House for Wild Things," *Frontiers*, February 1963.

"Wilderness Trail: Summer," *Living Wilderness*, Spring to Summer 1963.

"Deer Track—Wolf Track," *Audubon*, March–April 1964.

"Wilderness Trail: Autumn," *Living Wilderness*, Winter 1964–65.

"Nature Sketch Book—Groundhogs" (Helen and Adrian Hoover),
    *Golden Magazine for Boys and Girls*, February 1965.

"Big Cat, the Starving Lynx," *Audubon*, March–April 1965.

"Wilderness Trail: Winter," *Living Wilderness*, Spring 1965.

"Of Mice and Men," *Woman's Journal* (London), June 1965.

"Mrs. Mouse's Miracle," *Animals' Magazine* (London), September 1966.

"The White-tailed Deer," *Defenders of Wildlife News*, October–
    November–December 1966.

"Chipmunks—and More Chipmunks," *Golden Magazine for Boys and
    Girls*, March 1967.

"Flypaper and Other Toads," *Golden Magazine for Boys and Girls*, April 1967.

"The Bears Who Walk By," *Golden Magazine for Boys and Girls*, May 1967.

"There's Something about Bears," *Defenders of Wildlife News*, July–
    August–September 1967.

"The Visiting Lynx," *Golden Magazine for Boys and Girls*, October 1967.

## Serializations

"The Long Shadowed Forest," *Woman's Journal* (London), April, May,
    June, and July 1964. (The UK article did not include a hyphen in the
    title.)

"A Buck Called Peter," *Woman's Journal* (London), January, February,
    and March 1966.

"The Gift of the Deer," *The Animal World* (United Kingdom), February,
    March, April, and May 1968.

"A Place in the Woods," *My Weekly* (United Kingdom), April 11, 18, 25,
    and May 2, 9, 16, and 23, 1970.

## Under the Pseudonym J. Price

"Wolf at My Door," *Outdoor Life*, September 1958.

## Under the Pseudonym Jennifer Price

"Why the Robins Fly South in the Fall," *Humpty Dumpty's*, November 1960.

"Jake Rabbit Is Missing," *Humpty Dumpty's,* January 1961.

"Peter Whitetail's Day," *Humpty Dumpty's,* May 1961.

"Is He the Man for Me?" serial mystery, syndicated in *New York Daily News,* December 22, 1968–March 30, 1969.

## Adaptations, Anthologies, and Excerpts

"Mouse in the House," from *Nature,* in *Best Articles and Stories,* November 1958.

"Weasels Are Wonderful!," *The Audubon Book of True Nature Stories,* edited by John K. Terres. New York: Thomas Y. Crowell, 1958.

"Mrs. Mouse's Miracle," *This Is Nature: Thirty Years of the Best from Nature Magazine,* edited by Richard W. Westwood. New York: Thomas Y. Crowell, 1959.

"Mrs. Mouse's Miracle," adapted for *Defenders of Wildlife News,* December 1959.

"The Forest Family of Mrs. Helen Hoover," excerpt from *The Long-Shadowed Forest, Saturday Review,* April 4, 1964.

"Adventures at My Doorstep," adaptation of *The Long-Shadowed Forest, Grit,* September 13, 1964.

*The Audubon Nature Encyclopedia,* entries on bats (volume 1) and moose (volume 7). New York: Curtis Books, 1964, 1965.

"Spring Brings the Chorus of Frogs and Toads," excerpt from *The Long-Shadowed Forest, Defenders of Wildlife News,* April 1965.

"I Met a Wolf," excerpt from *The Long-Shadowed Forest, Defenders of Wildlife News,* April 1965.

"Enjoying Bears in Minnesota," excerpt from *The Long-Shadowed Forest, Defenders of Wildlife News,* April 1965.

"Mama and Her Twins," chapter excerpt from *The Gift of the Deer, Orion Nature Book Review,* September 1981.

"The Gift of the Deer," chapter excerpt from *The Gift of the Deer, McCall's,* December 1981.

"King Weather," chapter excerpt from *The Long-Shadowed Forest,* in *North Writers: A Strong Woods Collection,* edited by John Henricksson. Minneapolis: University of Minnesota Press, 1991.

# Notes

## 1. A Charmed Beginning: Ohio, 1910–1929

1. Frank Raymond Harris, *A Greene Countrie Towne* (Greenfield, Ohio: The Greenfield Printing and Publishing Company, 1954), 167.
2. Harris, *Greene Countrie Towne*, 170–71.
3. *Something about the Author: Facts and Pictures about Contemporary Authors and Illustrators of Books for Young People*, vol. 12 (Detroit: Gale Publishing, 1977), 101.
4. Harris, *Greene Countrie Towne*, 46.
5. Harris, *Greene Countrie Towne*, 49.
6. Florence Hart Carr, "Helen Blackburn Hoover: Scientist, Naturalist, Writer" (unpublished manuscript, 1993), 3; private collection, copy in author's possession. An abridged version is in the archives of the Minnesota Historical Society.
7. Carr, "Helen Blackburn Hoover," 3.
8. Helen Hoover, *The Long-Shadowed Forest* (New York: Thomas Y. Crowell, 1963), 204–5.
9. Carr, "Helen Blackburn Hoover," 3.
10. *Something about the Author*, 101.
11. Helen Hoover to Winnifred Hopkins, December 14, 1963, box 2, Helen Blackburn Hoover and Adrian Hoover Papers, Archives and Special Collections, University of Minnesota Duluth.
12. Hoover to Peggy Miller, February 2, 1983, box 2, Hoover papers.
13. Hoover, *The Long-Shadowed Forest*, 211–12.
14. Helen Hoover, *A Place in the Woods* (New York: Alfred A. Knopf, 1969), 45–46.
15. Hoover, *A Place in the Woods*, 45–46.
16. Carr, "Helen Blackburn Hoover," 7.
17. Carr, 7; and copies of pages from *The Dragon*, McClain High School, Greenfield, Ohio, 1927; private collection, copies in author's possession.
18. David E. Kyvig, *Daily Life in the United States, 1920–1940* (Chicago: Ivan R. Dee, 2004), 91–94.
19. Helen Hoover, "Chicago: Carpe Diem—Careers, Courtship and Culture, 1929–1954" (unpublished manuscript), 5, box 18, Hoover papers. The "Chicago" manuscript, an autobiography of Helen's life up to when she and Ade moved to Gunflint Lake, was written in the early 1980s.
20. Hoover, "Chicago," 31.

21.  Frederick Lewis Allen, *Only Yesterday: An Informal History of the 1920s* (New York: John Wiley & Sons, 1997), 73–74. See also Lynn Dumenil, *The Modern Temper: American Culture and Society in the 1920s* (New York: Hill and Wang, 1995), 114–16.

22.  Draft introduction to *The Long-Shadowed Forest*, not used, box 11, Hoover papers.

23.  Hoover, "Chicago," 30.

24.  Hannah Blackburn to Hoover, November 6, 1927, and May 4, 1928, box 2, Hoover papers.

25.  Hoover, "Chicago," 6.

26.  "Brian Andrews" is likely a pseudonym, as no record of a person with that name exists among Helen's college correspondence. This name was used in her "Chicago" manuscript.

27.  Hoover, "Chicago," 14.

28.  For a short but comprehensive summary of the run-up to the "Great Bull Market," see Allen, *Only Yesterday*, 219–41.

29.  Hoover, "Chicago," 4.

30.  Hoover, 4.

31.  Hoover, 4.

32.  Hoover, 4.

33.  Hoover, 4.

34.  Sinclair Lewis, *Main Street* (New York: Harcourt, Brace and Howe, 1920).

35.  Hoover, "Chicago," 4.

## 2. Grit and Perseverance: Chicago, 1929–1937

1.  Helen Hoover, "Chicago: Carpe Diem—Careers, Courtship and Culture, 1929–1954" (unpublished manuscript), 5, box 18, Helen Blackburn Hoover and Adrian Hoover Papers, Archives and Special Collections, University of Minnesota Duluth. Most of this chapter is drawn from this unpublished manuscript.

2.  Hoover, "Chicago," 6.

3.  Hoover, 6.

4.  Hoover, "Chicago," 10. It is not known if Helen used real names or pseudonyms for people. Where used here, they are taken from the "Chicago" manuscript.

5.  Hoover, "Chicago," 18.

6.  Hoover, "Chicago," 19.

7.  Hoover, 19.

8.  Hoover, "Chicago," 26. Helen related this story years later in correspondence to several people, validating that it was indeed true and not a fictional incident.

9.  Florence Hart Carr, research notes, n.d., private collection, copy in author's possession.

10.  Hoover, "Chicago," 26.

11.  Original notes and letters, box 2, Hoover papers.

12.  Hoover, "Chicago," 41.

13. Hoover, "Chicago," 42.
14. Hoover, 42.
15. Hoover, "Chicago," 46.
16. Hoover, "Chicago," 50.
17. Hoover, "Chicago," 54.
18. Hoover, 54.
19. David E. Kyvig, *Daily Life in the United States, 1920–1940* (Chicago: Ivan R. Dee, 2004), 232–33.
20. Kyvig, *Daily Life in the United States,* 220–23.
21. Hoover, "Chicago," 63–65.
22. Hoover, "Chicago," 68.
23. Hoover, "Chicago," 73.
24. Hoover, "Chicago," 76.
25. Addresses, box 14, Hoover papers; and Hoover, "Chicago," 77.
26. Writing examples are in box 18, Hoover papers.
27. Hoover to Alvin Tresselt, January 22, 1963, box 2, Hoover papers; and Hoover to Carol Brandt, September 17, 1967, box 14, Hoover papers. Helen never disclosed the topic of the story, only telling Brandt that it was "dreadful."

## 3. Marriage and Metallurgy: Chicago, 1938–1953

1. Helen Hoover, "Chicago: Carpe Diem—Careers, Courtship and Culture, 1929–1954" (unpublished manuscript), 83, box 18, Helen Blackburn Hoover and Adrian Hoover Papers, Archives and Special Collections, University of Minnesota Duluth.
2. A file of short stories written around 1938 is in box 18, Hoover papers. At the top of each story is a word count and her home address, which at this time was 1140 N. LaSalle, Chicago.
3. The Hoover papers include more than seventy canisters of movie film, shot from the late 1930s through World War II, and then after they purchased their car in 1966 and traveled around the country. Box 21, Hoover papers.
4. Here and below, Helen Hoover, "A Little Place in the Woods" (unpublished manuscript, 1956–58), 13–15, box 14, Hoover papers.
5. For background on Wisconsin's cutover land, see Robert Gough, *Farming the Cutover: A Social History of Northern Wisconsin, 1900–1940* (Lawrence: University Press of Kansas, 1997).
6. Hoover, "Chicago," 86–89.
7. Frederick Lewis Allen, *The Big Change: America Transforms Itself, 1900–1950* (New York: Harper & Brothers, 1952), 158–60.
8. Hoover, "Chicago," 91.
9. Hoover, "Chicago," 94.
10. Hoover to Carol Brandt, April 20, 1969, box 15, Hoover papers.
11. Hoover, "Chicago," 94.
12. Helen Hoover letters to and from Adrian Hoover, box 3, Hoover papers.
13. Film canisters, box 21, Hoover papers.

14. Hoover, "Chicago," 98.
15. Hoover, "Chicago," 99.
16. Hoover, "Chicago," 102.
17. Here and below, Hoover, "Chicago," 105–6.
18. Louise Dickinson Rich, *We Took to the Woods* (New York: J. B. Lippincott, 1942).
19. Betty MacDonald, *The Egg and I* (New York: J. B. Lippincott, 1945).
20. John J. Rowlands, *Cache Lake Country: Life in the North Woods* (New York: W. W. Norton, 1947).
21. Shandelle M. Henson, *Sam Campbell: Philosopher of the Forest* (New York: TEACH Services, Inc., 2001). This short biography of Campbell provides a good overview of his life and writings.
22. Steve Yahr, "Sam Campbell 'Philosopher of the Forest'" (Chicago and North Western Historical Society, 2008), 21–25, www.cnwhs.org/misc_pdfs/sam_campbell.pdf.
23. Sam Campbell to Hoover, June 24, 1947, private collection, copy in author's possession.
24. Here and below, Hoover, "Chicago," 110–12.
25. "FIN's Findings: Better Discs . . . or a Woman's Influence," *Farm Implement News*, March 10, 1958, 77, box 15, Hoover papers.
26. Helen Hoover, *A Place in the Woods* (New York: Alfred A. Knopf, 1969), 4.
27. John Henricksson, *Gunflint: The Trail, the People, the Stories* (Cambridge, Minn.: Adventure Publications, 2003), 21.
28. Hoover, "A Little Place in the Woods," 24–25. In this manuscript, the time of year is fall. Helen changes it to spring in her book *A Place in the Woods*. See also Henricksson, *Gunflint: The Trail, the People, the Stories*, 23.
29. Justine Kerfoot, *Woman of the Boundary Waters* (Minneapolis: University of Minnesota Press, 1994), 64.
30. John Henricksson, *The Gunflint Cabin: A Northwoods Memoir* (Edina, Minn.: Beaver's Pond Press, 2008), 48, 86.
31. Chilson D. Aldrich, *The Real Log Cabin* (New York: Macmillan, 1928). See also Chel Anderson and Adelheid Fischer, *North Shore: A Natural History of Minnesota's Superior Coast* (Minneapolis: University of Minnesota Press, 2015), 274–75.
32. A copy of the warranty deed is in a private collection, copy in author's possession. Reference to the $4,000 selling price is in Hoover, "A Little Place in the Woods," 32.
33. Hoover, "Chicago," 122–23.
34. Warranty deed dated January 28, 1949, selling lots to the Hoovers. They registered the sale with the county on May 18, 1949. Private collection, copy in author's possession.
35. Hoover to Brandt, April 20, 1969, box 15, Hoover papers.
36. Hoover, "A Little Place in the Woods," 36–37.
37. Hoover, "A Little Place in the Woods," 52.
38. Luana Brandt, et al., *A Taste of the Gunflint Trail* (Cambridge, Minn.: Adventure Publications, 2005), 70.

39. Grace Lee Nute, *The Voyageur's Highway* (St. Paul: Minnesota Historical Society Press, 1941), 5–10, 39.
40. Here and below, Hoover, "A Little Place in the Woods," 78–83. In the manuscript Helen uses "Larimers" as a pseudonym for the Morrisseys.
41. Hoover, "A Little Place in the Woods," 83.
42. Hannah Blackburn obituary notice, *Greenfield Times,* October 12, 1953, 4, accessed at www.newspapers.com.

## 4. Bears in the Basement: Gunflint Lake, 1954–1957

1. Helen Hoover, "A Little Place in the Woods" (unpublished manuscript, 1956–58), 88, box 14, Helen Blackburn Hoover and Adrian Hoover Papers, Archives and Special Collections, University of Minnesota Duluth.
2. Hoover, "A Little Place in the Woods," 88.
3. Hoover, "A Little Place in the Woods," 89.
4. Helen Hoover, *A Place in the Woods* (New York: Alfred A. Knopf, 1969), 43–44.
5. Hoover, *A Place in the Woods,* 44–46.
6. Hoover, "A Little Place in the Woods," 90–91.
7. Hoover, *A Place in the Woods,* 47.
8. Hoover, "A Little Place in the Woods," 91; and Hoover bank records, box 14, Hoover papers.
9. Employee record card for Helen D. Hoover, International Harvester Company, September 21, 1954, private collection, copy in author's possession.
10. Hoover, *A Place in the Woods,* 76.
11. Hoover bank records, box 14, Hoover papers.
12. Hoover bank records, box 14, Hoover papers.
13. Hoover, *A Place in the Woods,* 125–26.
14. U.S. Bureau of the Census, *Family Income in the United States: 1954 and 1953, Current Population Reports, Consumer Income* (December 1955), 1, www2.census. gov/library/publications/1955/demographics/p60-20.pdf.
15. Hoover, *A Place in the Woods,* 106.
16. Hoover, "A Little Place in the Woods," 161.
17. Hoover, *A Place in the Woods,* 125–28.
18. Hoover, *A Place in the Woods,* 182.
19. Hoover, "A Little Place in the Woods," 178–79.
20. Hoover, "A Little Place in the Woods," 240; and Hoover, *A Place in the Woods,* 214–15.
21. Hoover, "A Little Place in the Woods," 269–73. Hoover wrote more extensively about the photographer's visit in her draft manuscript but compressed the details for *A Place in the Woods,* not identifying him or the publication.
22. Hoover, *A Place in the Woods,* 182.
23. Helen Hoover, *The Years of the Forest* (New York: Alfred A. Knopf, 1973), 7.
24. Luana Brandt, et al., *A Taste of the Gunflint Trail* (Cambridge, Minn.: Adventure Publications, 2005), 251–53; and email from Sharlene LeTourneau to the author, May 12, 2024.

25.  Hoover, "A Little Place in the Woods," 293.

26.  Hoover check register, box 14, Hoover papers.

27.  Sharlene LeTourneau and Greg Gecas, interviewed by the author, April 30, 2022. LeTourneau is the daughter of Peggy Heston and owned Heston's Lodge after her mother; Gecas is her son and currently operates the resort with his wife. Both had interactions with the Hoovers.

28.  Hoover, *A Place in the Woods*, 252.

29.  The Hoovers' check register has an entry for a *Writer's Digest* subscription for $1.25 dated October 1, 1954, box 14, Hoover papers.

30.  Hoover's files indicate she sent a letter of inquiry to Fierst in May 1955; see box 10, Hoover papers. *Writer's Digest* magazines of this era carried Fierst's ad in the same position each month pitching his success at selling authors to publishers. See archive.org/details/pub_writers-digest, accessed February 15, 2023.

31.  Hoover to A. E. W. Johnson, International Harvester Company, August 12, 1955, box 14, Hoover papers.

32.  Ralph C. Archer, International Harvester Company, to Hoover, October 27, 1955, box 14, Hoover papers.

33.  Hoover, "The Fugitives from Our Laboratories" (unpublished article, n.d.), box 14, Hoover papers.

34.  Hoover, "From Field Failure to Factory: How Industrial Research Works for the Farmer" (unpublished article, n.d.), box 14, Hoover papers.

35.  Here and below, retail and wholesale catalogs of Hoover Handcraft, 1955 and 1957, box 13, Hoover papers.

36.  Summons and complaint, Russell Ueland v. Adrian Hoover, District Court, Eleventh Judicial District, n.d., box 16, Hoover papers.

37.  Hoover, *A Place in the Woods*, 143–47. Helen recalled details of the accident and the subsequent gossip in letters to their attorney, J. Henry Eliasen, who also served as the county attorney. Hoover to Eliasen, September 15, 1955, and October 19, 1955, box 16, Hoover papers.

38.  Hoover to Alvin Tresselt, May 20, 1962, box 16, Hoover papers.

39.  Hoover to Tresselt, May 20, 1962, box 16, Hoover papers.

40.  Hoover, *A Place in the Woods*, 282–89.

41.  Linda Lear, *Rachel Carson: Witness for Nature* (New York: Henry Holt, 1997), 199–200. See also Paul Brooks, *The House of Life: Rachel Carson at Work* (Boston: Houghton Mifflin, 1972), 122–24.

42.  Theodore Peterson, *Magazines in the Twentieth Century*, 2nd edition (Urbana: University of Illinois Press, 1964), 367–70.

43.  Eric Pace, "Alvin R. Tresselt, 83, Author, Wrote about Nature for Children," *New York Times*, August 3, 2000, national edition, B8, accessed at www.nytimes.com.

44.  Hoover to Tresselt, December 27, 1956, box 16, Hoover papers.

45.  Multiple letters between Tresselt and Hoover, 1957 and 1958, box 14, Hoover papers.

46.  Tresselt to Hoover, July 9, 1957, box 14, Hoover papers.

47. Resort owner Peggy Heston named deer and other animals that frequented her yard, so Helen might have picked up the practice from her.

48. Classified advertisement, *Audubon*, March–April 1957, 96; accessed at Kathryn A. Martin Library, University of Minnesota Duluth.

49. Gunflint Lodge burned down on June 28, 1953, and a Chicago youth staying overnight died in the fire. "Youth Dies in Gunflint Fire," *Cook County News-Herald*, July 2, 1953, 1, accessed on microfilm, Minnesota Historical Society; see also Justine Kerfoot, *Woman of the Boundary Waters* (Minneapolis: University of Minnesota Press, 1994), 111–13.

50. Hoover, *The Years of the Forest*, 54–56.

51. Manuscript ledger, box 10, Hoover papers.

52. Here and below, "A Little Place in the Woods," various pages.

## 5. The Buck with the Generous Heart: Gunflint Lake, 1958–1962

1. Helen kept track of early manuscript submissions on 3 × 5-inch index cards, noting dates of submission, acceptance or rejection, and payment information; box 10, Helen Blackburn Hoover and Adrian Hoover Papers, Archives and Special Collections, University of Minnesota Duluth.

2. Running accounts ledger, box 16, Hoover papers. The Hoovers produced catalogs for readers who answered their magazine classified ads and a wholesale catalog for gift shops and other specialty retailers in the area. It is unknown how many customers they had, as no complete business records exist. However, copies of many promotional catalogs are in box 13, Hoover papers.

3. Samples of various notepaper and custom and personal stationery are in box 13, Hoover papers.

4. Manuscript notes for Helen Hoover's *The Years of the Forest* (New York: Alfred A. Knopf, 1973), box 16, Hoover papers.

5. Hoover, *The Years of the Forest*, ix.

6. Alvin Tresselt to Hoover, February 28, 1958, box 14, Hoover papers.

7. *Outdoor Life*, September 1958, 10, accessed at Hennepin County Library.

8. List of submissions and rejections are in box 10, Hoover papers.

9. Hoover to Carol Brandt, April 20, 1969, box 15, Hoover papers; Hoover to Winnifred Hopkins, n.d., likely early 1960, box 2, Hoover papers.

10. The scurvy episode is described in box 16, Hoover papers. She also refers to this incident in *The Years of the Forest*, 77–78.

11. Hoover to Tresselt, March 2, 1959, box 16, Hoover papers.

12. Hoover, *The Years of the Forest*, 84.

13. Manuscript ledger, box 10, Hoover papers. The article, "Snow Country Thanksgiving," appeared in *Gourmet* November 1958.

14. "Hoover, Writer-Inventor, Lives on Gunflint Trail," *Cook County News-Herald*, May 8, 1958, 1, accessed on microfilm, Minnesota Historical Society.

15. Maps and correspondence about the proposed road are in box 10, Hoover papers.

16. Hoover to George A. Selke, October 11, 1958, Minnesota Department of Conservation, Commissioner's Office, General Correspondence, 1958–1959,

box 50 (location number 131.I.14.1B). State Archives, Minnesota Historical Society, St. Paul.

17. Tresselt to Hoover, July 2, 1958, box 14, Hoover papers. The column was eventually titled "Humpty Dumpty's Nature Page" with Helen's byline.

18. Details on submission and rejection dates are in box 10, Hoover papers.

19. Hoover to Tresselt, September 1, 1958, box 14, Hoover papers; see also *The Years of the Forest*, 88–89.

20. Helen Hoover, *The Long-Shadowed Forest* (New York: Thomas Y. Crowell, 1963), 35.

21. Scrapbook, box 18, Hoover papers.

22. Dorothy Gardiner to Hoover, December 18, 1958, box 15, Hoover papers.

23. Hoover to Hopkins, December 13, 1958, box 2, Hoover papers. Some words were typed incorrectly in the text.

24. Robert Kimber, introduction, *We Took to the Woods* (Camden, Maine: Down East Books, 2007), ix–xix.

25. Manuscript submission records on 3 × 5-inch cards, box 10, Hoover papers.

26. "Mr. Bear" folder, box 14, Hoover papers.

27. Helen Hoover, *The Gift of the Deer* (New York: Alfred A. Knopf, 1966), here and below, 9, 11–12, 14.

28. Hoover, *The Gift of the Deer*, 26–27.

29. Hoover, *The Gift of the Deer*, 24–26.

30. Hoover, *The Gift of the Deer*, 28–29.

31. A. L. Fierst to Hoover, January 20, 1959, box 14, Hoover papers.

32. Betty MacDonald, *The Egg and I* (New York: J. B. Lippincott, 1945).

33. Fierst to Hoover, January 20, 1959, box 14, Hoover papers.

34. Hoover to Hopkins, January 25, 1959, box 2, Hoover papers.

35. Hoover to John K. Terres, May 12, 1959, box 11, Hoover papers; and Russell Lynes to Hoover, September 1, 1959, box 10, Hoover papers.

36. Hoover to Hopkins, May 7, 1959, box 2, Hoover papers.

37. Interview with Sharlene LeTourneau and Greg Gecas, April 30, 2022. LeTourneau's mother was Peggy Heston, who with her husband Myrl owned Heston's Lodge. The Hestons were friends with the Hoovers. LeTourneau remembers local residents were surprised the Hoovers did not hunt or fish and were also concerned about their ability to keep warm in the winter.

38. Hoover, *The Gift of the Deer*, 45, 76.

39. Helen Hoover, "Wilderness Trail: Spring," *Living Wilderness*, spring 1959, scrapbook, box 18, Hoover papers.

40. Hoover to Hopkins, May 7, 1959, box 2, Hoover papers.

41. Hoover to John Lear, July 6, 1959, box 16, Hoover papers.

42. Hoover to Lear, August 9, 1959, box 16, Hoover papers.

43. Here and below, correspondence to state and federal officials about the budworm infestation, primarily 1961 and 1962, box 16, Hoover papers. Helen had also submitted a summary of a study about DDT that Justine Kerfoot used in her weekly column in the *Cook County News-Herald*, March 28, 1963, accessed on microfilm, Minnesota Historical Society.

44. Rachel Carson, "Silent Spring—II," *New Yorker,* June 23, 1962, www.newyorker. com/magazine/1962/06/23/silent-spring-part-2.
45. Hoover to Hopkins, August 14, 1959, box 2, Hoover papers.
46. Presentation remarks by K. U. Jenks, president, Metal Treating Institute, November 3, 1959, at the Metals Congress, Chicago, box 15, Hoover papers.
47. Hoover to Hopkins, August 14, 1959, box 2, Hoover papers.
48. Hoover, *The Gift of the Deer,* 71–72.
49. Hoover to Hopkins, January 25, 1961, box 2, Hoover papers.
50. Hoover, *The Gift of the Deer,* 76–77.
51. Hoover to Sigurd Olson, January 26, 1960, box 37, Sigurd Olson Papers, Minnesota Historical Society, St. Paul.
52. Hoover to Olson, January 26, 1960. See also Hoover to Selke, June 11, 1959, Minnesota Department of Conservation, Commissioner's Office, General Correspondence, 1958–1959, box 50 (location number 131.I.14.1B). State Archives, Minnesota Historical Society, St. Paul.
53. Olson to Hoover, December 30, 1959, box 37, Sigurd Olson Papers, Minnesota Historical Society, St. Paul.
54. Margaret E. Murie to Hoover, January 9, 1960, box 15, Hoover papers.
55. Manuscript ledger, box 10, Hoover papers.
56. Timeline notes for *The Gift of the Deer,* Helen Hoover papers, Children's Literature Research Collections, University of Minnesota Libraries.
57. Hoover to Hopkins, July 14, 1960, box 2, Hoover papers.
58. Hoover to Tresselt, March 25, 1961, box 16, Hoover papers.
59. Hoover to Tay Hohoff, June 10, 1961, box 2, Hoover papers. For more on Hohoff and her editing style, see Jonathan Mahler, "Invisible Hand That Nurtured an Author and a Literary Classic," *New York Times,* July 12, 2015, section C, 1, www. nytimes.com/2015/07/13/books/the-invisible-hand-behind-harper-lees-to-kill-a-mockingbird.html?searchResultPosition=3.
60. Peter Gzowski, "1961: Summer of the Angry Forest Fires," *Maclean's,* September 9, 1961, 18, archive.macleans.ca/article/1961/9/9/1961-summer-of-the-angry-forest-fires.
61. Hoover, *The Gift of the Deer,* 176–77.
62. Hoover, *The Years of the Forest,* 288–90. Helen fictionalized part of this story; the event appears in 1966 in *The Years of the Forest* but actually occurred in 1961. See Hoover to Hopkins, December 14, 1963, box 2, Hoover papers.
63. Original contract with Crowell dated November 13, 1961, is in box 15, Hoover papers.
64. Hoover to Hopkins, December 29, 1961, box 2, Hoover papers.
65. Hoover, *The Gift of the Deer,* 177.
66. Hoover, *The Long-Shadowed Forest,* 140.
67. Hoover, *The Years of the Forest,* 174–76.
68. Hoover, *The Years of the Forest,* 177.
69. Hoover, *The Years of the Forest,* 179.

## 6. The Restless Writer: Gunflint Lake, 1962–1965

1. Helen Hoover, *The Gift of the Deer* (New York: Alfred A. Knopf, 1966), 195–201.
2. Hoover to Carol Brandt, November 11, 1972, box 2; and Hoover to Angus Cameron, November 11, 1972, box 2, Helen Blackburn Hoover and Adrian Hoover Papers, Archives and Special Collections, University of Minnesota Duluth. Both letters, written ten years later, revealed what actually happened to Peter, in discussions they were having about edits to her book *The Years of the Forest.* Helen never wanted readers to know the true fate of Peter; in fact, she told her agent Carol Brandt that she never revealed to Ade the identity of who killed Peter.
3. Hoover to Winnifred Hopkins, April 22, 1962, box 2, Hoover papers.
4. Hoover to Alvin Tresselt, April 4, 1962, box 16, Hoover papers.
5. Mary Harris to Hoover, September 24, 1961, box 2, Hoover papers.
6. Helen Hoover, "With My Bow and Arrow," *Defenders of Wildlife News Bulletin,* n.d., but copyright 1962 by Helen Hoover, box 14, Hoover papers.
7. Hoover, "With My Bow and Arrow."
8. Hoover to Hopkins, April 22, 1962, box 2, Hoover papers.
9. Hoover to Hopkins, April 22, 1962.
10. Helen Hoover, *The Long-Shadowed Forest* (New York: Thomas Y. Crowell, 1963), acknowledgments.
11. Helen Hoover, *The Years of the Forest* (New York: Alfred A. Knopf, 1973), 191.
12. Hoover, *The Years of the Forest,* 195–96.
13. Hoover, *The Years of the Forest,* 198–99. "Moccasin wire" is slang for word-of-mouth, or informal communication among people in the area.
14. Manuscript ledger, box 10, Hoover papers. Helen's ledger indicates final manuscript was approved May 11, 1963.
15. Hoover, *The Years of the Forest,* 199.
16. Hoover, *The Years of the Forest,* 204–5.
17. Hoover to Tresselt, January 2, 1963, box 2, Hoover papers. Helen had actually tried her hand at writing short stories in 1938 and had sold one to an editor at the *Chicago Daily News,* but she rarely referenced these amateur efforts.
18. Hoover to Dorothy Gardiner, February 25, 1963, box 2, Hoover papers.
19. Hoover to Hopkins, June 14, 1963, box 2, Hoover papers; Hoover to Angus Cameron, November 21, 1965, box 14, Hoover papers.
20. Edward Tripp to Hoover, May 8, 1963, box 16, Hoover papers.
21. Hoover to Tripp, May 19, 1963, box 16, Hoover papers.
22. Hoover to Cameron, November 21, 1965, box 14, Hoover papers.
23. Patrick Barrett to Hoover, June 19, 1963, and Hoover to Barrett, June 22, 1963, box 16, Hoover papers.
24. Interview with Betsy Bowen, June 10, 2009. Bowen recalled meeting Helen at Leng's Fountain in Grand Marais in 1963 when Bowen was a teenager.
25. Hoover to Hopkins, September 27, 1963, box 2, Hoover papers. In *The Years of the Forest,* Helen takes creative license and has Tulip's death occur right after Peter was shot in 1962.

26. Mary Harris to Hoover, June 30, 1963, box 15, Hoover papers. Hoover's blind review appeared in *Defenders of Wildlife News Bulletin,* October 1963, 12, scrapbook, box 18, Hoover papers.

27. Helen Hoover, "Wilderness Trail: Summer," *Living Wilderness* (Spring–Summer 1963): 3, box 10, Hoover papers.

28. Margaret E. Murie to Hoover, September 25, 1963, box 15, Hoover papers.

29. Hoover to Murie, October 5, 1963, box 15, Hoover papers. The excerpts of *Two in the Far North* appeared in the November–December 1962 and January–February 1963 issues of *Audubon,* under the title "Arctic Honeymoon." Olaus Murie died on October 21, 1963; obituary in the *New York Times,* October 24, 1963, 33, accessed at www.nytimes.com.

30. David Backes, *A Wilderness Within: The Life of Sigurd F. Olson* (Minneapolis: University of Minnesota Press, 1997), 255.

31. Samples of both cards are in box 13, Hoover papers.

32. Hoover, *The Long-Shadowed Forest,* 169.

33. Luana Brandt, et al., *A Taste of the Gunflint Trail* (Cambridge, Minn.: Adventure Publications, 2005), 251. Heston named the deer Prince, Goldfine, Banjo Eyes, and Gentle Boy.

34. Hoover, *The Long-Shadowed Forest,* 17.

35. Hoover, *The Long-Shadowed Forest,* 154.

36. Gladys Taber, review of *The Long-Shadowed Forest, Family Circle,* October 1963, box 15, Hoover papers. Hoover, *The Years of the Forest,* 212; also *Cook County News-Herald,* October 31, 1963, 3, accessed on microfilm, Minnesota Historical Society.

37. Hoover to Tripp, February 5, 1964, box 16, Hoover papers.

38. John Barkham, review of *The Long-Shadowed Forest, Saturday Review,* syndicated in *Rochester Democrat and Chronicle,* January 15, 1964, scrapbook, 1963–1967, box 10, Hoover papers.

39. John Perry, review of *The Long-Shadowed Forest, Atlantic Naturalist,* January–March 1964, 70, scrapbook, 1963–1967, box 10, Hoover papers.

40. Scrapbook, 1963–1967, box 10, Hoover papers.

41. Pieter Fosburgh, review of *The Long-Shadowed Forest, Natural History,* August–September 1964, scrapbook, box 18, Hoover papers.

42. Hoover to Tripp, October 17, 1964, box 2, Hoover papers.

43. Alfred Knopf to Hoover, November 15, 1963; Hoover to Knopf, undated (likely mid-November 1963); Hoover to Knopf, December 1, 1963; Knopf to Hoover, December 5, all box 14, Hoover papers.

44. Hoover to Knopf, undated (likely mid-November 1963), box 14, Hoover papers.

45. Sally Carrighar, *One Day on Beetle Rock* (New York: Alfred A. Knopf, 1944). Carrighar wrote eleven nature books, including *One Day at Teton Marsh* (1947), a book similar to her first about observations of animals in the Tetons; *Icebound Summer* (1953), recording years of observations of animals in Alaska in the summer; and *Wild Heritage* (1965), her defense of ethology, which at the time was criticized for imposing human characteristics upon animals. This was a variation of the anthropomorphism for which Helen was also criticized.

46. Gladys Taber to Hoover, November 4, 1963, and Hoover to Tripp, February 5, 1964, box 16, Hoover papers.
47. Hoover to Hopkins, December 14, 1963, box 2, Hoover papers.
48. Hoover to Hopkins, December 14, 1963.
49. Hoover to Tresselt, November 24, 1963, and December 5, 1963, box 16, Hoover papers.
50. Tripp to Hoover, January 31, 1964, box 16, Hoover papers.
51. Knopf to Hoover, February 12, 1964, and Hoover to Knopf, February 15, 1964, both box 514.7, Alfred A. Knopf, Inc. Records (Manuscript Collection MS-00062). Harry Ransom Center, The University of Texas at Austin.
52. Doris S. Hatcher, review of *The Long-Shadowed Forest*, Book-of-the-Month Club catalog, February 1964, box 15, Hoover papers.
53. Hoover to Tripp, April 28, 1964, box 16, Hoover papers.
54. Tripp to Hoover, May 1, 1964, and Hoover to Tripp, May 10, 1964, box 16, Hoover papers.
55. Hoover to Hopkins, August 7, 1964, box 2, Hoover papers.
56. Hoover, *The Years of the Forest*, 212–13.
57. Hoover, *The Years of the Forest*, 245–46.
58. Hoover, *The Years of the Forest*, 246.
59. Hoover, *The Years of the Forest*, 272–73. Also recounted in working notes for the book, box 16, Hoover papers.
60. Hoover to Helen Finch, October 19, 1964, box 2, Hoover papers.
61. Manuscript ledger entry, October 10, 1964, box 10, Hoover papers; Finch to Hoover, October 29, 1964, box 14, Hoover papers. The story, titled "Of Mice and Men," appeared in the June 1965 issue of *Woman's Journal.*
62. Hoover to Finch, October 19, 1964, box 2, Hoover papers.
63. Hoover to Tripp, October 17, 1964, box 2, Hoover papers.
64. Hoover to Tripp, October 17, 1964, box 2, Hoover papers.
65. Leonard Lee Rue III, *The World of the White-tailed Deer* (New York: J. B. Lippincott, 1962).
66. Manuscript ledger entry, December 1964, box 10, Hoover papers.
67. Hoover to Tripp, November 4, 1964, box 2, Hoover papers.
68. Harrison E. Salisbury, "The Big Woods," review of *The Long-Shadowed Forest, New York Times,* December 24, 1964, 17, box 18, Hoover papers. It was interesting that Salisbury cited Fabre, perhaps an esoteric reference to Jean-Henri Fabre, a noted French naturalist and entomologist who wrote popular books on the lives of insects in the late nineteenth and early twentieth centuries. Or he may have meant Peter Farb, a naturalist who had written a popular series of guidebooks on insects and plants in the early 1960s. Actual sales figures for *Forest* were about twelve thousand, not the twenty thousand Salisbury cites, an error Helen was more than happy not to dispute.
69. Both newspaper clippings in scrapbook, box 10, Hoover papers.
70. Hoover to Tripp, May 2, 1965, box 11, Hoover papers.
71. Alvin Tresselt, "Humpty Dumpty Editor Goes Back to Nature," *Calling All Parents,* August 1965, 1, box 18, Hoover papers.

72.   R. Newell Searle, *Saving Quetico-Superior: A Land Set Apart* (St. Paul: Minnesota Historical Society Press, 1978), 220–21.

73.   Searle, *Saving Quetico-Superior*, 223–26.

74.   Hoover, *The Years of the Forest*, 228–29.

75.   Austin C. Wehrwein, "U.S. Plan for Canoe Park Divides Minnesotans," *New York Times*, May 30, 1965, 40, accessed at www.nytimes.com.

76.   Leonard Rue confirmed he corresponded with Hoover about the biology of deer; email to author, January 12, 2022. Helen recognized other experts in the Acknowledgments of *The Gift of the Deer*.

77.   Hoover to Bob Crowell, June 25, 1965, box 16, Hoover papers.

78.   Hoover to Crowell, June 25, 1965; and Hoover, *The Years of the Forest*, 266.

79.   Hoover to Tripp, August 27, 1965, box 16, Hoover papers.

80.   Hoover to Tressselt, December 5, 1965, box 16, Hoover papers.

81.   "Golden Anniversary of Excellence," *Life*, July 23, 1965, 37. For more on Alfred Knopf, see the website Literary Hub, October 1, 2015, "The Life and Times of Alfred A. Knopf," https://lithub.com/the-life-and-times-of-alfred-a-knopf/.

82.   Cameron to Hoover, August 11, 1965, box 14, Hoover papers.

83.   Hoover to Tripp, November 23, 1965; Hoover to Crowell, December 3, 1965, both box 16, Hoover papers.

84.   Hoover to Knopf, July 26, 1965, Hoover to Cameron, November 21, 1965; and Cameron to Hoover, December 14, 1965, all box 14, Hoover papers.

85.   Douglas Martin, "Angus Cameron, 93, Editor Forced Out in McCarthy Era," *New York Times*, November 23, 2002, 17, accessed at www.nytimes.com.

86.   Hoover to Tressselt, January 9, 1966, box 16, Hoover papers.

## 7. Paradise Lost: Gunflint Lake, 1966–1971

1.   Gladys Taber to Hoover, February 5, 1966, box 2, Helen Blackburn Hoover and Adrian Hoover Papers, Archives and Special Collections, University of Minnesota Duluth.

2.   Carol Brandt to Alfred Knopf, March 21, 1966, box 2, Hoover papers. From here on in the endnotes, the name "Brandt" by itself refers to Carol Brandt, Helen's agent. Correspondence with Carol's son Carl is indicated with the full name "Carl Brandt."

3.   Fierst to Hoover, January 20, 1959, box 14, Hoover papers; Hoover to Brandt, November 11, 1972, box 2, Hoover papers.

4.   Brandt to Hoover, April 27, 1966, box 2, Hoover papers.

5.   Manuscript record, March 25, 1966, box 960.1, Alfred A. Knopf, Inc. Records (Manuscript Collection MS-00062). Harry Ransom Center, The University of Texas at Austin.

6.   Manuscript record, March 25, 1966, box 960.1, Alfred A. Knopf, Inc. Records (Manuscript Collection MS-00062).

7.   Manuscript record, March 25, 1966, box 960.1, Alfred A. Knopf, Inc. Records (Manuscript Collection MS-00062).

8.   Hoover to Carl Brandt, May 1, 1966, box 2, Hoover papers.

9. Hoover to Brandt, March 27, 1966, box 2, Hoover papers.
10. Brandt to Kenneth Wilson, Reader's Digest Association, April 14, 1966, box 2, Hoover papers.
11. Carl Brandt to Carol Brandt, May 9, 1966, box 2, Hoover papers.
12. Brandt to Hoover, June 6, 1966, box 2, Hoover papers.
13. Hoover to Carl Brandt, May 3, 1966, box 2, Hoover papers; Helen Hoover, *The Years of the Forest* (New York: Alfred A. Knopf, 1973), 275.
14. Hoover to Brandt, May 31, 1966, box 2, Hoover papers.
15. Brandt to Taber, May 23, 1966, box 2, Hoover papers.
16. Brandt to Hoover, June 6, 1966, box 2, Hoover papers.
17. Charles Pick to Brandt, June 11, 1966, box 2, Hoover papers. *Ring of Bright Water* by Gavin Maxwell is a 1960 book about his life in a remote Scottish coastal town where he kept pet otters. As noted previously, Sally Carrighar was a popular American nature writer.
18. Hoover, *The Years of the Forest*, 277. Also, Brandt to Hoover, July 19, 1966, box 2, Hoover papers.
19. Brandt to Mark Hamilton, July 19, 1966, box 2, Hoover papers.
20. Ann McCutchan, *The Life She Wished to Live: A Biography of Marjorie Kinnan Rawlings, Author of "The Yearling"* (New York: W. W. Norton, 2021), 101. Brandt & Brandt was founded after World War I; Carol, Carl's wife, joined the firm from MGM in 1955. Carl died in 1957, and Carol remarried in 1961. Their son was also named Carl.
21. Albert Johnston to Angus Cameron, July 27, 1966, box 2, Hoover papers.
22. H. N. Swanson to Brandt, September 13, 1966, box 2, Hoover papers.
23. Copy of check dated July 22, 1966, box 14, 1960–75 bank records, Hoover papers. Film is in box 21, Hoover papers.
24. Hoover to Cameron, September 9, 1966, box 1378.2, Knopf papers.
25. Helen Hoover, *The Gift of the Deer* (New York: Alfred A. Knopf, Inc., 1966), 109.
26. Hoover, *The Gift of the Deer*, 206.
27. Hoover, *The Gift of the Deer*, 208–10.
28. Raymond E. Naddy, "Deer Are Neighbors Who Share Clearing," *Duluth News-Tribune*, October 9, 1966, scrapbook, box 10, Hoover papers.
29. Hoover to Diane Zeeman, Alfred A. Knopf, Inc., July 10, 1966, box 1378.2, Knopf papers.
30. "Hoover Book Gets Fine Reception," *Cook County News-Herald*, November 25, 1966, 1. Also, Hoover to Cameron, November 27, 1966, box 1378.3, Knopf papers.
31. Henry B. Kane, "Ways of the Wild," review of *Animals at My Doorstep*, *New York Times Book Review*, November 6, 1966, scrapbook, box 10, Hoover papers.
32. Hoover to Cameron, November 27, 1966, box 1378.3, Knopf papers.
33. Gun application from Brendamour's, Cincinnati, dated September 21, 1966, 3:10 p.m., box 18, Hoover papers.
34. Hal Borland, "Wilderness Friends," review of *The Gift of the Deer*, *New York Times Book Review*, November 13, 1966, 14–15, box 10, Hoover papers.
35. Hoover to Cameron, November 27, 1966, box 2, Hoover papers.

36. Ethel Jacobson, "Story of a Haunting Friendship," review of *The Gift of the Deer, Chicago Tribune,* November 6, 1966, and Victor H. Cahalane, review of *The Gift of the Deer, Defenders of Wildlife News,* October–November–December 1966, 386, both box 18, Hoover papers. Unsigned review of *The Gift of the Deer, Chicago Sunday American,* December 25, 1966, scrapbook 1964–70, box 10, Hoover papers.

37. Hoover to Hal Borland, March 3, 1967; Hoover to John Perry, March 27, 1967, both box 1378.2, Knopf papers.

38. Cameron to Hoover, November 18, 1966, box 14, Hoover papers.

39. Taber to Hoover, undated but likely October 1966, box 2, Hoover papers.

40. Margaret Culkin Banning to Hoover, October 20, 1966, box 2, Hoover papers.

41. Hoover to Knopf, September 9, 1966, box 1378.2, Knopf papers.

42. Helen Hoover, *The Years of the Forest* (New York: Alfred A. Knopf, 1973), 290.

43. Hoover to Cameron, February 25, 1967, box 1378.2, Knopf papers; Hoover to Brandt, March 14, 1967, box 2, Hoover papers.

44. Helen Hoover, *A Place in the Woods* (New York: Alfred A. Knopf, 1969), 11.

45. Hoover to Cameron, April 29, 1967, box 1378.2, Knopf papers.

46. Hoover to Brandt, February 16, 1967, box 2, Hoover papers.

47. Cameron to Hoover, February 2, 1967, box 14, Hoover papers.

48. Hoover to Cameron, June 20, 1967, box 1378.2, Knopf papers.

49. Hoover to Cameron, August 20, 1967, box 1378.2, Knopf papers.

50. Hoover to Tresselt, August 25, 1967, box 14, Hoover papers.

51. Hoover to Brandt, May 25, 1966, box 2, Hoover papers; Mary King, Chicago Tribune–New York News Syndicate, Inc., to Brandt, September 11, 1967, box 14, Hoover papers.

52. Hoover to Cameron, October 18, 1967, box 1378.2, Knopf papers.

53. Hoover to Brandt, October 29, 1967, box 2, Hoover papers.

54. Hoover to Brandt, September 24, 1967, box 2, Hoover papers.

55. Hoover to Cameron, November 8, 1967, box 1378.2, Knopf papers.

56. George A. Woods, "For Young Readers," review of *Animals at My Doorstep, New York Times Book Review,* December 3, 1967, scrapbook, box 10, Hoover papers.

57. Taber to Patricia Ayres, August 26, 1967, box 14, Hoover papers.

58. Hoover, "A Little Place in the Woods," box 14, Hoover papers. This is the manuscript that Hoover sent to literary agent A. L. Fierst in 1958 for his review and feedback.

59. Hoover, "A Little Place in the Woods."

60. Jim Kimball, "Author 'Born' in Cabin," *Minneapolis Tribune,* February 25, 1968, 49, accessed on microfilm, Minnesota Historical Society.

61. Hoover to Cameron, April 2, 1968, box 741.5, Knopf papers.

62. Cameron to Hoover, April 15, 1968, box 15, Hoover papers.

63. Hoover, *A Place in the Woods,* viii.

64. Sally Carrighar, *One Day on Beetle Rock* (New York: Alfred A. Knopf, 1944); Sally Carrighar, *One Day at Teton Marsh* (New York: Alfred A. Knopf, 1947).

65. Sally Carrighar, *Wild Heritage* (Boston: Houghton Mifflin, 1965).

66. Hoover to Cameron, May 26, 1968, box 741.5, Knopf papers.
67. Edna Moxley to Florence Carr, December 29, 1989, private collection, copy in author's possession. The motel was the Gas Lite, and the Hoovers would remain friends with Moxley until they moved to Laramie permanently in late 1977.
68. Hoover to Cameron, August 2, 1968, box 741.5, Knopf papers.
69. Hoover to Cameron, June 30, 1968, box 741.5, Knopf papers.
70. Brandt to Hoover, August 12, 1968, box 15, Hoover papers.
71. Cameron to Hoover, August 14, 1968, box 15, Hoover papers.
72. Hoover, *A Place in the Woods*, 190.
73. Hoover, *A Place in the Woods*, 213.
74. Hoover to Brandt, October 16, 1968, box 15, Hoover papers.
75. Cameron to Hoover, August 23, 1968; Hoover to Cameron, August 29, 1968; Hoover to Cameron, September 12, 1968, all box 15, Hoover papers.
76. Cameron to Hoover, September 5, 1968, box 15, Hoover papers.
77. Hoover to Cameron, August 29, 1968, box 15, Hoover papers.
78. Hoover to Cameron, October 16, 1968, box 741.5, Knopf papers.
79. Hoover to Cameron, January 1, 1969, box 741.5, Knopf papers.
80. Hoover to Cameron, January 1, 1969, box 741.5, Knopf papers.
81. *Greenfield Daily Times*, January 30, 1969, 1, scrapbook, box 15, Hoover papers.
82. Hoover to Brandt, January 7, 1969, box 15, Hoover papers.
83. Cameron to Hoover, October 6, 1967, box 14, Hoover papers. In the Reader's Digest Book Club arrangement, the book publisher and the author split the royalty evenly. This proved lucrative for Knopf as well.
84. Hoover to Brandt, April 20, 1969, box 15, Hoover papers.
85. Hoover to Brandt, April 20, 1969, box 15, Hoover papers.
86. Internal memo from Tony Schulte, Knopf publicity department, to Gene Rotenberg, Knopf Midwest sales manager, July 3, 1969, box 741.5, Knopf papers. Angus Cameron also wrote to Knopf colleague Dick Lieberman telling him "what a real selling job" Helen did during the interview. See also Hoover to Andre Norton, July 13, 1969, box 8, Andre (Mary Alice) Norton Papers, Special Collections Research Center, Syracuse University Libraries.
87. Cameron to Hoover, July 7, 1969, box 2, Hoover papers.
88. Hoover to Cameron, July 13, 1969, box 15, Hoover papers.
89. Hoover to Cameron, July 13, 1969, box 15, Hoover papers.
90. Hoover to Cameron, July 13, 1969, box 15, Hoover papers.
91. Will Muller, "Weasels Make the Best Friends," review of *A Place in the Woods*, *Detroit News*, July 6, 1969, scrapbook, box 10, Hoover papers.
92. Digby B. Whitman, "Week-end Books," review of *A Place in the Woods*, *Chicago Tribune*, July 4, 1969, scrapbook, box 10, Hoover papers.
93. Hal Borland, review of *A Place in the Woods*, *Natural History*, November 1969, 78–80, Hennepin County Library.
94. Borland, review of *A Place in the Woods*, 78–80.
95. Hoover to Cameron, January 10, 1970, box 12.8, Knopf papers.
96. Cameron to Hoover, January 19, 1970, box 2, Hoover papers.

97. Hoover to Anne Walentas, *Humpty Dumpty's,* August 12, 1969, box 15, Hoover papers. Hoover's backlog of columns continued through September 1970, with a few in 1971 and 1972. Ironically, nature writer and critic Hal Borland started writing the column in April 1972.

98. Hoover book jacket blurb for *The Winter of the Fisher* (New York: W. W. Norton, 1971), box 2, Hoover papers.

99. Hoover to Cameron, July 13, 1969, box 741.5, Knopf papers.

100. Hoover to Cameron, April 3, 1969, box 741.5, Knopf papers.

101. J. F. Carithers, Canyonlands National Park, to Hoover, December 12, 1969, February 19, 1970, and March 27, 1970, box 2, Hoover papers.

102. Hoover to Andre Norton, July 18, 1970, box 1, Norton papers.

103. Richard G. Lillard, "Books in the Field: Nature and Conservation," *Wilson Library Bulletin,* October 1969, 159, scrapbook, box 10, Hoover papers.

104. Borland to Hoover, November 23, 1969, box 14, Hoover papers.

105. Hoover, *The Years of the Forest,* 314–15.

106. Multiple letters from Gary C. Brown to Hoover, boxes 2, 14, and 16, Hoover papers. Hoover letters to Brown, private collection, copies in author's possession. Also, Gary C. Brown interview with author, May 3, 2023.

107. Hoover to unidentified fan, August 3, 1970, box 15, Hoover papers.

108. Cameron to Hoover, October 7, 1969, box 2, Hoover papers.

109. The *My Weekly* serialization ran in the April 11, 18, 25 and May 2, 9, 16, and 23, 1970, issues. Copies are in box 15, Hoover papers.

110. Hoover to Norton, May 10, 1969, box 8, Norton papers.

111. Hoover to Cameron, August 6, 1970, box 12.8, Knopf papers.

112. Helen Hoover, *Animals Near and Far* (New York: Parents' Magazine Press, 1970).

113. Hoover to Cameron, March 4, 1970, box 12.8, Knopf papers.

114. Hoover to Norton, July 2, 1970, and April 26, 1970, box 1, Norton papers.

115. Hoover to Cameron, August 6, 1970, box 12.8, Knopf papers.

116. The handwritten list was divided into two columns, with things to be done at the "Log House" and the "Large House"; box 16, Hoover papers.

117. Hoover to Cameron, March 4, 1970, box 12.8, Knopf papers.

118. Hoover to Cameron, August 6, 1970, box 12.8, Knopf papers.

119. Brandt to Hoover, April 15, 1971, box 2, Hoover papers. Also, Hoover to Norton, May 7, 1971, box 3, Norton papers.

120. Brandt to Hoover, May 14, 1971, box 17, Hoover papers.

121. Hoover to Brandt, June 1, 1971, box 17, Hoover papers.

122. Hoover to Norton, July 3, 1971, box 2, Norton papers.

123. Hoover to Norton, September 4, 1971, box 2, Norton papers.

124. Hoover to Norton, July 14, 1971, box 2, Norton papers.

125. Hoover to Norton, October 27, 1971, box 2, Norton papers.

## 8. Free to Roam: Florida and New Mexico, 1972–1977

1. Hoover to Andre Norton, February 18, 1972, box 3, Andre (Mary Alice) Norton Papers, Special Collections Research Center, Syracuse University Libraries.

2. Hoover to Carol Brandt, November 11, 1972, box 2, Helen Blackburn Hoover and Adrian Hoover Papers, Archives and Special Collections, University of Minnesota Duluth.

3. Brandt to Hoover, March 17, 1972, box 15, Hoover papers.

4. Angus Cameron to Hoover, April 20, 1972, box 15, Hoover papers.

5. Cameron to Hoover, April 3, 1972, box 15, Hoover papers.

6. Cameron to Hoover, April 20, 1972, box 15, Hoover papers.

7. Brandt to Hoover, April 3, 1972, box 15, Hoover papers.

8. Brandt to Hoover, April 26, 1972, box 15, Hoover papers.

9. Brandt to Hoover, August 5, 1971, box 2, Hoover papers.

10. Hoover to Norton, June 17, 1972, box 3, Norton papers.

11. Hoover to Norton, June 17, 1972, box 3, Norton papers.

12. Ray Bruess to Hoover, July 6, 1972, box 3, Hoover papers.

13. Hoover to Norton, July 28, 1970, box 1, Norton papers.

14. Brandt to Hoover, July 7, 1972, box 2, Hoover papers.

15. Brandt to Hoover, July 11, 1972, box 2, Hoover papers.

16. Hoover to Bette Alexander, Alfred A. Knopf, Inc., September 27, 1972, box 2, Hoover papers.

17. Brandt to Hoover, October 16, 1972, and October 30, 1972, box 2, Hoover papers.

18. Hoover to Cameron, November 11, 1972, box 2, Hoover papers.

19. Hoover to Brandt, November 11, 1972, box 2, Hoover papers.

20. Brandt to Hoover, October 30, 1972, box 2, Hoover papers.

21. Helen's passport was issued August 16, 1972, and Ade's was issued August 31, 1972. They were never used. Both are in box 10, Hoover papers.

22. Cameron to Hoover, October 9, 1969, box 2, Hoover papers. See also Sigurd Olson to Hoover, August 11, 1969, box 14, Hoover papers.

23. Cameron to Hoover, January 2, 1973, box 10, Hoover papers.

24. Hoover to Cameron, February 6, 1973, box 12.7, Alfred A. Knopf, Inc. Records (Manuscript Collection MS-00062). Harry Ransom Center, The University of Texas at Austin.

25. Hoover to Cameron, February 20, 1973, box 12.7, Knopf papers.

26. Cameron to Hoover, January 19, 1973, box 2, Hoover papers.

27. Helen Hoover, *The Years of the Forest* (New York: Alfred A. Knopf, 1973), 247.

28. Hoover, *The Years of the Forest*, 247.

29. Hoover to Cameron, May 29, 1973, box 12.7, Knopf papers.

30. Gerald Carson, "The Joy of Life to Be Found in the Wilderness," review of *The Years of the Forest, New York Times Book Review,* May 20, 1973, 51, box 10, Hoover papers.

31. Carson, "The Joy of Life," 51.

32. Anne Cawley Boardman, "The Wonderful 'Years of the Forest': a 'Place in the World,'" review of *The Years of the Forest, Minneapolis Tribune,* May 6, 1973, 10D, scrapbook, box 10, Hoover papers.

33. Hope Buyukmihci, "In the Wonderful, Waning Wilderness," review of *The Years of the Forest, Philadelphia Inquirer,* May 20, 1973, scrapbook, box 10, Hoover papers.

34. *Publishers Weekly,* February 26, 1973, 118, accessed at Wilson Library, University of Minnesota.

35. Review of *The Years of the Forest, Kirkus Reviews,* n.d., but likely early 1973, box 10, Hoover papers.

36. Christopher Lehmann-Haupt, "Andre Norton Dies at 93; a Master of Science Fiction," *New York Times,* March 18, 2005, 8, accessed at www.nytimes.com.

37. Chronology, box 14, Hoover papers.

38. Kenneth Wilson to NASA, July 20, 1973, box 2, Hoover papers.

39. Cameron to Hoover, September 5, 1973, box 12.7, Knopf papers.

40. Brandt to Hoover, September 14, 1973, box 14, Hoover papers.

41. Esther Jackson to Hoover, n.d., likely 1973, box 3, Hoover papers.

42. Helen Hoover, letter to the editor, *Cook County News-Herald,* October 18, 1973, 2, box 18, Hoover papers.

43. Powers newspaper advertisement, October 4, 1973, *Minneapolis Tribune,* 1B. Interviews resulting in stories included Ann Baker, *St. Paul Pioneer Press,* October 5, 1973; scrapbook, box 10, Hoover papers.

44. Cameron to Brandt, July 2, 1974, box 2, Hoover papers.

45. Hoover letter to unknown recipient, n.d., but likely 1971 or 1972, box 15, Hoover papers.

46. Calvin Rutstrum, *Greenhorns in the Southwest* (Albuquerque: University of New Mexico Press, 1972). For more on Rutstrum, see Jim dale Vickery, *Wilderness Visionaries* (Merrillville, Ind.: ICS Books, Inc., 1986), 160–87.

47. Hoover to Peg Miller, April 24, 1982, box 3, Hoover papers.

48. Helen Hoover, "The House of the Tarnished Shield" (unpublished manuscript), box 17, Hoover papers.

49. Folder "Cincinnati House," box 14, Hoover papers.

50. Hoover to Miller, April 24, 1982, box 2, Hoover papers.

51. Hoover to Norton, March 16, 1975, box 4, Norton papers.

52. Hoover to Brandt, February 22, 1975, box 15, Hoover papers.

53. Brandt to Hoover, March 4, 1975, box 15, Hoover papers.

54. Wilson to Brandt, March 20, 1975, box 15, Hoover papers.

55. Brandt to Hoover, March 21, 1975, box 15, Hoover papers.

56. Hoover to Norton, April 1, 1975, box 4, Norton papers.

57. Brandt to Hoover, March 17, 1975, box 15, Hoover papers.

58. Brandt to Hoover, April 16, 1974, box 14, Hoover papers.

59. Fabio Coen to Brandt, June 27, 1975, box 15, Hoover papers.

60. Hoover to Norton, August 18, 1975, box 4, Norton papers.

61. Hoover to Norton, August 18, 1975, box 4, Norton papers.

62. Jim Kimball column, *Minneapolis Tribune,* March 28, 1976, 1F, box 18, Hoover papers.

63. Here and below, letters generated in response to Kimball's column are in box 15, Hoover papers.

64. Jesse Lair to Hoover, n.d. but likely April 1976, box 15, Hoover papers. Lair wrote the best-selling self-help book *I Ain't Much Baby, But I'm All I've Got* in 1972.

65. Donald Zochert to Hoover, March 27, 1976, box 15, Hoover papers.

66. Hoover to Miller, April 27, 1976, box 2, Hoover papers.
67. Cameron to Hoover, April 2, 1976, box 15, Hoover papers.
68. Hoover to Heston, April 27, 1977, private collection, copy in author's possession.
69. Hoover to Miller, May 25, 1977, box 2, Hoover papers.
70. Hoover to Norton, September 25, 1976, box 6, Norton papers.

## 9. Looking for a New Hook: Laramie, 1977–1986

1. Helen Hoover to Andre Norton, September 2, 1977, box 6, Andre (Mary Alice) Norton Papers, Special Collections Research Center, Syracuse University Libraries.
2. "Cat Owners Collar Control Officers," *The Taos News,* December 8, 1977, 10, accessed at newspapers.com.
3. Hoover to Peggy Heston, December 9, 1977, private collection, copy in author's possession.
4. Edna Moxley to Florence Hart Carr, December 29, 1989, private collection, copy in author's possession.
5. Hoover to Norton, n.d., likely October 1977, box 6, Norton papers. Helen confirmed chartering a plane to Norton as well. Also, Albany County (Wyoming) Land Deed records, accessed October 24, 2022. The purchase price of the property was not disclosed as that is not public information in Wyoming.
6. Hoover to Angus Cameron, December 31, 1977, box 11, Helen Blackburn Hoover and Adrian Hoover Papers, University of Minnesota Duluth.
7. Gladys Taber to Hoover, September 13, 1978, box 2, Hoover papers.
8. Hoover to Cameron, December 31, 1977, box 11, Hoover papers.
9. Hoover to Heston, February 10, 1978, and March 6, 1978, private collection, copies in author's possession.
10. Hoover to Norton, May 1, 1978, box 8, Norton papers.
11. Manuscript for "The Princess and the Woodsman," box 15, Hoover papers.
12. Nancy Leeds Wynkoop to Hoover, March 19, 1978, box 2, Hoover papers.
13. Charles Schlessiger to Hoover, June 27, 1978, box 15, Hoover papers.
14. Cameron to Hoover, July 31, 1978, box 2, Hoover papers.
15. Hoover to Heston, October 10, 1978, and November 12, 1978, private collection, copies in author's possession.
16. Schlessiger to Hoover, February 20, 1979, box 2, Hoover papers.
17. Schlessiger to Hoover, May 18, 1979, box 2, Hoover papers.
18. Gladys Taber to Hoover, September 13, 1978, box 2, Hoover papers.
19. Hoover to Heston, October 12, 1979, private collection, copy in author's possession.
20. Rendering and bid by Comin Construction, Laramie, for cattery, August 24, 1979, box 10, Hoover papers.
21. Orville Gilmore to John Henricksson, September 19, 2008, private collection, copy in author's possession.
22. Hoover notes for Ohio University event, May 22, 1979, box 2, Hoover papers.
23. Hoover to Heston, May 30, 1980, private collection, copy in author's possession.

24. Hoover to Peg Miller, January 30, 1980, box 2, Hoover papers.
25. Carol Brandt to Hoover, March 19, 1980, and March 28, 1980, box 2, Hoover papers.
26. Carl Brandt to Hoover, December 2, 1980, box 2, Hoover papers.
27. Carl Brandt to Hoover, December 2, 1980, box 2, Hoover papers.
28. Hoover to Miller, January 30, 1980, box 2, Hoover papers.
29. Hoover to Miller, October 1981, box 2, Hoover papers.
30. Joseph Reiner, Bonanza Books, to Hoover, December 5, 1978, box 2, Hoover papers.
31. James L. Mairs to Hoover, September 29, 1980, box 2, Hoover papers. Mairs had an interesting Minnesota connection. Born and raised in St. Paul, he attended Dartmouth College and went to work for W. W. Norton after graduation and spent his entire career there. His father was an investment firm executive in St. Paul and enjoyed spending time in northern Minnesota, which is mentioned in this letter.
32. Toinette Lippe, reprint rights director, Alfred A. Knopf, Inc., to Brandt, March 14, 1980, box 2, Hoover papers. Brandt told Hoover that six other trade publishers had turned down the opportunity before Houghton Mifflin agreed. Part of the reluctance was due to economic challenges in the paperback market at that time.
33. Houghton Mifflin published only *The Gift of the Deer;* the others were not reprinted. Susan Steinway, Houghton Harcourt archivist, email to the author, August 24, 2023.
34. Schlessiger to Hoover, June 17, 1981, box 2, Hoover papers. Clip of *Orion Nature Review* article in box 10, Hoover papers.
35. Hoover to Miller, October 1981, box 2, Hoover papers.
36. Brandt to Hoover, October 9, 1981, box 11, Hoover papers.
37. Brandt to Hoover, October 9, 1981, box 11, Hoover papers.
38. Bobbie Bristol to Hoover, May 21, 1982, box 2, Hoover papers.
39. Hoover to Miller, October 1981, box 3, Hoover papers.
40. The "Chicago" manuscript is in box 18, Hoover papers. Biographer Florence Hart Carr transcribed Helen's handwritten pages, which are in Carr's private papers. A copy of her transcription is in the author's possession.
41. "Chicago" manuscript, box 18, Hoover papers.
42. Norton to Adrian Hoover, October 1, 1984, box 3, Hoover papers.
43. Hoover to Miller, February 2, 1983, box 2, Hoover papers.
44. Karen Nelson to Hoover, December 27, 1967; Hoover to Nelson, September 16, 1968, both box 15, Hoover papers.
45. Moxley to Carr, December 29, 1989, private collection, copy in author's possession. .
46. Hoover to Robert Brome, March 14, 1982, private collection, copy in author's possession.
47. Richard A. Hennig to Florence Carr, December 6, 1989, private collection, copy in author's possession. Hennig was the Hoovers' estate lawyer in Laramie.

48. "Helen Hoover, Nature Writer and Metallurgist, Dies at 74," *New York Times,* July 7, 1984, 14, box 3, Hoover papers.

49. Letters, *Cook County News-Herald,* August 2, 1984, 2, box 3, Hoover papers.

50. Adrian Hoover to Heston, July 8, 1984, private collection, copy in author's possession.

51. Brandt to Adrian Hoover, July 18, 1984, box 3, Hoover papers.

52. "CAROL BRANDT," *New York Times,* October 27, 1984, 33, accessed at www.nytimes.com.

53. Cameron to Adrian Hoover, July 14, 1984, box 3, Hoover papers.

54. Richard Reilly to Adrian Hoover, July 3, 1984, box 3, Hoover papers.

55. Sister Noemi Weygant to Adrian Hoover, n.d., but likely July 1984, box 3, Hoover papers.

56. Diana Owen to Carr, November 28, 1989, private collection, copy in author's possession.

57. Norton to Adrian Hoover, August 29, 1984, box 3, Hoover papers.

58. Norton to Adrian Hoover, August 29, 1984, box 3, Hoover papers.

59. Owen to Carr, November 28, 1989, private collection, copy in author's possession.

60. Norton to Adrian Hoover, August 29, 1984, box 3, Hoover papers.

61. Norton to Adrian Hoover, October 21, 1984, and Richard Reilly to Adrian Hoover, November 1, 1984, both box 3, Hoover papers.

62. Norton to Adrian Hoover, December 10, 1984, box 3, Hoover papers.

63. Norton to Adrian Hoover, December 10, 1984, box 3, Hoover papers.

64. Last Will and Testament of Adrian E. Hoover, n.d., private collection, copy in author's possession. The contents of the James S. Copley Library, which had more than two thousand manuscripts, books, letters, pamphlets, and maps in its collection, were sold by several auction houses after it closed in 2010. The Minnesota Historical Society purchased the typed manuscript of *The Long-Shadowed Forest* and later all of the drawings Ade created for Helen's Knopf books when they appeared on the market.

65. Last Will and Testament of Adrian E. Hoover, n.d.; and Carl Brandt to Carr, November 30, 1989, private collection, copy in author's possession. Also, William Kimok, Ohio University, email to author November 1, 2007.

66. Hennig to Carr, December 6, 1989, private collection, copy in author's possession.

67. Henricksson interview with the author, September 15, 2008. See also Carla Arneson, "A Place in the Woods," *The Boundary Waters Journal,* Fall 1993, 46–48.

68. Hoover, *The Years of the Forest,* 318.

# Selected Bibliography

This bibliography includes books and articles by Helen Hoover and by other nature writers, as well as autobiographies and biographies of some of those writers. It is by no means a definitive list, but it is intended as a reference regarding authors and books mentioned in the text or used as sources.

Arlen, Alice. *She Took to the Woods: A Biography and Selected Writings of Louise Dickinson Rich.* Camden, Maine: Down East Books, 2000.

Arneson, Carla. "A Place in the Woods." *The Boundary Waters Journal,* Fall 1993.

Backes, David. *A Wilderness Within: The Life of Sigurd F. Olson.* Minneapolis: University of Minnesota Press, 1997.

———. *A Private Wilderness: The Journals of Sigurd F. Olson.* Minneapolis: University of Minnesota Press, 2021.

Banning, Marjorie Culkin. *Mesabi.* New York: Harper and Row, 1969.

Becker, Paula. *Looking for Betty MacDonald: The Egg, the Plague, Mrs. Piggle-Wiggle, and I.* Seattle: University of Washington Press, 2016.

Brandt, Luana, Sharon Eliasen, Sue Kerfoot, Jo Ann Krause, Kathy Lande, Bette McDonnell, Sue McDonnell, et al. *A Taste of the Gunflint Trail.* Cambridge, Minn.: Adventure Publications, 2005.

Brooks, Paul. *The House of Life: Rachel Carson at Work.* Boston: Houghton Mifflin, 1972.

Buyukmihci, Hope Sawyer. *Unexpected Treasure.* New York: M. Evans and Company, 1968.

———. *Hour of the Beaver.* Chicago: Rand McNally and Company, 1971.

Campbell, Sam. *Nature's Messages: A Book of Wilderness Wisdom.* Chicago: Rand McNally and Company, 1952.

Carr, Florence Hart. *Helen Blackburn Hoover: Scientist, Naturalist, Writer.* Roseville, Minn.: self-published, 1993.

Carrighar, Sally. *One Day on Beetle Rock.* New York: Alfred A. Knopf, 1944.

———. *One Day at Teton Marsh.* New York: Alfred A. Knopf, 1947.

———. *Wild Heritage.* Boston: Houghton Mifflin, 1965.

———. *Home to the Wilderness: A Personal Journey.* Boston: Houghton Mifflin, 1973.

Carson, Rachel L. *The Sea around Us.* New York: Oxford University Press, 1951.

———. *Silent Spring.* Boston: Houghton Mifflin, 1962.

Freehafer, Nancy. "Helen Hoover (1910–1984)." In *American Nature Writers,* volume 1, edited by John Elder, 389–99. New York: Charles Scribner's Sons, 1996.

Henricksson, John. *A Wild Neighborhood.* Minneapolis: University of Minnesota Press, 1997.

———. *Gunflint: The Trail, the People, the Stories.* Cambridge, Minn.: Adventure Publications, 2003.

———. *The Gunflint Cabin.* Edina, Minn.: Beaver's Pond Press, 2008.

Henson, Shandelle M. *Sam Campbell: Philosopher of the Forest.* New York: TEACH Services, Inc., 2002.

Hoover, Helen. *The Long-Shadowed Forest.* New York: Thomas Y. Crowell, 1963; Minneapolis: University of Minnesota Press, 1998.

———. *Animals at My Doorstep.* New York: Parents' Magazine Press, 1966.

———. *The Gift of the Deer.* New York: Alfred A. Knopf, 1966; Minneapolis: University of Minnesota Press, 1998.

———. *Great Wolf and the Good Woodsman.* New York: Parents' Magazine Press, 1967; Minneapolis: University of Minnesota Press, 2005.

———. *A Place in the Woods.* New York: Alfred A. Knopf, 1969; Minneapolis: University of Minnesota Press, 1999.

———. *Animals Near and Far.* New York: Parents' Magazine Press, 1970.

———. *The Years of the Forest.* New York: Alfred A. Knopf, 1973; Minneapolis: University of Minnesota Press, 1999.

Jaques, Florence Page. *Snowshoe Country*. Minneapolis: University of Minnesota Press, 1944.

Kerfoot, Justine. *Gunflint: Reflections on the Trail*. Duluth, Minn.: Pfeifer-Hamilton Publishers, 1991.

———. *Woman of the Boundary Waters*. Minneapolis: University of Minnesota Press, 1994.

Kimball, James W. *The Spirit of the Wilderness*. Minneapolis: T. S. Denison, 1970.

Langford, Cameron. *The Winter of the Fisher*. New York: W. W. Norton, 1971.

Lear, Linda. *Rachel Carson: Witness for Nature*. New York: Henry Holt, 1997.

Liers, Emil E. *An Otter's Story*. New York: Viking Press, 1953.

MacDonald, Betty. *The Egg and I*. New York: J. B. Lippincott, 1945.

Maxwell, Gavin. *Ring of Bright Water*. New York: E. P. Dutton, 1961.

McCutchan, Ann. *The Life She Wished to Live: A Biography of Marjorie Kinnan Rawlings, Author of "The Yearling."* New York: W. W. Norton, 2021.

Murie, Margaret E. *Two in the Far North*. New York: Alfred A. Knopf, 1962.

Nute, Grace Lee. *The Voyageur's Highway*. St. Paul: Minnesota Historical Society Press, 1941, 2002.

Olson, Sigurd F. *The Singing Wilderness*. New York: Alfred A. Knopf, 1956; Minneapolis: University of Minnesota Press, 1997.

———. *Listening Point*. New York: Alfred A. Knopf, 1958; Minneapolis: University of Minnesota Press, 1997.

———. *The Lonely Land*. New York: Alfred A. Knopf, 1961; Minneapolis: University of Minnesota Press, 1997.

———. *Open Horizons*. New York: Alfred A. Knopf, 1969; Minneapolis: University of Minnesota Press, 1998.

Rawlings, Marjorie Kinnan. *The Yearling*. New York: Scribner's, 1938.

Rich, Louise Dickinson. *We Took to the Woods*. New York: J. B. Lippincott, 1942; Camden, Maine: Down East Books, 2007.

Rowlands, John J. *Cache Lake Country*. New York: W. W. Norton, 1947; Woodstock, Vt.: The Countryman Press, 1998.

Rue III, Leonard Lee. *The World of the White-tailed Deer.* New York: J. B. Lippincott, 1962.

Rutstrum, Calvin. *Greenhorns in the Southwest.* Albuquerque: University of New Mexico Press, 1972.

———. *Once Upon a Wilderness.* New York: Macmillan Co., 1973; Minneapolis: University of Minnesota Press, 2002.

———. *The Wilderness Life.* New York: Macmillan Co., 1975; Minneapolis: University of Minnesota Press, 2004.

Searle, R. Newell. *Saving Quetico-Superior: A Land Set Apart.* St. Paul: Minnesota Historical Society Press, 1977.

Vickery, Jim Dale. *Wilderness Visionaries.* Merrillville, Ind.: ICS Books, 1986.

# Illustration Credits

**Dale Carlson**
Page viii (photograph by Mauritz and Elsie Westmark)

**Helen Blackburn Hoover and Adrian Hoover Papers, Archives
and Special Collections, Kathryn A. Martin Library, University of
Minnesota Duluth**
Plates 1, 2, 4, 5, 7, 10, 11, 14, 17, 27, 28, 30, 31 (photograph by Ray Naddy,
*Duluth News Tribune*), 32

**Main Street Downtown Greenfield**
Plate 3

**Photography Collection, The New York Public Library**
Plate 6

**John Fredrikson and Gunflint Lodge**
Plate 8

**Minnesota Historical Society**
Plates 9 (photograph by Monroe P. Killy), 22 (map by Adrian Hoover)

**Records of the Forest Service, U.S. National Archives**
Plate 12 (photograph by Ray E. Bassett)

**Bobby Don Brazell Collection, Gunflint Trail Historical Society**
Plate 13

**John P. Marquand Collection, Yale Collection of American Literature, Beinecke Rare Book and Manuscript Library, Yale University**
Plate 15

**Kevin Cameron**
Plate 16

**Cook County Historical Society, Grand Marais, Minnesota**
Plate 18

**Archives and Special Collections, Kathryn A. Martin Library, University of Minnesota Duluth**
Plate 19 (photograph by *Duluth News Tribune*)

**Photographs by Earl Seubert, *Minneapolis Tribune*; copyright Star Tribune Media Company LLC. Reprinted with permission; all rights reserved.**
Page vi, Plates 20 (Hoover Papers), 21, 23 (Hoover Papers), 24, 25 (Hoover Papers), 26 (Hoover Papers), 29, 33

# Index

## Abbreviations

AH   Adrian Hoover
AT   Alvin Tresselt
AC   Angus Cameron
CB   Carol Brandt
HH   Helen Hoover
*Forest*  *The Long-Shadowed Forest*
*Gift*   *The Gift of the Deer*
*Place*  *A Place in the Woods*
*Years*  *The Years of the Forest*

132–33; foreign editions of, 129; idea for, 96, 116; importance of to HH, 127, 137; magazine excerpts of, 192; premise of, 116–17; promotion of, 133, 134; sale of to Knopf, 127; sale of to Reader's Digest, 128; reviews of, 133–36; sales of, 136, 137; summary of, 126; television pitch of, 131; UK serialization of, 122, 124, 125

Gilmore, Orville, 188

Glass Block department store (Duluth), 148

Gomersall, Bruce (uncle), 50, 62, 70, 175; death of, 131

Gomersall, Claire (aunt), 26, 82

Gomersall, Edward (uncle), 26

Gomersall, Robert (uncle), 50, 70, 131, 175; death of, 147

*Gourmet*: submissions to, 79–80; Thanksgiving story, 78, 79, 80

Grand Marais, Minnesota, ix, 37, 79, 106, 131, 172, 195; BWCA public hearings at, 120; HH regret of promoting, 134

Grand Marais Chamber of Commerce: and border road proposal, 91

"Great Bull Market," 7

Great Depression. *See* Depression

*Great Wolf and the Good Woodsman* (book), 198; Brooklyn Art Books for Children citation for, 181; early attempts to sell, 92; publication of, 140; reviews of, 140

"Great Wolf and the Good Woodsman" (article): sale to *Humpty Dumpty's*, 74; writing of, 67–68

Greenfield, Ohio, 1, 9, 27, 34, 199; HH attitude about, 2; later visit, 147; temperance revolt, 1–2

*Greenhorns in the Southwest* (Rutstrum), 174

Gunflint Lake, ix, 119, 186, 195, 201, 202; border crossing controversy, 79, 91; budworm problem at, 88; changes to, 96, 99, 163–64, 181; concerns about DDT in, 88; first impression of, 38;

inability to return to, 181, 187; moving away from, 134, 139; moving to, ix–x, 47, 49; promotion of, 166; sense of loss over, 155, 158, 187; vacations to, 41, 42

Gunflint Lodge, 58, 59, 71, 78; fire at, 70, 84; first visit to, 38; Thanksgiving story about, 78

Gunflint Trail, ix, 37, 43, 51, 52, 79, 80, 195, 202

guns: father teaching use of, 4; HH purchase of, 134; HH shooting hawk, 4; use of to scare hunters, 90, 103, 134

*Harper's*, 66, 75, 85

health of HH: anxiety from International Harvester, 85; asthma, 184; cataracts, 194; depression, 158, 162; emotional drain following deer deaths, 100; exhaustion after *Years*, 171; flu and pneumonia, 185; Hong Kong flu, 147, 148; illness from Crowell interactions, 121, 122; impact from moves, 194; low iron, 77; miscarriage, 41; "muscular myolitis," 100; nervous collapse, 41; obesity, 194; peritonitis, 195; pneumonia, 41; scurvy, 77; weight gain, 115, 148; weight loss, 103, 115.

Henry Paulson Company, 13, 14, 55; HH dispute with owner, 16

Heston, Myrl, 58

Heston, Peggy, 58, 110, 180, 186–87, 195, 224n37

Heston's Lodge, 58, 59, 92, 224n37

high school. *See* education

Hohoff, Tay, 93–94, 225n59

homes: apartments in Chicago, Illinois, 12, 15, 26; Greenfield, Ohio, 1, 3; Laramie, Wyoming, 183, 188; Ranchos de Taos, New Mexico, 175, 177. *See also* cabins

Hoover, Adrian (husband): ability with cars, 16–17, 104; art director at Scott, Foresman, 34; aspirations to be an

The text of this book is set in Adobe Caslon, a digital version based on the original typeface created by London typesetter William Caslon, circa 1728. The type became popular in Europe and the American colonies and was used prominently by Benjamin Franklin. The first printings of the U.S. Declaration of Independence and the Constitution were set in Caslon. Its revival is due, in part, to its readability and visual comfort, as well as being welcoming and unpretentious.

**David Hakensen** is a public relations consultant and former board president of the Minnesota Historical Society. He has written for *Minnesota History, Mpls./St. Paul,* and *Twin Cities Business.*